The Lost Magic of Christianity

Celtic Essene Connections

Michael Poynder

GREEN
MAGIC

Published by Green Magic

First published in 1997 by Collins Press, Ireland

© Michael Poynder

This edition published in 2000 by Green Magic
BCM Inspire, London WC1N 3XX

A catalogue record for this book is available from
The British Library

Typeset by Academic and Technical, Bristol
Printed and bound by Redwood Books, Trowbridge, Wiltshire

Jacket Design by Michael Poynder

ISBN 0 9536631 0 8

Contents

Colour Plates

About the Author

Michael Poynder was born in London of Anglo Irish parents and has lived much of his life in the west of Ireland, currently near Westport, Co. Mayo.

He paints landscape, has published poetry and has a Ph.D. in Alternative Medicine.

His earlier book 'Pi in the Sky – A Revelation of the Ancient Celtic Wisdom Tradition' is widely acclaimed.

Acknowledgements

I would like to thank the following people for their information, support and friendship in putting this book together: Duncan Hopkins, Glastonbury, for his graphics and artwork; Barbara Duffy, Niall Herriott and Anne Crowley of Westport, Co. Mayo, for their help in preparation; Peter Dawkins of the Francis Bacon Research Trust (F.B.R.T.) and the Gatekeeper Trust; Philip and Stephanie Carr-Gomm of the Order of Bards, Ovates and Druids (O.B.O.D.); Colin Bloy and Fountain International; Geoffrey King, Maurice Cotterell, Clair O'Kelly and Michael Herity. I am also indebted to the staff of the Commissioners of Public Works (Parks & Monuments), Dublin; the Irish Ordnance Survey and the National Museum of Ireland for their constant help.

Grateful acknowledgement is made to Mark Paterson and Associates for permission to quote from *The Passover Plot* by Hugh J. Schonfield.

But most particularly, the invaluable help and support in the past both of the late Clive Beadon, Ben McBrady and Bruce MacManaway, during their lifetimes, who taught me so much.

The second edition of this book has been put together by Roma Ann Harding, Weymouth, Dorset, and I offer her my sincere thanks and appreciation.

This book is dedicated
to the
'LOVE'
That fills the void
When the
'centre cannot hold'.

Introduction

It is at Christmas that Christianity comes into many millions of homes around the world and especially in north-west Europe. It is a time when people cast aside their differences and celebrate the family, thinking of the birth of a boy child in Bethlehem 2,000 years ago. The Christ child, Jesus of Nazareth – the Nazarene.

So why this book – where does it arise from?

Myself – I grew up in the wartime years of 1940–45 and the lean times after its end. My memories are certainly not ones of joy and plenty; indeed my father had died after a long illness in 1943 and my mother, already well into middle age, found it very hard to make ends meet. So Christmas, although celebrated as best we could, was in rented houses during stringent times without the joy or togetherness of a big family as there was only the two of us.

To be alone a lot of the time as the child of middle-aged parents was not a happy experience and I remember at boarding school, amidst the physical abuse of the stick and tight discipline, slipping away as often as I could into the woods to talk to Jesus and ask for help to face up to the system I had been born into.

So Jesus on a personal level came into my life at an early age as someone external, far away and seemingly quite uselessly unhelpful, yet 'someone' to talk to on a tearful level. I would mention in passing, since introductions of books are generally personal statements, (unless the book is an 'I' book), that my family on both sides had a long history of service through the army and the church; my father's family particularly were evangelical Christians, being part of the Clapham sect in the early 1800s. This was the time of Wilberforce and the abolition of slavery, and an Act of Parliament, pushed through by my great-great-grandfather, banning the practice of 'Suttee' in India – the ritual burning of the wives at the death of their husband. We were an Anglo-Irish family of traditional Protestant stock, middle-class and fully used to the idea of service to King and country, and the practice of Christianity. Without question this was a lifestyle of travel and early death in distant parts of the Empire, particularly India. My great-grandfather, a parson to the Indian army, married an Indian Christian lady in 1848.

Many years later, living in Ireland and having begun to question the basis of my Christianity – the Crucifixion – the Resurrection and the Ascension – allowed me to put the so-called truths of my faith to the test. Amongst the ancient cultures that are so essentially part of this beautiful island, Ireland, I was to find the origins of many of the Christian stories as part of the Stone Age mythology from millennia before the birth of Jesus. It was a shattering experience, although adding greatly to its own richness, to discover that the birth of Jesus on Christmas Day, 25 December, had absolutely no foundation in the Bible. There is no reference in any of the Gospels or the Acts to substantiate this event. For what reason therefore do we celebrate 25 December formally as Jesus' birthday?

My interest and study of ancient civilisations inevitably led me to the great cairn of Newgrange, built about 3000 B.C., and recognised as the centre of the Stone Age culture in Ireland. It is said to be the home or 'hostel' of 'Dagda', the great God of the Sun, still a place of annual pilgrimage for many Christians interested in their earlier Paganism.

The layout and structure of the great cairn deliberately allows the path of the rising Sun's rays to beam through the skylight above the entrance door and penetrate into the centre of the cruciform chamber deep within the circular cairn. This shaft of polarised sunlight comes from the rising Sun only at the Winter Solstice when the Sun is at its lowest on the horizon, at the shortest day of the year, 21 December. At this time the Sun seems to stay at that point for three days – just as it does on the longest day of the year, (mid)Summer Solstice, 21 June.

Three days after the Winter Solstice, the Sun starts to move back along the horizon as the days begin to lengthen again and the annual renewal of the Earth and all on and within it in the northern hemisphere begins to rejuvenate accordingly. That Jesus said he would rise from the dead three days after the Crucifixion is very significant.

That three day standstill point after 21 December takes us up to 25 December, i.e., the new beginning, the rebirth of the Sun itself, the rebirth of a new year and the 'Christ-mass'; a time of great celebration and joy. That day, 25 December, in the Druidic or Pagan calendar was of immense significance.

The Christian Church did not become the recognised faith of the Roman Empire till the third century A.D., i.e., nearly 300 years after the birth of Jesus. In order to take over and make the Christian calendar acceptable to the Pagan countries of north-west Europe, Rome decided to make the old Pagan solar and lunar festivals the new Christian festivals. The most pertinent and obvious start to the calendar was the birth of Jesus. So it is reported in 273 A.D. that the Church declared that the birth of Jesus took place on 25 December, in order to anchor that date to the rebirth of the Sun itself, the giver of life, the divine rebirth of the Son of God – Ogma of Dagda, the great God of 'Burgh na Boinne'.

The solar and lunar cultures of the ancients were then rehashed and reported as 'Divine', incorporating the Sun as the masculine energy, the male of the priesthood. The Moon, no longer 'the Goddess' of old, was seen as the female or Mary, the Virgin Mother of the Divine Child. Venus was always the consort of the Sun, since it rises helically, and was seen as either the Holy Ghost or 'the Son', the one begetting the other.

Deep within the recesses of the great cairn of Newgrange is engraved the enigmatic trinity of the triple spiral, celebrating the triple conjunction of the divine bodies seen through the skylight to penetrate the very womb of matter. The triple spiral therefore represents both male and female and the balance or birth from the union of that duality; the Divine new Son or Sun of the new millennium.

We now know from the work of Maurice Cotterell in *The Mayan Prophecies* that the ancient metaphysical priests used Venus as a gauge to table the sunspot cycle of fertility, a cycle on a mini-scale of 187 years and on a mega-scale of 5,125 years. The Sun therefore was, and has always been, seen as totally vital to the continuance of life on Planet Earth. That Jesus, an obscure prophet from the Middle East, was birthed to this cycle was a deliberate intellectual decision in order to marry the ancient metaphysical beliefs, subsequently ridiculed, to the new religion to give it substance.

To realise that Jesus wasn't born on Christmas Day and the reasoning behind this myth was a pretty shattering event in my life and started me on a track of investigation, meditation and intuition into all aspects of Christianity in relation to the cultures, specifically here in Ireland, that preceded it.

It is the result of my study, covering the past fifteen years, that I have attempted to convey in this book. The purpose of writing is essentially not to dismiss Christ as a lie, but to show how the Church, through dogma encapsulated in the patriarchal system and dominated by the male sexual ego, has deliberately taken away from us our personal inner mythology. The Church itself has begun to be seen as redundant and we, as individuals, are lost in a sea of uncertainty and spiritual insecurity. By taking away our connection to everything natural we have become separated from ourselves and therefore 'the Christ'. The cosmic eternal soul Christ within ourselves has been lost in clouds of materialism and spiritual manipulation by a debased male priesthood.

I hope sincerely that within these pages you may find some of the answers and reassurance you need to repair your faith in yourself and all that Christianity once practised. Because today, suddenly at this 'end of times', exactly the same situation arises that the Jews found themselves in, in 5 B.C., the year of Jesus' birth on perhaps 15 September. We are now expecting a 'second coming' when in fact it could be a 'first coming' or a 'hundredth coming'. And yet such incarnations are already amongst us through the lives of illumined beings of this age such as Mother Meera, Sathya Sai 'Baba' and the Dalai Lama. These people walk the earth and express all the attributes of the truly divine cosmic Christ. It is to them, and all the miracles of love and healing they daily perform for us, that I humbly offer this book.

CHAPTER I

The Stone Age Legacy

In the Beginning

Forty thousand years ago a man and a woman made love in a cave somewhere out there on the tundra, or in the forests of Europe. You and I are the result of that union. We were not found under a gooseberry bush and the stork didn't lower us down the chimney. Today we are concerned with our ancestry – 'my grandfather was such and such, my father is this or that', because we need reassurance of our 'birthright' to establish ourselves in a fractured society. We have forgotten our distant past and the wealth of our inner mythology.

Forty thousand years is not a long time in the evolution of Planet Earth. Certainly the Aborigines of Australia have a direct genetic link back through, we are now told, 80,000 years or 3,200 generations from the start of their culture. Within their spirituality and folk memory there is timelessness and a sense of 'One-ness' and 'Being' that makes the convolutions of modern religions, Christianity in particular, seem bizarre. The way Stone Age Man (S.A.M.), in north-west Europe integrated with nature, and the relationship between himself and the seasons and the animals in order to survive, let alone prosper, meant that an inner sense of connectedness was built up through all the senses. This intuition developed into a state of total awareness of body, mind and spirit through the interaction of water, earth, air and 'fire' – the Sun. Wo-man did not feel separated or superior from the rest of life or nature, for indeed that 'mind' was aware and used the subconscious.

Today in our emerging struggle towards understanding natural physics and our part in the rescue of the planet, we are just beginning to realise our responsibility for the future. Through 2,000 years of religious dogma and hard-nosed patriarchy we have been parted from our birthright, made to feel emotionally guilty, and yet superior and in 'control' of Mother Earth.

That Stone Age sense of inner being is still available to us today; a few people are born with it and some develop it through hard work and inner discipline. It is called clairvoyance and clairaudience – the ability to see 'innerly' through time and space into the hologrammatic expressions of past, present and future lateral relationships and events, and to hear an inner voice of the higher connected self in all creations.

12

To understand Christianity and the magic that is inherent in it, we need to explore the legacy of earlier times – the way S.A.M. lived and thought – because that legacy was brought forward and integrated into early Christianity as an easy transition between the Bardic and Druidic ways of the middle Iron Age, and into the science of the later Christian monks. The previous religious practices of the Druid priests were included and then discarded, being labelled as Pagan in order that the suspicious people of mainly rural countries could be brainwashed into accepting the idea of 'One God Omnipotent', through the teachings of Jesus of Nazareth. This idea could only be brought through a human messenger directly from God 'Himself' in the form of the Messiah of an obscure Roman province. The extraordinary thought behind this that we will address in the Stone Age legacy is that the people already knew 'the One' instinctively deep within their metaphysical mythology; their culture and their buildings reflected the principle of 'no separation' in sacred architecture. Subsequently, the gentiles of north-west Europe were easily 'converted' to the early Christian ways.

Let us go back in time to the period just after the Ice Age which ended in north-west Europe in approximately 9000 B.C. Gradually wo-man returned to the wastelands as the herds of game found new pastures to graze after the ice had retreated and the climate warmed up.

Water in the earth is the same as blood in our veins, the essential juice that allows life to pulsate in the body. We are a water planet and without water we have no growth in the kingdom – animal, vegetable and mineral, or in the womb.

Animals instinctively followed the tracks of unseen energy lines from underground water-flows across the wasteland because they had, and still have, natural clairvoyant sight. They knew that the underground flows forming invisible tracks would eventually lead them to a conjunction or surface spring and therefore to a supply of the Earth's life-blood – water.

Next, men – hunting the animals – followed their tracks (diagram 1) and so eventually, millennia later, these tracks became roads and the conjunctions became cross-roads, places of tribal gathering – villages, and, as the population increased, towns.

These underground water-flows are easily defined with twigs or a pendulum as many people have what is called the dowsing and divining ability. An underground flow can be annotated as to direction, strength and depth, because the flow shows five side-bands through to the surface either side

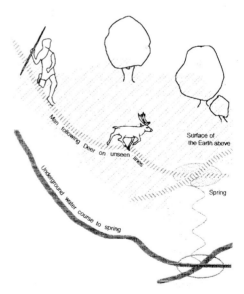

Diagram 1. *Wo-man following deer along a water track line.*

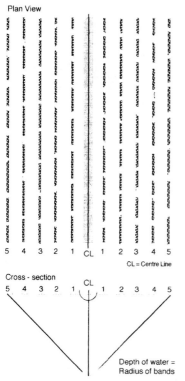

Plan View

5 4 3 2 1 CL 1 2 3 4 5

CL = Centre Line

Cross - section

5 4 3 2 1 CL 1 2 3 4 5

Depth of water =
Radius of bands

Diagram 2. *Underground water course and 'side' bands.*

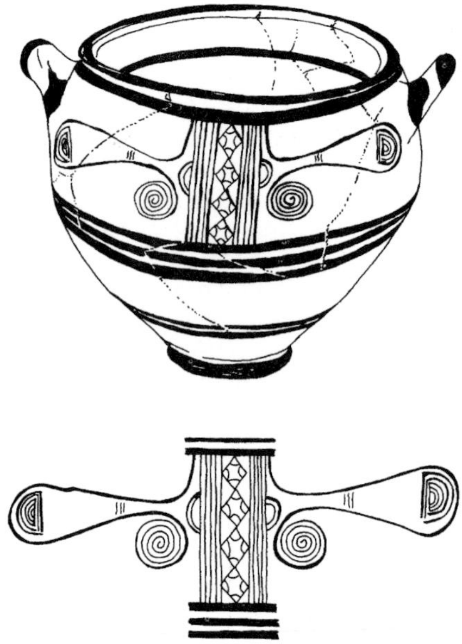

Diagram 3. *Water vessel showing the underground water patterns relating to a human torso, c.1300 B.C.* (**Cyprus Museum, Souskiou**).

of the track's centre-line. These bands are natural vibrations unseen by the normal eye (diagram 2).

The depth of the central flow will be the same as the radius of the side-bands on the surface. Water has always been so essential to survival that the ability to locate it has been part of all native cultures. The diviner, dowser, priest, shaman or even witch-doctor was the local 'seer' and held in great respect. 'Water' and 'Mother' were synonymous principles since both involved fertility and birth. The water pot was the sacred vessel of the family, a sort of universal grail.

The little pot, shown in diagram 3, lies unrecognised in a provincial Cyprus museum, clearly telling us that these people of 1300 B.C. understood the banding and spiralling of underground water and its relationship to the fecundity of the human female body. Here the five side-bands enclose the lozenges of sacred geometry and the arms spread wide above the right and left-hand spiral of the human female, depicting her life-giving breasts, even suggesting the Fallopian tubes!

Where a flow crosses another flow, i.e., at an underground conjunction point, a force-field sets up a circular pattern on the surface of five concentric rings at a point above the underground crossing point. Where the water does not come through to the surface, this point is known as a blind spring or energy 'riser'. These points were marked with standing stones by S.A.M. (diagrams 4, 5, and 6).

14

Plan View

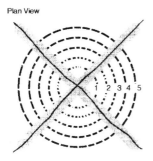

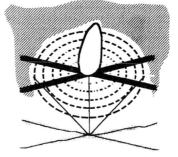

Two underground water courses crossing - produce energy patterns in circles on surface known as a 'riser' or blind spring

Standing stone placed over blind spring to control energy spiral

Diagram 4. *Underground water conjunction.*

When the water from an underground conjunction breaks through the surface as a spring or when a flow issues through rock to form a pool or 'grotto', then in early Christian times these became the Holy Wells. If the water had a strong chemical content some healing attribute was applied, offering seemingly miraculous cures. These wells were often attributed to the Virgin Mary as representing birth and the feminine or to various Saints, female or male.

The Sun's energy changes the polarity of the underground water-flows from day to night, positive to negative, on a mini scale, and from week to week on a larger scale. The Moon also causes changes, with similar influences such as on the tides in the sea; from springs to neaps, high to low water on

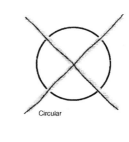

Circular

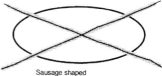

Sausage shaped

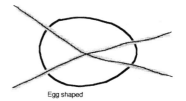

Egg shaped

The conformation of the underground water lines dictate the shape of the energy field in the surface hence the different shapes found at stone circles (Plan View)

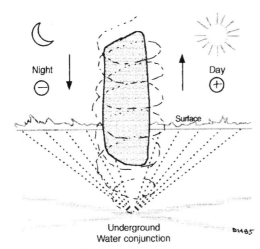

Night ☾ ⊖ ↓

Day ☀ ↑ ⊕

Surface

Underground
Water conjunction

Diagram 5. *Standing stone spiral energy.*

Diagram 6. *Underground water conjunctions producing different shaped energy fields.*

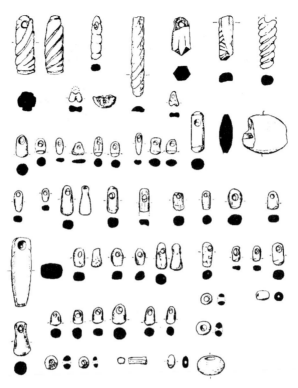

Diagram 7. *Stone Age pendulums from the Irish temple cairns; note spiral engraving* (**Michael Herity**).

a 'moonthly' time-table. All these changes can be easily checked with a pendulum, just as S.A.M. did in the Stone Age to lay out his circles and erect his stones on major energy power points (diagram 7).

As he dowsed a circle of energy, so he was able to build it on the ground with a ring of stones or a bank of earth, now known as a stone circle or a ring fort. At the same time he often incorporated a series of stones in alignments to the rising and setting Sun, known as 'avenues', and also over incoming water lines or magnetic flow lines. By doing this he was able to read the annual cycle and create a calendar to help him in his agricultural and seasonal development, a real Sun and Moon dial.

The late Professor Thom spent his life drawing complex geometric diagrams to fit the shape of these circles. However, he was not a dowser so failed to understand that these shapes were based on round circles and flattened circles or 'egg' shapes and had been effectively dowsed by S.A.M. with his pendulum from confirmation of the patterns of invisible surface energy. These forces form into invisible spirals that perform as energy vibrations from day to night and help to build the grid of the atmosphere. It is these energy vibrations that the dowser picks up – the unseen atomic patterns that surround us all the time in gravity.

Energy builds up in the clouds as electricity $(+)(-)$ and is released as lightning. The Stone Age standing stones and circles acted as conductors, attracting the electricity down into the underground water and activating the

16

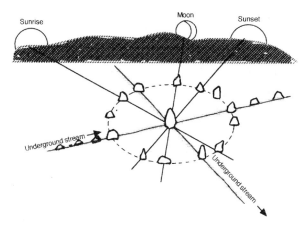

Diagram 8. *Solar and lunar dialling.*

Earth's life-blood. When the water energy became too strong, in turn excess energy naturally flowed back into the atmosphere from the earth to the sky. This 'balancing' of natural energy is fundamental to the fertility of the planet – true metaphysics. This was one way the Druid priests controlled the weather. The energy from underground water rises through S.A.M.'s structures and performs in spirals, from day (+) to night (−), Sun and Moon (diagrams 8 and 9).

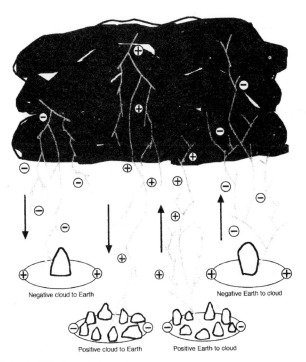

Diagram 9. *S.A.M. using lightning to balance the ecosystem.*

17

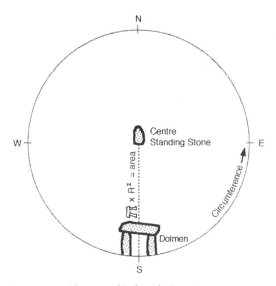

Diagram 10. *The origin of Pi from the Stone Age.*

Colour plate 5 shows the structure of an Earth Star. These natural interconnecting spherical patterns cover the surface of the Earth and can be described as showing the vibrational structure of the atmosphere. When S.A.M. intuited these patterns with his pendulum he often sited a structure at the centre point, perhaps a cairn, standing stone or stone circle. From this centre point he would dowse outwards to the perimeter of the circle and at the southern-most point, the 12 o'clock midday point all year, he would place a 'dolmen'.

The shape of the dolmen as the doorway was later taken into the Greek alphabet as the letter 'Pi' or π. As we know from our education, Pi defines a circle with the equation of Pi $\times$ radius^2 = area (diagram 10). This surely helps us now to comprehend the extraordinary natural ability of our Pagan ancestors to live within the concept of creative unity that has nothing to do with Jesus of Nazareth, yet is an aspect of *'One-ness'*.

Spirals

A spirall, (spelt here with a double 'l' deliberately) looks like this ⊚, and is found engraved over or by water points at ancient sites all over the world. The pendulum will swing in a double spirall thus ⊚⊚: or to the answer of 'yes' or 'no' to any question. Amongst dowsers many different types of pendulums are thought to be effective, from brass to wood and porcelain to plastic, but almost anything will do.

The use of the pendulum is considered by the Christian Church today to be Pagan, yet it was once an essential part of the Christian wisdom tradition; now misunderstood and therefore vilified – although deep within the few true healing ministries of the Church there are still priests who use the pendulum and fully appreciate its God-given gift. If we think of the word 'spirall', it is no more than the double spiral turned vertically to give us the letter S, 'Pi' for the circle fraction, Ra the Sun or giver of life, and 'LL' the Roman numerals for 50/50 or the balance of $(+)(-)$, ⊚, π, ✿, LL.

The Origin of Pendulums

How do we know S.A.M. had any knowledge of the pendulum? Regularly small pendants or pieces of Stone Age 'jewellery' have been found amongst the sparse artefacts removed from megalithic cairns and dolmens. These little pendants are cut and carved in such a way that their use as pendulums is obvious to anyone interested in dowsing. Some of them are even carved with spirals around their body, and when suspended the movement of the positive and negative energy swings the pendulum in circles.

S.A.M. even managed to use natural rock crystal in its true hexagonal form to produce pendulums, as found in dolmens at Carrowmore in Co. Sligo. He usually made his pendulums of steatite, a soft, easily worked form of soapstone or serpentine which has a talc base and is found on the western seaboards of the Atlantic coastline. For the technically minded, the chemical composition of steatite is $Fe_2Mg_3(SiO_4)$. Perhaps it is also significant that the original scarabs of Ancient Egypt – the carvings of the sacred beetle – were made out of this material. The Egyptians used the Ankh and Christians the Cross as pendulums.

Pendulums were used by the priests to plot, measure, geometricise and lay out their structures. In Egypt these instruments were called Merkhets or 'instruments of knowing'. The standard measurement of Neolithic times is now accepted as the megalithic yard of 0.829 metres or 32.64 inches. Later, after the discovery of metal, various measurements were established with the use of peridot, the origins of which are obscure, but peridotite, serpentine and steatite are all of the same material 'family'. Peridot, a crystal of olivine, was mined in Egyptian times on Zogotra (Socotra, S. Yemen) in the Red Sea, later known as St. John's Island in early Christian times.

It seems that the chemical content of steatite, and its next evolutionary crystalline structure as peridot, has built within it a strong basic dowsing force. This unique vibrational response when used in conjunction with various common metals, and put to the vibrations of underground water, produces a beat from the pendulum of various 'spaces'. These spaces have come to be measured and over the millennia have been used by different civilisations as their specific unit.

In the field, by holding a piece of steatite/peridot and the different metal in the left hand and dowsing outwards from the centre line; a centre point of an underground water-flow or conjunction, a response will occur with the pendulum at the appropriate distance. This is a natural dowsing phenomenon and was most secretly held by the ancient priests.

There are seven metals which when used with peridotite give the origins of measurement:

1. **Peridot and gold (Sun)** gives one megalithic yard or 32.64 inches and dowses on white vibrations.
2. **Peridot and silver (Moon)** gives one metre or 39 inches and dowses on red vibrations.
3. **Peridot and tin** gives one Greek foot or 12.15 inches and dowses on yellow-green vibrations.
4. **Peridot and iron** gives one 'remen' or 0.370 metres and dowses on red vibrations.
5. **Peridot and lead** gives one royal cubit or 0.524 metres and dowses on yellow and red vibrations.

6. **Peridot and bronze** gives half a metre or 19.4 inches and dowses on black vibrations.
7. **Peridot and copper** gives the Golden Mean proportion or 1/1.618, demonstrated on the Fibonacci scale of 1.1.2.3.5.8.13.21 etc. Copper dowses in spirals.

Peridot and still water dowses 31.141 metres or Pi × 10.

Peridot and one dewdrop dowses 0.31141 metres or Pi ÷ 10.

On the map, these measurements are achieved by holding the piece of metal and peridot in the left hand and dowsing outwards from the exact centre of the water line to the next swing of the pendulum, or by putting a piece of metal and the peridot on the start of a ruler and a piece of peridot in the left hand and dowsing along the ruler until the next swing indicates a stop point. The 'distance' then read on the ruler will signify the relevant measurement.

Medieval alchemy suggested that the green stone turned base metals into gold – the Philosopher's Stone. The analogy here is that the green stone, peridot, was used in the ancient world as a source of wonder and magic since it produced measurement and therefore facilitated one of the secrets of geometry. Gold has always been a word denoting 'knowledge' in mythology. Hence, 'dross into gold' means turning ignorance into knowledge.

CHAPTER II

The Breath of God

How and Where it all Starts

Let us begin with the origins of our mythology and magic. The Sun is the star of our planetary system, symbolically denoted by a dot within a circle ⊙, representing the source of all life. There are nine major planets orbiting it, of which the Earth is one. Moving outwards from the Sun, the planets in order of distance are as follows: Mercury, Venus, Earth, Mars, Jupiter, Saturn, Uranus, Neptune and Pluto. Each of the planets moves round the Sun with different elliptically shaped orbits and therefore at varying distances (diagram 11).

As the Sun produces heat and light, so it also produces electro-magnetic fields of enormous strength. Each planet travels its own particular path because of these fields and the combined forces of gravity.

The Sun is a ball of thermonuclear atomic fusion brought about by the interaction of hydrogen and helium. On a predictable cycle it releases varying amounts of energy from different areas of its mass, known as sun flares and sunspots; they create the solar wind – the 'Breath of God' in the Book of Genesis.

The beautiful stained glass window from the thirteenth century (colour plate 1) shows 'God' holding the Sun in the shape of an egg in His left hand, the origin of the 'orb' in regalia. With an open right hand, the hand of giving, He blows His creative breath around a plot of the swirling cosmos showing the signs of the Zodiac. This clearly tells us of the Church's interest and understanding of astrology as a part of the ancient mysteries.

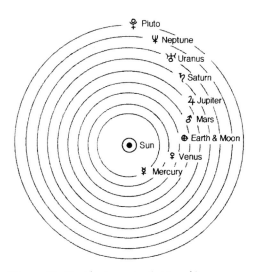

Diagram 11. *Our planetary system (not to scale).*

21

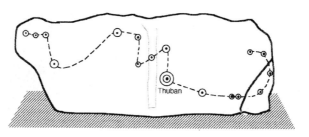

Diagram 12. *The North Star at the time of Newgrange – constellation of 'Draco the Dragon'.*

The relative positions of the planets at the time of our birth must affect life too. Hence the relevance of natal and conceptual astrology. It would be much simpler to comprehend if the Sun was static in the universe, but it is not. The Sun moves in a gigantic orbit pulling its revolving planets along with it. The relationship of the movement of the Sun and the movement of the planets around it as it curves through space is another aspect of the ancient mysteries.

This is such a vast concept that the only way S.A.M. was able to obtain astrological reference points was to choose constellations that were lying far out around the seemingly static periphery of the night sky. So the twelve constellations of the Zodiac became part of the calendar. In 1998 A.D. the Pole Star, Polaris, is our semi-permanent true north reference point, but in S.A.M.'s time, in 3000 B.C. when Newgrange was built, it was in the constellation of Draco, the Dragon (diagrams 12 and 13). This change is due to the movement of the Earth around the Sun combined with the natural tilt of the Earth's axis, and the Sun's movement through the heavens. This causes what is called cyclic precession; each completed cycle around the celestial pole, from start to finish taking 26,163 years.

S.A.M. was aware of this. In 3000 B.C. he engraved the alignment on the back stone of Newgrange with cup (star) marks, to show that at that time the North point was in the constellation of Draconis and that its brightest star was Thuban. We now know that the Egyptians aligned the Great Pyramid to the constellation of Orion, and we will see how the early monks years later also aligned their little churches to star risings and settings. Astronomy was essentially part of the initiation and esoteric training of the priesthood down the millennia.

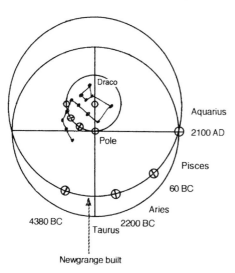

Diagram 13. *Precession and the Zodiac.*

Let us now examine how the Sun affects us here on Earth. As

B&W plate 1. *Newgrange lintle stone – solar rays (**Commissioners of Public Works, Dublin**).*

it rotates, so energy is given off in the form of a solar wind consisting of positive and negative particles that take approximately 48 hours to reach the Earth. Solar wind particles are a by-product of magnetic activity, which arises due to the differential rotation of the polar and equatorial fields.

The Earth is also rotating once round the Sun every 365.242 days. So it has been calculated that every seven days, due to this differential rotation, the Sun's energy hits us with alternating polarity, i.e., positive to negative every week. It is interesting to note that because of this, underground water energies seemingly change polarity every seven days too. This is particularly noticeable along Stone Age 'alignments'.

The Sun's rays contain the necessary energy from within the solar wind to generate life and rebirth throughout the planet. S.A.M. often aligned his ancient structures to the seasons of the Sun – solstices and equinoxes – to 'capture' this energy in his structures and re-energise the earth itself. He engraved the rays of the Sun on his lintle stones with lovely zigzag lozenge wavelength pictures telling us of this (black and white plate 1).

When these rays penetrated deep into the chamber of the cairn they were engraved as the triple spiral of Newgrange. This beautiful engraving (diagram 14) is of the Trinity of the creative breath itself. In India this is drawn as the sign and meditative sound of 'OM', being the three aspects of the Trinity:

Diagram 14. *The Triple Spiral, Newgrange cairn* (**Commissioners of Public Works, Dublin**).

Brahma the creator, Vishnu the holder of reality, and Shiva the destroyer and rebirther.

In Ireland we have a silent secret language called 'Ogam', pronounced 'OM', depicting the same principle (diagram 15). In scientific terms the triple spiral denotes the interweaving DNA up and down the spine – the Kundalini in Eastern mythology. It also denotes the forces of electricity (the Sun), magnetism (the Earth) and light, all interacting as the creative forces of electro-magnetism. In later Christian terms the triple spiral became the Trinity of 'Father, Son and Holy Ghost', whereas it should have been 'Father, Mother and Holy Ghost'; the latter referring to divine 'light'. It also symbolises the conjunction of Sun, Moon and Venus through the sky-light of the cairn.

A change is occurring now, understood and acknowledged by many individuals and groups around the world. This is concerned with the 'New Age', the changeover date reckoned to occur before the end of this century or shortly afterwards – indeed many different cultures have predicted it in their mythology, not least our own with the predictions of early saints such as Malachy and Patrick. This change concerns sunspot cycle activity that happens in intermediate multiples of approximately 1,250 years

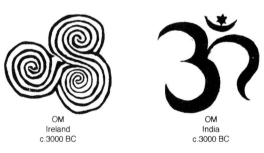

OM
Ireland
c.3000 BC

OM
India
c.3000 BC

'Ogham' or 'Ogam' (the silent 'language') is
pronounced OM in the Irish language

Diagram 15. *The Triple Spiral and the sound of 'OM'.*

24

and is reported in history as the return of a 'comet', known by the Aztecs and Incas as Quetzalcoatl or Kukulcan; even in Irish mythology as the return of the King 'Cuchulain' (1997, Hale Bopp). But perhaps this comet also represents the sudden explosive activity occurring when the solar magnetic fields shift and change positions? Then subsequently the solar wind and flare activity erupts to blast Planet Earth with uncontrollable disruption to the Earth's deep structured fold lines, to the tectonic plates and the earthquake stratas, causing vast fires and explosions – the seeming return of a vengeful 'God'.

Geologists and Astronomers calculate that every 3,500 years the Sun changes its polar tilt or angle of axis – currently $23\frac{1}{2}°$, and we, being directly controlled by solar magnetism, have to follow suit. Planetary pole shifts have occurred theoretically in 1500 B.C., 5100 B.C., 8600 B.C. Mesolithic, 12,150 B.C. Magdalenian II, 15,690 B.C. Magdalenian I, etc., etc., back through time.

The Moon

The Moon is a neutral satellite of the Earth, its path following that of the Earth, and is held in orbit by the strength of gravitational forces. It is a ball of negatively charged volcanic rock, a quarter of our size, about 239,000 miles away, turning on its axis at the same speed as we turn. Hence we only ever see the same face towards us.

The Moon, being the consort of the Earth, reflects the light of the Sun like a solar mirror, and it is the varying amount of sunlight reflected towards the Moon as we both revolve that gives us the different lunar phases during one complete orbit of the Earth. We call this a month or 'moonth' (diagram 16).

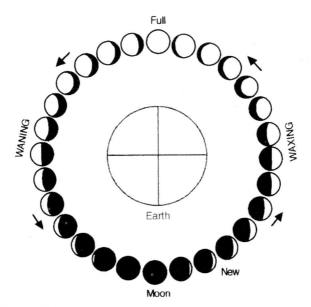

Diagram 16. *The Lunar Cycle.*

As the Sun controls us during the day, so the Sun reflected off the negative Moon influences us at night. Seemingly controlling the night-time growth of nature and the cycles of growth and decay, it also influences the water energies on Earth, the ebb and flow of the tides being obvious examples, as well as female menstruation on a moonthly cycle. When the Moon becomes full, the night-time energy reaches its peak, for the Moon is acting as a full-faced mirror reflecting as much of the power of the Sun as is possible, and for life on Earth this becomes a time of expansion. After a full Moon, the energy drops away, or wanes, towards the next detractive new Moon. These phases are easily calculable.

In mythology, the Moon governs both positive and negative forces because of the effect these phases have on energy levels, and is known to affect electricity, fertility, conception, growth, decline, decay and death, thereby influencing the natural cycles.

Lunar eclipses occur from two to five times a year, when the Moon passes into direct shadow of the Earth with the Sun directly behind it. This is a time of strong negative activity on Earth and lasts for about three and a half hours.

The Sun and Moon Relationships

In mythology, the Sun is masculine and represents the positive male force; the Moon being feminine and negative, represents the female. Both, when working together, nurture and influence the Earth with balance – a duality of energy accepted as pervading all life forms on Earth. This is expressed in the double spiral engravings in Ireland, and as the *yin* and *yang* by the Chinese. The Sun's energy manifests as gold and the Moon's as silver.

The female, or lunar, aspects of life were always seen and appreciated in terms of the fertility of the land and the continuance of the family and the tribe. Hence the glorious fat Rubenesque female figures from the caves of Ice Age France – the vast breasts and the mountainous thighs that suggest infinite resources of power and generation, the Goddess. But unfortunately, somewhere along the lines of time, 'She', the lunar female, has been replaced by the Sun in splendour; the male warrior priest, with his sword of light and shield against the evil of darkness and the Devil – or woman herself. Hence the scheme of patriarchy and male dominance in every walk of life since the last great upheaval, or Sun flare/Sunspot explosions that disrupted our balance in Neolithic times, around 3500 B.C.

The 'Sun God' flared up in power and rage, and the Earth suffered retribution and devastation. As a result we gave the Moon away, pushed her into oblivion and started to worship the Sun to appease it. So the calendar, the annual calculation of the year changed. We and the ancients knew that the Earth takes 365.242 days to travel one orbit of the Sun – a solar year. But this number is impractical to divide up in months, and the twelve months we have now are ridiculously awkward. Possible representations of the solar cycle are illustrated in diagrams 17 and 18.

Diagram 17. *The Fuller Brooch, Anglo Saxon, c.ninth century A.D.* **(British Museum)**.

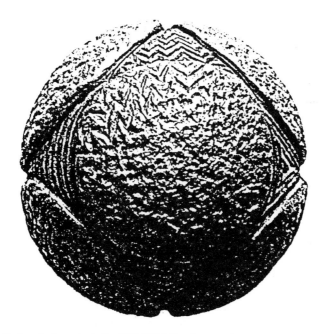

Diagram 18. *Replica of a Stone Age ball, c.3000 B.C.* **(Aberdeen area)**.

The alternative calendars as used by the Ancients, 364, and the Egyptians, 360, were easier and more useful. For example, Robin Heath in *Sun Moon Man Woman* tells us:

The 360 Day Calendar
Egyptian 'Solar' Calendar   360 Implied Structure
12 'Solar' months of 30 days (12 × 30 = 360)
51.428571 weeks of 7 days
36 weeks of 10 days (Egyptian 'Decan' Calendar)
4.28571 weeks in a month
5 intercalary days (6 in a leap year)
A 30 day month approximates to the 29.53 lunation
4 seasons (each 12.857142 weeks) of 91 days
ADVANTAGES: All whole number relationships if used with a 10 day week.

The 364 Day Calendar
Ancient 'Lunar' Calendar   364 Implied Structure
13 'Lunar' months of 28 days (13 × 28 = 364)
52 weeks of 7 days
4 weeks in a month
1 intercalary day (2 every fourth year)
A 28 day month approximates to the lunar orbital period
4 seasons (each 13 weeks) of 91 days
ADVANTAGES: All whole number relationships.

The 365 Day Western Calendar
Roman Gregorian 'Solar' Calendar   365 Implied Structure
12 'Solar' months of average length 30.4166 days
Variable month lengths: 28, 30, 31 days
52.142857 weeks of 7 days
4.34523 weeks in 'average' month
4 seasons (each 13.057 weeks) of 91.25 days
Leap year day (1 every fourth year)
No relationship to the Moon
ADVANTAGES: Only a good alignment to the solar cycle.

It will be seen therefore that the 364 day/night calendar has major recommendations within it, the 28 day month being a happy compromise between the lunation period, 29.53 days and the lunar orbital period of 27.32 days (diagram 19).

Most importantly, the Moon was seen to influence the tides in an extraordinary way, and no doubt the early peoples of north-western Europe on the Atlantic seaboards were able to observe this phenomenon closely. Twice a month, approximately every 14 days, the tides fulfil their cycle of highs and lows in accordance with the phases of the Moon, and twice in 24 hours the tides rise and fall in a constant rhythm. This, coupled with the feminine

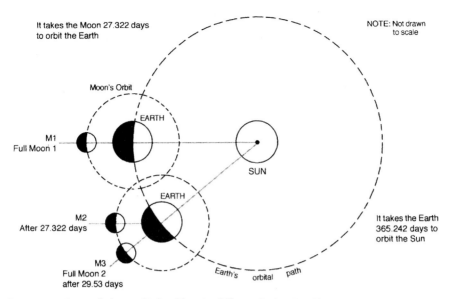

It takes the Moon 27.322 days
to orbit the Earth

NOTE: Not drawn
to scale

Moon's Orbit

EARTH

M1
Full Moon 1

SUN

EARTH

M2
After 27.322 days

It takes the Earth
365.242 days to
orbit the Sun

M3
Full Moon 2
after 29.53 days

Earth's   orbital   path

Diagram 19. *Reasons for lunar orbital and lunation differences* (**Robin Heath**).

menstrual cycle, was accepted as a fundamental natural duality within the feminine psyche, intimately connected to procreation – hence the worship of the woman Goddess of fertility and life. *But* the Old Testament tells us of changing times – times of expulsion, power, and the might of the Assyrians sweeping through the Middle East in the period 1500–500 B.C. – the Greeks and then the Romans.

The old calendar was suppressed and the cult of the Sun: Mithras the Bull, power, might, male domination and control took over, and the irrational and illogical 365 day Roman calendar was imposed. The cult of the 'Messiah', the male saviour as an aspect of a male God, became the idea of salvation to the Jewish people, and Jesus, the Nazarene, took up the challenge.

However, do not think that Jesus did not have a deep knowledge of the mysteries within, as a result of his initiation and training amongst the Essenes. Remember the twelve Disciples represented the annual cycle with 'the Master' as the 13th element of salvation.

There were 12 months (Moons) in the Roman 365 day solar calendar and 13 months (Moons) in the 364 lunar calendar. In numerology, 5 is the marriage of the male (Adam – 3) with the female (Eve – 2), making the 5 vibrations of water and birth on Planet Earth. The resulting triangle is known as the Lunation Triangle (diagram 20). Here, the right-angled triangle has a

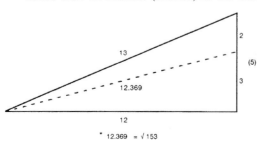

13

2

(5)

3

12.369

12

* 12.369 = √153

Diagram 20. *The Lunation Triangle* (**Robin Heath**).

base of 12 (solar months), a rise of 13 (lunar months) and an end of 5 (2 + 3) The hypotenuse has a value or length of 12.369, which equals the square root of 153.

This is remarkable within itself but now we can appreciate the words of the Gospel:

> **Matthew 18:20** – *For where two or three are gathered together in my name there am I in the midst of them.*

But it should read: 'for where two *and* three are gathered together . . . ', to tell us that Jesus was expressing the principle of the lunation (feminine) triangle and the Ancient calendar rather than the Roman calendar of 365 days in the year.

This makes sense when we also recall *John 21* and the mathematics of Pythagoras. Jesus is on the shore (land) and five named disciples are in the boat. Jesus tells them to cast their net to the right side of the boat – the right side of the brain – the intuitive, feminine side of spirituality and lunality. The net, with its mesh of squares suggests the square root of the 153 (fishes). Two hundred cubits perhaps refers to the Hebrew sacred cubit of 25 inches, so 200 would be 5,000 inches. Remember the feeding of the 5,000 with five loaves and two small fishes with 12 baskets to contain the scraps! (there are two unnamed disciples in the boat as well).

The fact that the 12, 13, 5 (2 + 3) triangle is integral to the construction of Stonehenge, c.2700 B.C., means that the writer of St. John's Gospel had a fine knowledge of metaphysics, as had Jesus himself! (Robin Heath, *Sun Moon Man Woman*).

Planetary Geometry

The paths of the planets together make schematic geometric patterns that seem to conform to the structures of crystals. That the atmospheric imprint and the earthly imprint are both part of our whole creative geometry is not surprising, but the implications of this are stimulating. S.A.M. was aware not only that the planets and the Sun seemingly went around in the heavens, but of planetary alignments at significant points in time.

We know that the completion of a grand cycle of the Sun, beginning at Aries takes approximately 26,163 years. This equinoctial point also marks the start of the annual orbit of the Earth around the Sun through the Zodiac. The planets each have their own corresponding paths and respective distances from the Earth, the Moon being the closest body to our planet, as we have seen taking a lunar moonth, and Pluto, with its uniquely oblique orbit, being the furthest away, taking 248 years to move around the Zodiac.

Saturn, the second largest planet to Jupiter, completes a full circuit every 28 years and 167 days. Jupiter takes about a year to move through one of the signs, and therefore about twelve years to make a complete cycle of the Zodiac. So it moves faster inside Saturn's orbit and is seen to come into line, or conjunction, with Saturn at regular intervals. These two planets represent the two great balancing forces, conservatism and expansion, acting as a link between the inner and outer planets. Diagram 21 shows three Saturn/Jupiter conjunctions

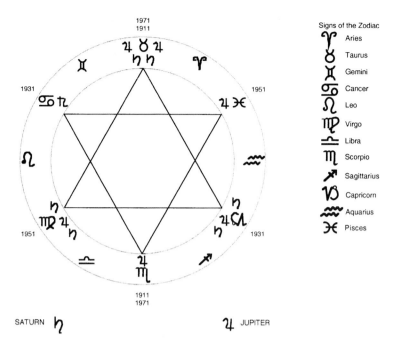

Signs of the Zodiac

♈ Aries
♉ Taurus
♊ Gemini
♋ Cancer
♌ Leo
♍ Virgo
♎ Libra
♏ Scorpio
♐ Sagittarius
♑ Capricorn
♒ Aquarius
♓ Pisces

SATURN ♄   ♃ JUPITER

Diagram 21. *Saturn/Jupiter conjuncts (**Keith Critchlow**).*

taking place in the 'earth' signs at 20 year intervals, as illustrated by Keith Critchlow in his book *Time Stands Still.* It is interesting that we refer to a young man 'coming of age' in his twenty-first year.

CHAPTER III

In the Image of God

Pi and the Vesica Pisces

Whereas Pi (π) defines a circle and was used from the earliest times by S.A.M., so Phi (ϕ) – the Golden Mean proportion – defines the conjunction of two inter-locking circles, the centre of each being the perimeter of the other. When these two circles are put side by side, the overlap between the centres forms an ovoid shape. The shape of this overlap suggests an idea of unity expressing the joining of two worlds between which there is a state of 'One-ness' (diagram 22). The actual proportion is expressed as a fraction, 1/1.618 derived from the one overall conjoining circle shown by the radius of the oblong holding the ovoid. Fibonacci, a thirteenth-century A.D. mathematician, developed this fraction into a pro-gressive expanding spiral scale 1.1.2.3.5.8.13.21.34.55.89.144.233.377.610., etc. After the series has commenced with 1.1 the other numbers are obtained by adding the preceding two together to achieve the next number.

The Fibonacci series as a function of Phi predominates in the growth patterns of nature, plants, shells, flowers; even in the human body itself – for all is ONE. Maurice Cotterell in *Astrogenetics* explains how Phi is the procreative solar fraction. In *Sacred Geometry*, Robert Lawlor says:

> *It is the most intimate relationship, one might say, that proportional existence – the universe – can have with Unity, the primal or first division of 'One'.*

For this reason the ancients called it 'Golden', the perfect division. Christians have related this proportional symbol to the 'Son of God', known as the 'Man-dorla', where Jesus is placed within the ovoid (diagram 23).

However, if we turn the diagram vertically, the central ovoid becomes horizontal – the only way a fish can swim! For now the ovoid gives us the definition of the Vesica Pisces – the fish with its tail swimming from left to right from intellectual-ism towards spirituality – left brain to right brain into 'unity' (diagram 24). Being a fish, it can generally swim in the other direction as well.

Jesus is closely identified in Christian mythology with 'The Fisherman' and in our zodiacal precession we note we are just now passing out of the era of Pisces, the fish, into the New Age of Aquarius due to commence, as has been predicted, sometime early in the next millennium – if precession is correct, in 2126 A.D.

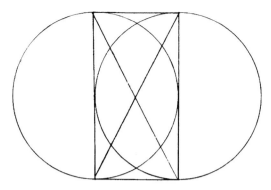

Diagram 22. *The Vesica Pisces.*

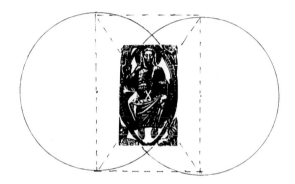

Diagram 23. *The Vesica Pisces with Christ.*

But many predictions have it that the return of the 'Divine' or a higher consciousness will change Planet Earth in 2012 A.D., the so-called 'second coming' or return.

In Irish mythology, there is the magical tale of Fin McCool and 'Fintan', the silver salmon of knowledge (Divine One-ness), and the nine hazelnuts of wisdom – nine being the number of divine inspiration and illumination in esoteric (geometric) lore. The hazel kernel and nut represented the cranium of the brain and are found regularly in Stone Age burials, burnt and broken open, symbolising the release of the soul from the imprisonment of the cycle of life. The soul thus returns, back through fire to 'God', the creative force, the cosmos, divine resurrection and ascension.

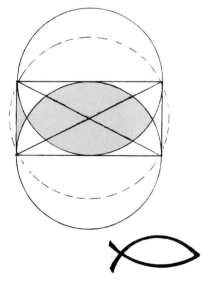

Diagram 24. *The Vesica Pisces – 'The Silver Salmon of Knowledge' and New Age Christian symbol.*

33

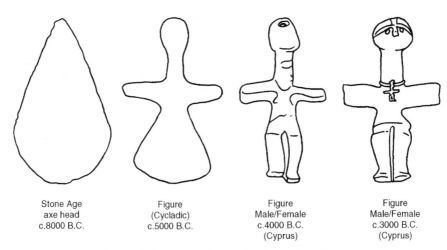

| Stone Age axe head c.8000 B.C. | Figure (Cycladic) c.5000 B.C. | Figure Male/Female c.4000 B.C. (Cyprus) | Figure Male/Female c.3000 B.C. (Cyprus) |

Diagram 25. *The development of 'figures' in ritual objects from the simplest axehead.*

Through many civilisations the expression of divinity, fertility and knowledge has been built into 'cult' figures, as the archaeologists call them. If we can unravel the secrets that those figurines contain, sometimes we can arrive at strange discoveries, showing a startlingly sophisticated consciousness from the past, brought forward into later societies (diagram 25).

Aphrodite, 'Hermaphrodite' of Paphos

Aphrodite, the Goddess of Love, from the Greek 'foam being', originated out of the sea, one of 'her' titles being Anadyomene (rising from the sea). Her attributes were said to be those of the ram, the he-goat, the dove, certain fish, the cypress, myrtle and pomegranate; the animals being a symbol of fertility and the plants a symbol of sterility – a formidable selection of characteristics. In the *Iliad*, Aphrodite was the daughter of Zeus and Dione; in the *Odyssey*, she was the wife of Hephaestus. She was associated with the Moon, fertility of the soil, gardens and seductive beauty.

As usual, behind every myth there is a basic truth hidden from uninitiated sight or understanding. Within the figurines of Aphrodite of early Cyprus lies a beautiful sacred geometry that depicts to the trained eye the basics of form and esoteric science, and the relationship between the circle and the square. These figurines, called Cycladic from the Greek Islands, go back in civilisation to 6000 B.C. in their simplest forms. The figure illustrated (diagram 26) is of limestone, 39.5 cm in height, and dates to 2500–2000 B.C. Found in Cyprus, it is said now to reside in a private collection in Germany. However, there are many less sophisticated figurines in Cyprus museums of a similar style, many of them much older and dating in their cruder, simpler form to the earliest Cycladic figures of 6000 B.C.

It was noted that this figurine had a deeply significant inner meaning beyond the obvious male-female form – the essence of Aphrodite being associated with the Moon as the female aspect and the Sun as the male, symbolising the Earth. This suggests an inherent secret built into the shape of the object. Peter Dawkins, an architect and brilliant draughtsman, also an elder of the Gatekeeper Trust, stepped in to help and his interpretation of the Hermaphrodite of Paphos is set out for us in Appendix A. Similarly, the Moon's intimate geometric connection with the Earth is also built into the proportions of the Great Pyramid of Cheops (diagram 27).

Let us go back to the Vesica Pisces in vertical dimension and superimpose upon it the 'woman' figure similar to the figure of a man, drawn by Leonardo da Vinci, with arms outstretched within a circle. If we use the base of the body as the centre of the lower circle and the crown of the head as the centre of the higher circle, the body of 'woman' fits neatly into the horizontal ovoid of the 'Salmon of Knowledge' – the body of illumination (diagram 28).

Next, impose the pyramidic proportion of the Moon and the Earth over the figure using the head as the Moon, and we see how wo-man reflects the feminine principle in the head of the figure, just as in 'Hermaphrodite'. Surely this helps us to recognise the feminine capacity for compassion and fertility as the balancing energy to the male sexuality encapsulated in the base of the spine and actuated in life through the male (sexual) ego. Both aspects are inherent in each gender, but

Diagram 26. 'Hermaphrodite' of Paphos – limestone cruciform figure from Cyprus (**Private collection**).

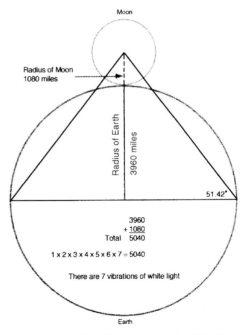

Diagram 27. *The Pyramid proportions* (**John Michell**).

35

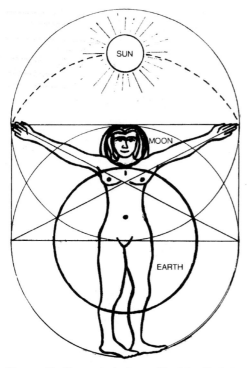

only work happily together through self-realisation of divine responsibility and unity.

Sun and Moon, male and female – hermaphrodite indeed.

Human Energy Fields – The Aura

Much has been written about the invisible energy field that surrounds the human body and the bodies of all living things. A book much quoted from is *Hands of Light*, depicting how this energy field fluctuates with physical, emotional and mental activity, and states of health. The shape of the aura around the upright wo-man is similar to the ovoid of the upright Vesica Pisces and so was used in Christian symbology around the Christ figure as we have noted.

Diagram 28. *Wo-man in the image of Sun/Moon/Earth proportions.*

Kirlian photography is the photography of unseen energy fields that emanate from the human body either as the aura or, as here (diagram 29), the 'feathers' of energy that extend from the fingers of activated hands;

Diagram 29. *'Healing Hands' (**Kirlian photography**).*

36

perhaps in 'blessing' or the 'laying on of hands' in Christian healing terminology. Ideally these 'feathers' should all extend the same length and be unbroken around the fingers and palms. Where there are 'spots' of energy rather than 'feathers', this denotes small concentrations of toxins in the hands and therefore reflects the whole body. These can be eliminated and transmuted by perhaps change of diet and physical exercise. The 'feather' energy can be transferred from one person, the healer, to another, the patient, by good intent in the elimination of pain, emotional or mental stress, and in a purely physical way to alleviate the growth of tumours or septic wounds. The possibility of renewal was practised by Jesus in the healings recorded in the Bible, and today, everyday, by enlightened beings throughout the globe. Herein lies the infinite reassurance of the divine powers of the cosmic Christ energy that a human being can facilitate (diagram 30). It is this complete miracle healing that all healers aspire to and that lies dormant within us all, as we are all 'of God'. In humility, 'we' ask for grace to help others, to repair others, to heal others, but it is only with no expectation, i.e., no ego, that results are possible, and often the results are totally unexpected anyway.

The human energy field is subject to many levels of interpretation depending on the ability of the clairvoyance of the observer. Basically, it consists of three levels out from the physical layer of the skin (diagram 31). The first level is normally about six inches deep in a healthy person. This is called the pranic or physical level, and reflects the physical state of the person. The next level is the emotional aura, extending beyond the pranic, usually by about a further foot

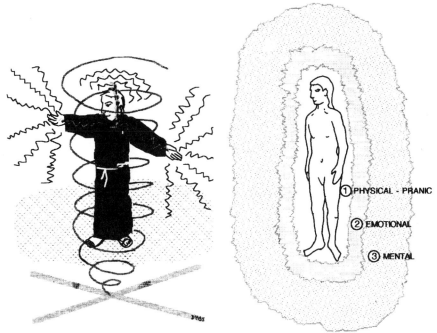

Diagram 30. *'Priest blessing his flock' standing on blind spring energy 'riser'.*

Diagram 31. *The human aura.*

to eighteen inches, and this reflects our general sympathetic state – happiness, unhappiness, relationships (not least with ourselves), hopes and desires. Outside this, and stretching to the limits of our own envelope, is the mental aura, extending a further two to three feet outwards. Here, our conscious mind actuates our thinking processes, and the higher and lower principles of how we lead our lives. This includes our belief patterns, faith and higher aspirations. Outside this is Atma-universality. The three envelopes, although defined and seen separately for diagnostic purposes, are of course intimately connected and interweave within themselves. They can therefore be seen as just one field of varying colours or spectrums at different points of the body, denoting perhaps an area of ill health or potential disease.

A deeply clairvoyant observer will be able to read much more obscure and sensitive aspects of a person's 'history' through time, from birth to present age; even possible future events as well as retrospectively into past incarnations. This is because within the spectrum of the aura is imprinted the current physical history of this lifetime on a conscious level and previous existence of the soul on the sub-conscious level. There is nothing clever in this as it is just another gift 'of God' available to all human beings, through objective love and pure spiritual practice, and is not exclusive in any way to Christians.

The Chakra System

Within this auric field of the human envelope lie the energy centres of the body itself, centres that again reflect the state of being of wo-man. There are seven energy centres, directly related to the seven vibrations of light that we see in the rainbow, or the splitting of white light, sunlight through a prism or crystal. These centres (diagrams 32 and 33) from the base chakra upwards are:

1. **Red** – of spine sexual areas and evacuatory systems.
2. **Orange** – stomach area and digestion.
3. **Yellow/Gold** – solar plexus, the reflection of the Sun itself in our digestive areas.
4. **Green** – heart and chest, reflecting the whole of the nature aspect of unconditional love.
5. **Blue** – throat area where we communicate our thoughts.
6. **Indigo** – forehead at the frontal lobes of the brain (pineal gland).
7. **Violet** – crown or top of the head in the area of the anterior fontanel (pituitary gland).
8. **White/Clear** – when all these centres are working together in harmony, then this raised consciousness manifests as a field of white light above the head.

These energy centres appear to clairvoyant sight as swirling vibration, standing out from and within the physical body. They tell us of the state of each of the organ centres they represent and may appear clear, sparkling or translucent, or perhaps show a dull, grimy, lifelessness, denoting the nature of the ill health of the individual. We can change each of these centres individually (or collectively) to improve our state of health and general 'well being', obviously through diet

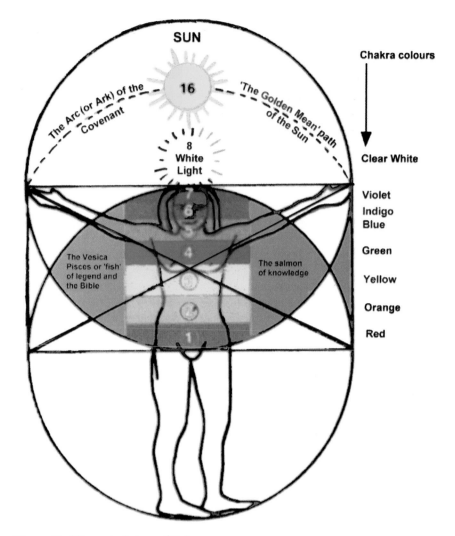

The following labels appear in the diagram:

SUN

16 (within the sun)

The Arc (or Ark) of the Covenant

'The Golden Mean' path of the Sun

8 White Light

Chakra colours

Clear White

Violet
Indigo
Blue

Green

Yellow

Orange

Red

The Vesica Pisces or 'fish' of legend and the Bible

The salmon of knowledge

Diagram 32. *'Wo-man in the image of God'.*

and abstinence from alcohol, drugs, nicotine, coffee, tea or any mood altering substance. Emotionally we can undo the knots of stress we create through our relationships, our jobs and social life. Similarly, when in tune mentally with both the preceding states, we can connect to our higher chakras through our expression of thought, word and deed. When all the seven 'internal' or body centres are cleaned up and working well, and our aura and envelope is also showing a healthy, happy prism, then we will be in good health, with optimum energy levels, happy in ourselves, and will feel good and generally stand out from our fellows. Hence the parable of the Seven Wise and Seven Foolish Virgins and their (chakra) lamps, Salome and the Dance of the Seven Veils, Snow White and the Seven Dwarfs, etc.

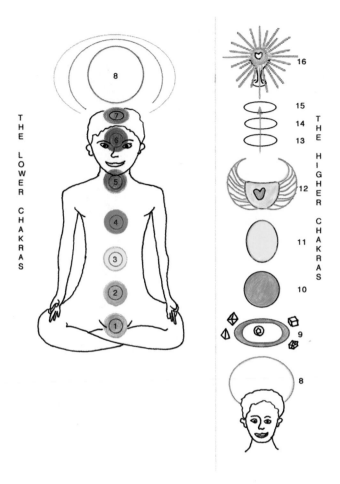

Diagram 33. *The chakras of wo-man – the eight-fold path of enlightenment/Kundalini* (**Fountain International, Amsterdam Group, Holland**).

These chakras have been drawn in Eastern philosophy with many different geometric shapes. Here in the West, in our early Christianity, we drew them reflecting a pattern directly from the Stone Age and Druidic lineage as the spiral or the double spiral, showing a balance of positive and negative force. The highest vibration is the open crown, depicted as the triple spiral, again suggesting both positive and negative and balance.

Kundalini Energy

When we look at the swirling energy rising and falling through the early standing stones, we see how the spiral of positive and negative actuates from the Sun and Moon every day and night – thereby creating a balance in the weather and the natural realms. Similarly, the chakra system of the human body walking

40

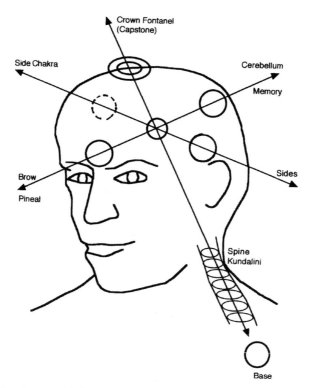

Diagram 34. *Three-dimensional chakras.*

upright like a standing stone actuates in the same way. The base chakra of our spine contains a pool of cerebrospinal fluid that, when activated through right practice and meditation, courses up the body; up the spine to flood the brain or crown chakra with shattering vibration (diagram 34).

This energy in Eastern terminology is the Kundalini or the rising entwined snake, both positive and negative, that normally lies trapped in the base. Most people only experience a very limited aspect of this sensation in their whole lives through sexual activity at orgasm, as most orgasms only take place in the base area. However, this Kundalini energy is like the release of a massive vibrational event that floods the whole being or body with a shattering experience. It can be likened to the rise of the phoenix, the primal fire of the deep inner 'self', and often gives the individual an incredible sensation of power and wonder.

The beautiful Christ figure (cover and diagram 35), follows directly the form of Aphrodite from 3,500 years previously. It is taken from a small Christian bronze Psalter cover in the National Museum of Ireland, dating from about 700 A.D. Here we see the double spiral of the solar plexus, the heart and the throat; even the tiny lamp of the heart between them, clearly showing us that the early Celtic Christians understood and worked with the chakra system and the Kundalini energy. But really startling is the triple spiral above the

41

Diagram 35. *Christ and the Triple Spiral* (**National Museum of Ireland**).

open crown, telling us that those early monks had a direct connection with the principles of their Stone Age ancestors. Early Christianity and the Stone Age were not therefore separated by dogma or centralised Roman power. It is clear that the principle of 'OM', the breath of God, was understood and used as a symbol to describe creation and action in daily life.

This work of art is perhaps one of the most important pieces from the early Christian era, as it gives us a direct key into the thinking and healing practices of those times.

About seven years ago, a group of social workers in the Orkney Islands of Great Britain accused several families of 'Satanic practices' and forcibly removed some seventeen small children from their parents, on the premise that these children were at risk of Satanic abuse. The reason for this traumatic action was the discovery in their homes of a plastic replica, simulating black Irish bog oak, of this little Christ figure. It seems that no-one in the Health Authority had any idea as to the figure's deep Celtic Christian origin. Had this been the case, perhaps the resultant pain and distress caused by such ignorance might never have taken place. Subsequently, several years later, the authorities returned the unhappy children from 'care' to their deeply bewildered and angry parents. Further comment seems irrelevant now.

When Adam and Eve were innocent in the garden of Eden, no doubt sexually aware in a normal 'animal' sense, they were tempted by 'the snake', the rising Kundalini energy, depicted in Genesis, the ancient book of beginnings, as an offering of the fruit of the tree, symbolised by the 'apple'; as a fruit of beauty, richness, colour and, through its seeds, procreative potential. Suddenly, the sexual act became a source of immense beauty and power as a man and a woman were able to make love, for reasons other than

ADAM   **EVE**

Diagram 36. *Adam and Eve, the Tree, the Snake and the 'Apple'.*

procreation, and together enjoy the incredible fulfilment of the rising Kundalini, thereby achieving that wondrous mutual loving event of a joint crown chakra orgasm. The snake had risen – the Kundalini released, and wo-man became aware of both the duality and the singularity of the creative impulse of the 'Gods'. Wo-man became 'One'. The snake is depicted even now as the sign of Mercury or Hermes, the Messenger of the Gods, and on the staff of the medical profession as the Caduceus rising to a winged figure – the release of energy from the base to the crown into the cosmos itself (diagram 36).

When a man and a woman – a wo-man – achieve such a gift through chance or right practice, their lives change as they become aware of their deep responsibility in sexual practice and the fundamental truth of marriage as monogamous – something not to be played with or wasted superficially – the virgin relationship of monogamy. Beyond duality, it is said of spiritual marriage, 'one plus one do not make two – but ONE'.

Virgin birth has always fascinated people, particularly concerning the birth of Jesus and the Virgin Mary. As Peter Dawkins tells us:

Virginity referred to the growth of a boy or girl, i.e., before puberty. It could refer to the unmarried state or to a marriage of pure love between both partners. The ideal marriage therefore was considered to be a virgin marriage – a marriage of pure, fulfilled love.

43

There was the idea of virginity as being that of a girl who had not yet attained puberty. Her virginity would thus end in menstruation, her first period. If the first blood had not appeared when the girl was betrothed or married, even after sexual intercourse, she remained technically a virgin. Many girls were married before puberty was reached. If the girl bride then conceived a child on her first ovulation, that is without ever having had a menstrual period, then her child was known as the child of a virgin conception, and when born, as the child of a virgin birth.
(Peter Dawkins, *The Virgin Ideal.*)

Eastern religions practice sex deliberately to use the Kundalini energy as a way to achieve heightened spiritual awareness and also to connect with the principles of reincarnation. This practice is called Tantra, the act sometimes depicted as sexual 'art' between the 'Prince' and the 'Princess' mutually offering each other food and drink (sacrament) whilst making love. It is based on the concept of aspiring consciously to the yin/yang levels of expression, ascending through the seven chakras by way of sensual pleasure ultimately to reach a synthesis with the divine.

This principle is fine in essence if it is indulged in with mutual love and understanding. But unfortunately many people in the West have discovered the use of hallucinatory drugs and chemical damaging substances that distort the sexual appetite and the functions of the brain, to the extent that we now read regularly of gross and horrific crimes of a sexual style being perpetrated in groups or on children. This drug related release of the Kundalini is obviously not the force of the God-given love we are meant to enjoy to further the divine objective expression of life. It is simply the instant gratification of our lower self through the exercise of the male orientated sexual ego, demonstrated in its most gross form. It is this aspect of our sexuality that received the wrath of God when 'it', addressing the snake said, 'on thy belly shall thou go all the days of thy life' – the ultimate karmic punishment of regressing in evolutionary terms to our basic instincts. When St. Patrick banished the snakes out of Ireland, the purpose was to stop the Druidic practice of raising the Kundalini in order to achieve power. After Patrick, this was a privilege for the ordained priesthood only.

Now perhaps the reasons for the vow of celibacy within the more recent priesthood are explainable. It is possible for a man or a woman in isolation to raise the Kundalini energy up their spine through controlled sexuality, i.e., masturbation, thereby exploding personal energy up to, and through, the crown chakra. But this singularity and self-indulgence is not acceptable to the principles of 'Divine Inspiration' through the principles of duality and ulti-mately into *Trinity* – positive and negative balance – the 'Triple Spiral' and the 'Om' of creation.

Self-gratification through masturbation, either male or female, priest or nun, was therefore considered to be devilish and punishable with dire disciplinary action in the early monasteries, yet at the same time has always been a common, human and 'priestly' practice. The lie that the Church has perpetrated through many centuries of its personal God-realised chastity has been hideously exposed in the last few years through the media in the West. We have repeatedly been told of defiling sexual practices within the priesthood, in total default of ordained vows. It is not necessary to detail any of the style of these common abuses that have occurred with regularity down many centuries, for they are well proven and the Church's karmic debt is now being paid as it falls from grace.

The cover-up has been continued from one generation of Christian priests to the next, because the 'sins of the Fathers' were vested in the subsequent 'Fathers'. It is only now that the karmic law of 'an eye for an eye and a tooth for a tooth, vengeance is mine', saith the Lord, is being worked out, and all those years of pain and original sin are being finally exposed. The Church cannot excuse it, or plead human weakness, and will not survive it, because together with its financial and social shenanigans, it is now seen to be a very rotten apple.

Once the Kundalini is raised up through the crown chakra, through, by comparison, the cap-stone of the cairn or cranium, then meditative energy can begin to meld with universal consciousness and the Christ consciousness. However, it must be totally understood that the Christ consciousness is not exclusive in any way to Christians. It is the consciousness of the principle of cosmic 'One-ness' that is available to any human being of any colour, race or creed, religion or atheism; for it is the energy of life itself and never exclusive.

This energy even pulsates through the standing stones, which in their own way have a consciousness, as does anything existing by virtue of its very God-given existence, activated by the Sun and the Moon from day to night. The engraving shown in diagram 37 is on a standing cross near Colon in Co. Louth. It clearly shows an Eastern connection – the hand held up in blessing surrounded by nine spirals of the Sun with the Trinity of the three heads on the upright area, entwined with the two coiling snakes of the Kundalini. This picture could well have been taken straight off the wall of a Hindu temple, depicting the divine principle that pervades all things.

This concept has nothing to do with the later Christian dogma of Paganism, guilt and sin, or the

Diagram 37. *Standing cross-rising Kundalini snakes, three heads and the Hand of God, c.eleventh century (**Monasterboice, Co. Louth, Ireland**).*

45

worship of the tortured body of a man on a Roman Cross. We might just as well worship the emaciated victim of a Nazi concentration camp and be made to feel guilty for the excesses of that hideous regime. For what reason do we still perpetuate the horror of the Cross when the whole principle of Jesus' path to the Cross was an expression of his love and personal sacrifice as the return of 'the Messiah' to fulfil a Jewish prophecy? Behind all the misinterpretations and screens that the early writers and translators have deliberately pulled over our eyes, is the abiding principle of love. As found in all of nature, He asks us to express this love through 'ourselves', to recognise 'One Kingdom' in humble simplicity and forgiveness.

Diagram 38. *St. Andrew Santiago de Compostella – jewelled aura.*

The cloud of white energy shown in colour plate 2, is the Kundalini released through the capstone of the human skull 'cairn', the cranium of the brain where the release point is the fontanel. This little doorway to the realms of the upper chakras is normally closed-over six months after birth, when the baby has built-up its armour of light, its 'aura', as a self-protecting shield against external psychic attack, and as a natural energy field emanating from the physical body outwards (diagram 38).

Once the energy of the Kundalini has risen and opened our crown chakra, then we can invite the energy of higher consciousness or 'guidance' as it is termed, to enter into us. That is when it is necessary for wo-man to start consciously asking for 'help': an audience, voice, vision or telepathic communication. If we sit in meditation, the highest point to which we can raise our Kundalini, until it is fully open, is to the eighth chakra; into that swirl of white or clear energy seen as a halo.

The Eighth Chakra and Beyond

Above the eighth chakra is a ladder of higher chakras that are a recapitulation of our eight chakras, descending from the divine source of the 16th Chakra to the eighth, i.e., to meet in this sphere of our earthly vibration. Neither standing stone nor wo-man will start to operate as catalyst or guardian between

46

Heaven and Earth until this 'traffic' is in two-way flow, up and down, joining to and from the very essence of life itself.

The higher chakras rise up above the crown, beginning with the eighth chakra, and on up 'the ladder' as it was called in early Christianity (diagram 33). This ladder has always been there, ever since Adam and Eve erected it by eating the apple and opening the door. It has been called 'Jacob's ladder', and is depicted as the pathway to heaven. As we progress in meditation, so we experience each of these chakras in turn, and can begin to use them as an energy force in healing – personal, physical, emotional, mental and planetary.

Perhaps an older couple, man and woman not able to have children due to age, but still wishing to express their love-making in cosmic terms, but not in a sexual way, can raise their energies up through the chakras and envisage the birth of an etheric, or cosmic child. This birth of an angelic vibration that is conceived in love, above the necessity of physical union, is activated by the longing to join once again to the cosmic realms through meditation.

In the Old Testament we are told of the prophets ascending to the mountain top to commune with 'God'. Also, in the New Testament, Jesus goes to the top of the mountain into 'the clouds' to receive instruction from 'my Father which is in Heaven'. Although many hermits and spiritual people have ascended mountains to seek enlightenment, this climb is only an analogy of the individual entering into trance meditation and raising the Kundalini into the 8th and 9th chakras. The cloud of knowing (perhaps 'unknowing') is the auric field released by this meditation through which the participant can begin to talk psychically with his or her aspect of 'God'.

Each year, in the west of Ireland on the last Sunday in July, Garland Sunday, many thousands of Catholics make a devout pilgrimage to climb the Holy Mountain, Croagh Patrick, in Co. Mayo. This journey represents 'the outward expression of (seeking) an invisible truth', by way of 'the path'. It is the expression of an internal discipline no longer taught by the Church; we have been taught to think of God as external, at the top of an inaccessible place where penance has to be observed in the approach. Hence many pilgrims climb bare-footed to receive Mass at the summit. Again, the Church sets itself up as the higher authority, inaccessible in its mystery and magic. We mere mortals have to suffer pain to approach the Deity.

When Jesus went into the desert for forty days and forty nights (probably to Qumran) he went to be instructed and initiated by the Essenes into the realms of 'God', and to practice trance meditation into the 8th, 9th and higher chakras. Forty days are forty positives, forty nights are forty negatives. Forty divides a circle (the circle of reality) into ninths. Nine is the number of higher initiation. Likewise St. Patrick supposedly climbed Croagh Aigle, the mountain of the eagle (the royal kingly bird), to meditate for forty days and nights. Do not think for a moment this was an expression of time and physicality – it is the biblical way of disguising truth and esoteric teaching in the riddle of what is called a *pesher*, as Barbara Theiring tells us in *Jesus the Man*.

The eighth chakra is represented by an eight-pointed star, and was used by the Knights' Templar as an emblem and symbol of their initiatory and belief

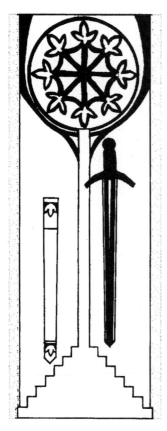

Diagram 39. *The Grail Cup and Sword*
(Andrew Sinclair).

patterns of knowledge and wisdom. They called the eight-pointed star within that energy field 'The Grail Cup' – enlightenment achieved by the knight through his vows of poverty, obedience and chastity within the strictures of the order of Christian chivalry. The order had been founded supposedly to recapture the holy city of Jerusalem from the infidel, the Moslems, and to restore the holy of holies back into the faith. The Crusades were mounted from Europe to achieve this in the twelfth and thirteenth centuries A.D. Each knight started at the lowest grade of initiation, but as he progressed and earned his way up the ladder of initiation, so he was taught the higher mysteries on a spiritual level.

We have a picture of the 'Grail Cup' and the eight-pointed star, with its central rose representing the sacred heart of the Virgin Mary, together with the ladder of initiation, as seen on the grave slabs of Templars in the thirteenth century (diagram 39).

The Grail Cup has a stepped base. Sometimes three, but usually seven steps, representing the base of one of the pillars of the original Temple of Solomon – the ancient hall of wisdom pre-dating Christianity. The seven steps also denote, mythologically and spiritually, the seven chakras from base to crown, represented by the stem or spine of the cup rising straight up the centre of the slab. On the right of the cup is the knight's sword, unsheathed, and pointing downwards. This signifies the shaft of divine light that enters the crown chakra to fill the knight with divine wisdom and knowledge of 'God' and the Kingdom. The sword, as a brand of light from above, shines into the realms of the density of this worldly state of ego and chaos to dispel ignorance and, in this case, the Infidel.

The sword, known also as a 'brand', also refers to a torch. In the Iron Age, the chieftain, or local 'king', always had a brand burning outside, or in his 'hall' or 'hostel', to demonstrate with fire that he was alive and in residence. When the king died, the brand was extinguished, just as after King Arthur died his sword, Excalibur, was thrown into the lake. But this is only an analogy to the extinguishing of his brand. In fact, his *torch* was thrown into the lake to put out the light, denoting his death. The name Excalibur, so Flavia Anderson tells us in *The Ancient Secret*, is a derivation of Ex-Kylie-Pur, which translates into 'out of a cup – light'. Once again the Grail Cup becomes a means of producing divine or celestial light – fire – out of the polished bowl of the silver chalice,

Plate 1. *'Breath of God', c.thirteenth century A.D. church window (Suffolk).*

Plate 2. *The eighth open crown chakra (author).*

Plate 3. *The Nanteous Cup (Private collection).*

Plate 4. *The Ardagh Chalice, Irish, c.eighth century, A.D. (National Museum of Ireland, Dublin).*

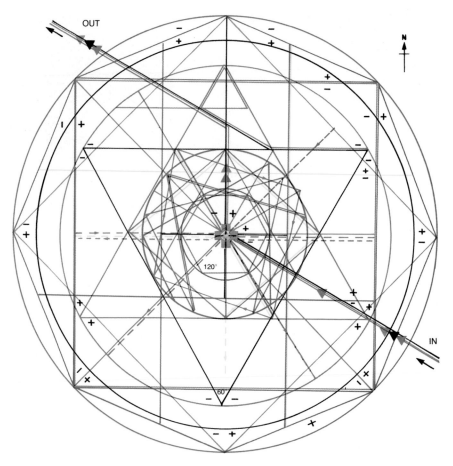

Plate 5. *The Earth Star complete – atomic 'squaring' of the circle (Clive Beadon)*.

Plate 6. *An example of open head side chakras (author).*

Plate 7. *The Gallarus Oratory, Co. Kerry, Ireland (Insight Photographic).*

Plate 8. *The Tara Brooch (National Museum of* Ireland, Dublin).

Plate 9. *'The Arrest of Christ' (Book of Kells,* Board of Trinity College, Dublin).

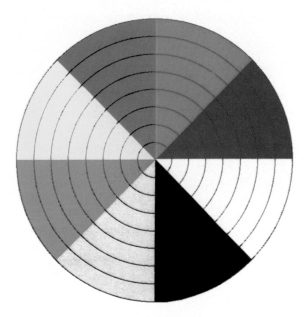

Plate 10. *The Majer Colour Wheel (Henri Majer).*

Plate 11. *The Spiral of Tranquility & Pendant (Clive Beadon, Geoffrey King* and Michael Poynder).

made deliberately into a parabolic shape. It can direct and concentrate the Sun's rays, seemingly magically and invisibly, to kindle a fire, or the candles on the Easter altar, from the Sun's rays beaming through the window.

The populace viewed the priest's ability to produce fire using such a lens, reflector, or mirror, as an act of great magic and power, demonstrating his high initiated status. The drawn sword therefore represented the power of the illuminated server and the divine light of, in this case, the Christ – a weapon indeed.

On the left of the diagram, the scabbard is shown open and empty – the knight has been initiated, drawn his sword and embarked on the journey of Christian spiritual purpose that he and his fellow Templars see as divine and unassailable. Through following the Jesus story in the Bible, their great journey to rescue the holy shrine and the relics of the Crucifixion is paramount. They must find and bring away the cup, the shroud and the lance, all so precious, to validate their order. The fact that the Moslems were also embarking on a similar march of their armies to defend the rock at Jerusalem because they, in their worship of Allah, felt the same way, was unfortunate and perhaps today we'd say unnecessary. But in those days there was no communication system and West and East were in no way reconciled any more then than they are today, 800 years after the Crusades – Christianity and Islam, both defeating themselves through fundamentalism.

Another revelation of the eight-pointed star is that it represents the Tibetan Wheel of the year and the seasons – the annual cycle of nature that gives us our food and crops, our sunshine and rain. The longest and shortest day of the year, the equinoxes – the days of equal sunlight and darkness, and the four inter-mediary quarter days that are the eight formative points in the cycle of nature. So not only is the Grail Cup the open human eighth chakra, but it is also the cycle of nature that we, as human beings of any race, culture, religion or creed, are inseparable from.

The higher chakras have been dowsed, felt by hand and seen psychically and clairvoyantly. The dimensions, colours and distances between the chakras are different for each person, but are in general similar. All chakras have a three-dimensional form, and extend beyond the third dimension into timelessness (diagram 33). The higher chakras can be described as follows:

8th Chakra – The chakra of the Higher Self, the Spirit, the Christ conscious-ness. A sphere of blue-white light with hundreds of points in all directions. First manifested as a three to twelve-pointed star, and the eight-pointed star of the Knights' Templars. Out of this chakra, healing through pure love is possible.

9th Chakra – A golden, oval ring, with the longer sides wider than the shorter sides. Inside the ring, three-dimensional forms appear, one at a time, represent-ing the five elements. The form pictured within the ring represents spiritual power, the binding element, the essence, the dodecahedron. Around the ring the other elements are drawn: earth, water, air, fire. According to some, this chakra is the archetype of the self. Psychics can see a damaged ring in case of illness or ailment. Spiritual healers can apply healing here. The five Platonic solids (tetrahedron, octahedron, icosahedron, cube and dodecahedron) represent the building blocks of reality and the life force.

10th Chakra – Round this sphere, blue cord-like shapes are moving in a jerky way. This chakra is considered the archetype of the Earth, and suggests our unbreakable connection with Mother Earth and our responsibility for 'her', for Gaia – the Goddess.

11th Chakra – An opaque yellow egg. The archetype, symbolising one's connectedness and relationship to the ubiquitous cosmic consciousness. Does this egg perhaps announce the birth of a cosmic wo-man?

12th Chakra – This golden winged chalice form reminds us of the legendary Grail, which is supposed to represent the synthesis of the male and female principle, the alchemistic idea of the androgyn, a hermaphrodite. Only when a man accepts the female counterpart in his being, or a woman the male counterpart, may access be gained to the higher chakras and the consciousness levels belonging to them.

13th, 14th & 15th Chakras – These were seen in November 1987 as oval shapes, black interior with small blue-white star pinpoints flashing on and off. At the beginning of 1988 the forms were filling in, in a magnified way.

13th Chakra – In this oval with an outer tooth-like structure, 21 petals or feathers can be found, surrounding another similar oval with a multi-coloured Sun in the centre. This chakra is seen as the female creative energy of Earth's reality, revered in all religions as the Goddess-Mother. We are genes of Isis, or Genesis. This aspect is the archetype of 'all that was and will be'. Thus the ancients knew her as Isis, goddess with the thousand names: Astarte, Athena, Diana, Quan Yin, etc.

14th Chakra – This chakra seems to represent the paradise of an un-corrupted state of wo-man. We interpret this as the Ideal, the perfect form of Being.

15th Chakra – This chakra would represent the Adam and Eve state of man, but now as a unity before the separation of the sexes. According to the evangelist Philippus, it was this separation that brought us death. The 13th is associated with Isis, while the 15th is associated with Nephthys, her sister in the Egyptian Pantheon. Think of the myth of Osiris, hacked to pieces, and Isis bringing all the parts together except for one.

16th Chakra – A white, light-emitting sphere, with bright rays. This chakra would represent the force that creates reality and maintains it. By bringing consciousness to this level, wo-man is supposed to be able to participate in influencing karma, in unison with the totality of the cosmos in all dimensions.

So Osiris is complete again, and creates the Grail Cup, overflowing with light and love.

Meditation therefore provides the gateway to our inner spiritual self, leaving the ego behind. Sometimes we sit patiently, week by week, raising our energy up the spine, up the Kundalini pathway through our crown chakra. This is the normal state of meditation through which many people find great help in stabilising their emotions.

However, as we have seen, there is a higher realm with chakras nine to sixteen. This is the connection to our higher consciousness – where human and

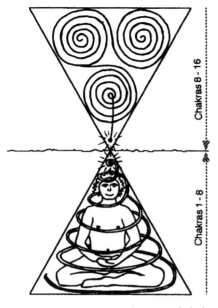

Diagram 40. *Wo-man in meditation with higher powers.*

Diagram 41. *Wo-man 'illumined' – 'I and my Mother/Father are One'.*

universal realms meet at a level between chakras eight and nine (diagram 40). It is a sort of barrier that can only be crossed when we 'ask' for further help by way of teaching and learning. Awaiting us in this realm are the guides and soul energies that have already passed on through death into 'light'. They cannot come down to us as they are lighter in vibration than our physical form, restrained by its earth-bound disrupted magnetic density. We therefore have to aspire to and create the necessary 'lightness' in our meditation to ask 'them' to join 'us'. They can then descend through sixteen, into eight-seven-six-five-four-three-two-one, into our very being to instruct, help and heal us.

When inner illumination occurs, we seem to be connected to a shaft of white light that descends through our crown chakra and floods our inner self (diagram 41). This is 'the road to Damascus' experience of the 'Divine' entering into our being; the shaft or sword of light – light into matter – that begins our own personal illumination and heralds a new phase in our spiritual understanding and work of service to others. At this stage, we lose all sense of attachment and ego and communication can begin between the lower and higher selves, either through symbology or direct voice:

'I and my Father/Mother are ONE'
or 'As above, so below'.

51

CHAPTER IV

Magical Gemstones

Quartz and Rock Crystal

Quartz is a white stone looking like hunks of gleaming white cheese that occurs in blocks and seams in granite. Sometimes it also contains wisps of gold within its cracks – quartz and gold are called gold ore. Quartz has been found throughout the world and has been incorporated in many ancient structures. S.A.M. used blocks of it in the construction of Newgrange, the great Irish Cairn in Co. Meath, and often in his circles and burials. It grows from this white translucent rock into 'rock crystal' like the root of a tooth into its crown – for the crystal is clear, colourless and of perfect atomic structure. The chemical composition of quartz is SiO_2. It has a particular growth pattern with a structure, either right-handed or left-handed, in spiral form. This is said to be a helical growth pattern, from the Greek 'Helios', the Sun.

We have seen how the Sun and the Moon produce positive and negative spirals from an underground spring. In a like way, rock crystal, energised from the Sun and Moon, has grown in patterns over endless centuries giving off minute vibrations of energy. This energy manifests as pyro-electricity when subjected to variations of temperature and piezo-electricity when subjected to changing pressures. We can say therefore that the changing energies of day to night and season to season allow rock crystal to become alive. S.A.M. knew this and used this intuitive knowledge to energise his early structures to help the soul consciousness of his ancestors in their eternal travels in the cosmos.

Quartz also has a unique property in the whole of the gemstone world, in that when polarised light (sunlight directed as a beam), is passed through it, it refracts or bends that light through $45°$, i.e., it turns it. In doing so, it displays the hidden vibrations of white light or sunlight through its component parts; the seven rays of the body of light we see visually in the rainbow and psychically in the chakras of the human body. Also, this bending produces a balance between electricity and magnetism; the energy that with consciousness makes up the triple procreative spiral forces of Planet Earth. It is not surprising that the light image of the 'figure' produced by directing polarised light through quartz onto a 'plate' is the same in cross-section as the DNA – the cerebro spinal fluid that courses up and down the spine to give us our own personal

52

illumination. Rock crystal also conforms to the hexagonal/trigonal gem structure which gives us an expression of six-fold symmetry (diagrams 42, 43 and 44).

Within the structure of DNA is also found the shape of the six-pointed star, referred to as the double helix. However, it is now being suggested by scientists that it has many more 'strands', which when unravelled may tell us the blueprint of life. It would be interesting if the double helix in its next exposure were shown to be a triple helix, as it would then match the triple spiral of the Stone Age.

It is not therefore remarkable to see so many early Christian artefacts adorned with rock crystal as an energiser of the 'Word'; both of the article itself and its contents, such as a cross, chalice, or even saints' bones! An example of an early Christian shrine with crystals is shown in diagram 45, illustrating the Shrine of Cathacht.

Many different gemstones were also used to glorify early Christian artefacts: chalices, monstrances, shrines, altars and crosses. But remember, in those early days, gemstones were a considerable rarity – such stones as diamonds, rubies, sapphires and emeralds were virtually unknown in the West until the Middle Ages – and they had to come all the way along the tortuous endless caravan routes from

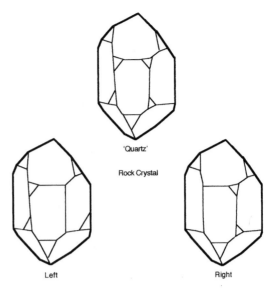

'Quartz'

Rock Crystal

Left   Right

Diagram 42. *Quartz Crystal structure.*

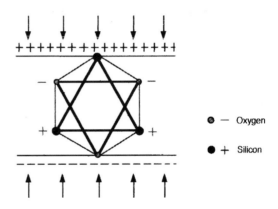

⊗ — Oxygen

● + Silicon

Diagram 43. *Quartz atomic structure SiO₂* (**Robert Webster**).

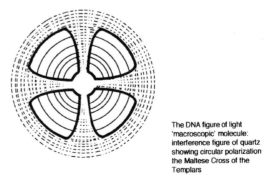

The DNA figure of light 'macroscopic' molecule: interference figure of quartz showing circular polarization the Maltese Cross of the Templars

Diagram 44. *Interference figure of polarised light* (**Robert Webster**).

Diagram 45. *The Shrine of Cathacht, c.eleventh century. A.D. (**National Museum of Ireland**).*

India. It was obvious that many of the very earliest stones used were those that could be found locally in the West, including the British Isles – such stones as rock crystals and amethysts from Cornwall, Wales, Scotland and Ireland, and agates and carnelians off our beaches, as water rolled pebbles to be polished up as cabochons.

The use of mounted rock crystal and quartz was essentially to enliven an object, such as a bishop's ring – an amethyst was mounted and required to be kissed as an act of spiritual homage in audience with 'the great man', through which hopefully personal favour would flow and grace be given. Amethyst being mauve represented the higher vibration of the crown chakra, symbolising divinity and spiritual intellectualism. Clear 'white' crystal, as we have seen, represented the eighth chakra and the halo of saintly illumination.

We know that S.A.M. used quartz a great deal in the construction of his circles, dolmens and standing stones. These places were often chosen because they were not only over an underground water conjunction, but also because there was an Earth Star centre there too. If a piece of rock crystal or quartz was placed in the centre of an Earth Star, the pattern changed from natural chaos to a natural symmetry, particularly if the quartz had been activated by the Kundalini of the priest. They would both be resonating at the Schumann brain level of 8–12 Hz (see Appendix C).

The Star pattern lines changed to a red-black and white line running east–west, and a violet and black line running north-south, thereby forming a cross at the conjunction point of the altar. If the priest now stood at this point, which in Christian times would be in *front* of the altar, sited in his church deliberately to encapsulate this energy, and gave his blessing, violet energy (spiritual light) will then flow through his hand from his higher chakras. This can be greatly enhanced if at the same time he was wearing an amethyst in a

54

gold ring. Indeed, this was the very reason for the bishop's traditional ring of amethyst and his purple robes – a fact long forgotten today.

The Use of Gemstones and Metals

Many people today wear jewellery. Since we live in an age of affluence and have so many luxuries at our disposal in the West, it is not at all unusual for any woman to have a collection of gemstones, rings, earrings, necklaces and brooches, set in gold, platinum, silver or even copper. But how many people have ever stopped to think of the effect of those individual stones or combination of different stones lying innocently on the chest, or adorning a finger or two? Jewellers, having to sell as many stones as they can have never stopped to study the effect of putting different stones together in a piece of jewellery or the result that those stones may have on the wearer, which of course will vary from person to person.

Some years ago, the author and a very psychic friend, a seer, carried out a series of experiments using different gemstones to try and get an idea of what happened to the 'aura' of the wearer. The author held a stone in his left hand – the hand we receive into, and transferred his Kundalini energy down into the stone, whilst the observer noted how his aura changed.

The illustrations in diagram 46 show a small sample of results with some of the better known stones:

Diagram 46 (1a, b & c)
1. **Quartz**
   (a) At start, white flower in crown;
   (b) growing through crown;
   (c) into a red flame through a mantle of white 'flowers'.
   (black and white plate 2)
Photograph of the Bothisahva 'Enlightened One' with flaming open crown chakra.

Diagram 46 (2, 3, 4 and 5)
2. **Rock Crystal**
   A silver mushroomed shape appeared with a gold aura around the head and shoulders.
3. **Diamond**
   Crown chakra opened enormously with golden light and a silver triangle, downwards, appeared in the third eye.
4. **Sapphire**
   Brilliant goldy/amber light all round the head, out of the third eye and into a rising cone out of the crown chakra – a really bright positive opening force. Of all stones examined, sapphire produced the most positive and expansive energy. Note that the early bishops used sapphires in gold stirrup rings – called their 'undress rings'.
5. **Sapphire and Rock Crystal**
   Pale blue cone with double image of the head – not thought to be very beneficial.

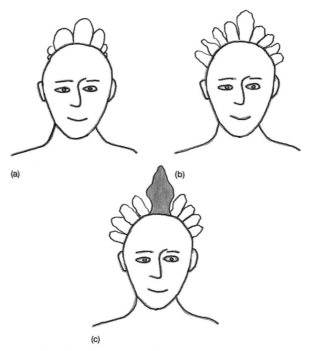

Diagram 46. *Diagrams of crystal consciousness (a) (b) & (c).*

B&W plate 2. *Open crown chakra 'flame' – Bothisahva – Thailand (**Private collection**).*

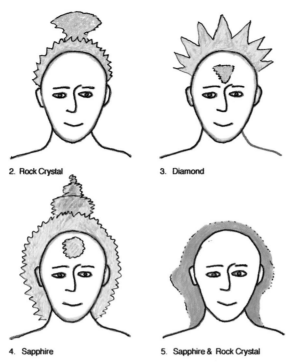

2. Rock Crystal

3. Diamond

4. Sapphire

5. Sapphire & Rock Crystal

Diagram 46. *Diagrams of crystal consciousness (2, 3, 4, & 5).*

Diagram 46 (6, 7 & 8)

6. **Emerald**

   Light seemed to fold inwards with this stone, and it was not thought to be advantageous.

7. **Ruby (Indian)**

   Seemed to be a lightener of 'burdens' around the shoulders, particularly the base of the neck; perhaps helps communication and self-expression.

8. **Amethyst**

   Affects the third eye – opening it into a rising violet cone of 33° and lightening the crown chakra. This was seen as an initiatory stone, to help perceptions and intuition. (not illustrated)

9. **Opal**

   Affects the heart chakra, slowing it down and should not be used with anyone emotionally down or sad.

10. **Peridot**

    Affects the heart chakra – speeding and opening it up, also a strong white aura from the opening crown.

11. **Moonstone**

    Does not have any effect on the aura and only dimly produces energy up to the solar plexus – of no value esoterically as it tends to hold down energies.

12. **Garnet**

    Affects the root/base chakra and acts as a depressor or grounder of energy.

6. Emerald 7. Ruby (Indian)

8. Amethyst 13. Amber

Diagram 46. *Diagrams of crystal consciousness (6, 7, 8, & 13).*

Diagram 46 (13)

13. **Amber**

Produces two triangles just overlapping on the head and shoulders and a fountain of gold light through the crown – a good material.

14. **Turquoise**

Free flow through the chakras with a golden light – a nice energy.

15. **Lapis Lazuli**

Energised the duodenum and the solar plexus, i.e., the centre of the body; a good healer of that area.

Diagram 46 (16)

16. **Nephrite**

Crown chakra swells into a large, pale-blue aura – pleasant and comfortable.

Diagram 46 (17a, b & c)

17. **Crystal in Cairn**

This experience is discussed on page 62.

All these stones were held alone – i.e., they were not mounted and set in metal, gold or silver. Several stones were then tried with gold and in each case the energy was either markedly depleted or changed; it was reckoned that perhaps a silver mount or chain was less active. If an owner insists on 'wearing' the stone, it is suggested that it should be worn in a special pouch at the throat,

58

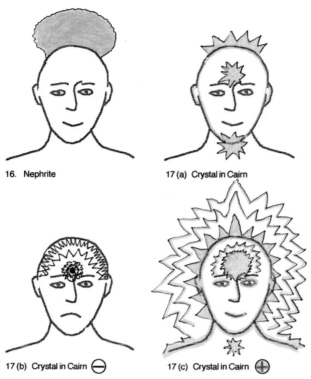

16. Nephrite

17 (a) Crystal in Cairn

17 (b) Crystal in Cairn ⊖

17 (c) Crystal in Cairn ⊕

Diagram 46. *Diagrams of crystal consciousness (16, 17(a), (b), & (c)).*

chest, or in a pocket. To adorn oneself with gemstones is in general an expression of the material/spiritual ego.

Every natural material, animal, vegetable and mineral on the planet has its own dowsing fingerprint – a response particular to itself that can be annotated with the use of the colour rosette (see Appendix B) and the pendulum. All things have a response of four colours. The first response is an anti-clockwise swing of the pendulum, the second clockwise, third anti-clockwise, and fourth clockwise. These four responses are consistent with the inherent four colours of a human being as shown by his/her unique chemistry, physical (pranic), emotional and mental auras (see Chapter III) – for everything is created on the same principle and nothing is separate from 'God', the creative universal force.

This concept is important when considering gemstones and jewellery. Since each person has four colours and each gemstone its own four colours, it is obvious that we have to cross-match positive and negative and balance ourselves to our appropriate stone if we are going to receive benefit and harmony from that stone. This can help us in so many ways towards better health. It is vital to understand this principle and find the stone, or combination of stones, that suits us on a metaphysical level, as each gemstone has its own chemical composition and refractive index (the way it bends light). Interestingly, the celestial city, 'Camelot', derives from the words Camu + lot, meaning 'bent light' in our mythology, but is ultimately a secret of crystallography or 'magic'.

The converse is also important, as any stone detrimental to our well-being worn, say on our heart chakra or on our ears, as earrings either side of the brain, can cause deep, subtle imbalance. Worse still, consider how our materialistic greed today draws us to jewellers shops to buy items of many different stones mixed up together, and then mounted in different precious metals. A combination of different stones can set up a very disruptive force-field which we then carry around, thinking it's beautiful, and show off as a symbol of our wealth and status.

There is a practice today in the New Age therapy field that is applied through ignorance and emotional stupidity. It is the extensive use of many different crystals – gemstones – being placed over the body of a 'client' or 'patient', often on the chakras in circles and lines, mixing up many different highly potent but latent, volatile structures that can undoubtedly do a great deal of damage to the subtle aura of the individual. Usually the practitioner of such therapies has taken some expensive course in gem therapy and been issued with an impressive certificate. The practitioner then launches out on his or her practice, inadvertently causing further harm in a most well-meaning way, using – we are told – 'intuition' as to which stone suits 'you'. The practice of this style of gem therapy is dangerous and should not be used.

The author was for 30 years a dealer in antique jewellery and gemstones in London. Often a client would bring in a collection or piece of jewellery, such as a ring set with a single stone, or a brooch perhaps with a combination of many different gems such as diamonds, rubies, amethysts and peridot – each of greatly varying 'vibrations'. Sometimes at the end of a day's work, an unexpected energy would seem to overtake him and he'd feel pain, perhaps in his stomach, or unreasonable sadness, anger, or – rarely – joy! In essence, he was picking up the energy from the item that had interacted with the owner and taken on his/her emotions through the stones. If an owner had had cancer through extreme stress, one wonders how long it might have been for someone to have the same disease transferred through wearing the same jewel?

The metals used in jewellery are also contributory to energy change, particularly and uniquely gold, so widely sought after and robbed throughout many centuries. Yet on enquiry to the Professor of Archaeology at Dublin's University College as to the incidence and whereabouts of burials and hoards of gold objects, it was surprising to learn that 'no gold object from the Bronze Age has been found in conjunction with a burial or a corpse, so the objects therefore must have some ritual purpose'.

Gold was not originally used for adornment. It was not considered necessary to wear jewellery to express worth or ego. Primarily, gold, as the Sun metal, was used to make solar and lunar calculators for the use of the early priesthood (see *Pi in the Sky* by the author, Chapter XI).

Pure gold has eleven magnetic variations that give it a peculiar energy that fluctuates wildly and seemingly irrationally in its polarity from moment to moment, hour to hour, sunrise to mid-day to sunset; therefore at any time. Perhaps it is activated by the subtle electrical emanations of the human brain itself, but certainly by the Sun and the Moon's influence from day to night to day – and we wear it. Not only do we wear it by itself as, for example, a 22ct gold wedding ring on the third finger of our left hand, thereby screwing up that meridian through the body, but we even put all those disruptive combinations of gemstones together in fancy 18ct gold settings. No wonder greed – the greed of wealth and personal show-off – so often leads to unaccountable stress, illness and separation.

Perhaps you saw the beautiful video made by the B.B.C. on the Khogi Indians of Colombia. They say categorically that pure gold should be revered and remain in the ground, as an aspect of the fertility and the might of the Sun.

Table 1 gives a list of some popular gems and their subtle four-fold colour dowsing fingerprint.

TABLE 1   Examples of Material Dowsing Responses with the Pendulum (Clive Beadon)

	anti-clock ☽ (−)	clock ☾ (+)	anti-clock ☽ (+)	clock ☾ (+)
1. White Agate	Blue/Green	Blue/White	Violet/Black	Grey
2. Peridot	Yellow/Red	Blue/Green	Violet/White	Black/White
3. Opal	Grey	Black	Blue/Green	Blue
4. Rock Crystal	Blue/Green	Yellow	White	Grey
5. Quartz	Blue/Green	Yellow	White	Grey/Black
6. Gold	White	Violet	Yellow/Red	Green
7. Silver	White	Grey	Blue/Green	Red
8. Copper	Blue	Red	Grey	Grey/Black

Note: The personal four colours actuate on the fourth circle of the colour wheel.

The author, loving gemstones, particularly sapphires, was surprised to find (dowse) his personal four colours as:

1. Red ☽   2. Green ☾   3. Violet/Black ☽   4. Violet/Blue ☾

which happen to cross-reference the colours of flint!

The implication of the four-colour personal vibrational fingerprint is on a very subtle dowsing level. It has certainly been known about in ancient India, as Indian jewellers put together combinations of gems in their jewellery that are beneficial to the individual wearers. In the West we have no knowledge of this now, nor had we in the past, except with rock crystal and quartz as an energiser from the Stone Age.

To sum up, the use of gemstones to enhance energy on a personal level can be very detrimental if used without clairvoyance and knowledge of dowsing and the four-colour imprints. The correct combination of gemstones to balance and enhance energy fields as explained in Chapter VIII, was made as **The Spiral of Tranquility** by the late Clive Beadon, and is now promoted by Michael Poynder (see Appendix D).

More about Pendulums

Gemstones were worn by the priesthood in early Christian times but the stones available, both in the Middle East and north-west Europe, were sparse. Rock crystal and quartz are the most widely spread stones throughout the planet, and rock crystal having a latent, inbuilt energy, was used from the Stone Age until today – you will have noted the Stone Age crystal pendulum from Carrowmore, c.4000 B.C. in *Pi in the Sky*, page 42.

Can we really imagine Jesus, in his simplicity, wearing gemstones or decking himself out like some golden Christmas tree, as do the egotistical, materialistic clergy of today! It just wasn't, and isn't, necessary in order to teach love.

Many people, especially dowsers, choose to use a pendulum made out of some favourite gemstone and hang it from a chain of metal. It is suggested by *The British Society of Dowsers* that their standard pendulum, made out of plastic and suspended on a nylon cord, is best, as it has no inherent energetic property to meld with the user, and so confuse questions asked inwardly.

When dowsing, often answers are confused by peripheral energy. If a rock crystal is held in the left hand and the Kundalini energy poured into it, and then raised up through the chakras to the 12th chakra, the stone will take on a special property, activating the higher chakras and energising the stone in such a way that it cuts out much of the 'fudge', or extraneous information that often crowds in to confuse us. This enhanced energy will also cross-fertilise to other rock crystals nearby, thereby activating them in a way of 'absent healing', stone to stone. It is from the 12th chakra that *love* flows freely.

The author experimented with holding a rock crystal in his left hand in the centre of a cairn at Carrowkeel, i.e., in structured space over an energy riser. Taking us back to diagram 46 (17a, b & c), which shows varying levels of consciousness and corresponding changes to the aura, the results were as follows:

17(a) Just sitting at rest in the cairn. This created a flame alight in the pituitary gland and crown chakra.

17(b) Squeezing the crystal to a minimal size in the hand and in the mind. This created a black hole and inward aura in the centre of the head (pituitary gland).

17(c) Expanding the crystal to an enormous size in the hand and in the mind. This created a vast expanding, uncontrolled energy field of flashing light that disappeared, i.e., a white hole.

It was in this way, by changing consciousness, that the early clairvoyant priesthood of S.A.M.'s time used their Kundalini to activate the whole structure of the cairn, i.e., the auric cairn body of light in combination with the human consciousness that then allowed astral travel. The energy fields combined and expanded, and resulted in another 'vehicle' to transport the individual priest into other realms. It allowed wo-man to know 'God', or 'the Gods' of the cosmos, as the human form transcended gravity through the acceleration of the unfolding, unwinding spiral together with the melding into the universal mind. This opening of the mind through time enables 'seeing' in the fullest sense of prophecy, as well as the control of natural abilities and phenomena. It is this energy that allows a fully Christed Being – an Avatar – to express the principles of Omnipresence and Omnipotence, as do illumined mystical teachers in their constant appearances to individuals and groups all over the world at the same time.

CHAPTER V

The Path to the Cross

The Last Times

Here we are almost 2,000 years after the birth of Jesus of Nazareth and in astrological terms about to enter a New Age. In many parts of the world, particularly in the West, people of different religious and cultural systems believe and even predict the advent of a leap in consciousness that will be divinely inspired. This prediction encapsulates the thoughts and hopes of not only deeply religious people of conservative and intellectual persuasion but also the fringe cultures of alternative, 'hippie', anti-establishment 'drop outs' following free-living Paganism, much reviled by so-called straight thinkers. In between these extremes are many many people fed up with patriarchal authority and the outdated dogma and practices of the Church, together with the controlling, fundamentalist, anti-feminism of Christianity and Islam. The idea of a New Age, a time of enlightenment, seems to come round on a cyclical basis as the Earth turns around on its wobbling axis from age to age, as indicated by the constellations of the signs of the Zodiac. The names of the constellations were chosen in ancient times, pre-dynastic Egypt and Sumaria of 3000 B.C., as a gauge to the progress of the planet; the precession through the signs anti-clockwise as our star – the Sun – pulls us along on its path through the Milky Way.

At the time Stonehenge was built, about 3000 B.C., i.e., 5,000 B.P. (before present), the North Star was Thuban and we were in the zodiacal sign of Taurus the Bull. In 2200 B.C. Planet Earth moved into the sign of Aries the Ram where it remained until 60 B.C., a significant date as we'll see, and then on into Pisces the Fish. Now in 1997, just before the turn of the millennium, always a time of emotional and spiritual question marks, we are nearing the end of Pisces, in 2100 A.D., and will be moving into the sign of Aquarius the Water Carrier. It is a time of great expectation, a change of many ideas, aspirations and human patterns, or so we expect. At the same time, enlightened people, mystics and scientists suggest that due to solar activity, again on a cyclical basis, the Sun is due to change its angle of inclination, or 'tilt'. If this happens, as has happened before, then Planet Earth will also change its alignment. The last time, around 11,000 B.P., the changing angle allowed the ice of the Ice Age to melt, due to the sudden influx of warm water from the mid-Atlantic flooding into the northern hemisphere and created the northern flow of the Gulf Stream.

Whenever the end of an age or era is predicted, civilisations automatically seem to turn to 'God', whoever that may be in their culture, to save, rescue or help that tribe to survive, praying for the gift of some special 'grace'. In isolation, this suggests a deep fundamental spiritual ego – an attitude of 'we are the chosen ones' that immediately becomes separatist and therefore misses the whole point of the 'One God', 'One Creation' principle that is Planet Earth.

This was the situation and current thinking in Palestine around 60 B.C. and was known then as 'The Last Times', 'The End of Days', 'The Day of The Lord' – a time of great expectation that at last the Jewish people would be lifted up into a realm of godliness that was their special place in the evolution of 'the World'. This concept had been handed down through a succession of Babylonian and Persian teachings – for as we think now, so it was then thought that the forces of good and evil would contend with each other, reaching a climax in 'the penultimate age', followed by an age of peace and glory. Before this could happen, the forces of evil would finally have to be defeated and overcome. At that time, the arrival of a Messiah was anticipated to save and instruct the 'chosen' Jewish people.

In Christian terms, we call this the 'second coming', referring to the idea that Jesus might walk among 'us' again. In England, this expectation is so deep-rooted that British fundamental Christians expect that 'coming' to be centred in Anglicanism at Glastonbury. In Ireland, Roman Catholicism expects it at some special shrine, where visions have been seen – perhaps at Knock, Co. Mayo, or in Europe at Lourdes or Fatima.

The End of Days

As far as the Jews of 60–4 B.C. were concerned, they were under the yoke of the Roman conquest of their lands, whom they rightly considered, through cruel experience, to be the evil they had to contend with before the Messiah arrived to lead them into their expected New Age.

Jesus accepted his life as dedicated to the idea of the Messiah returning to give hope and faith to his people. His training and teaching was one of simplicity, honesty and love –founded on truth, right-living and forgiveness, for he was an Essene priest. It was Jesus who chose the way. He constructed and manipulated the last weeks before the path to the Cross, deliberately allowing those close to him to accept and believe that he was the 'Chosen One', the Messiah.

Of the disciples, Jesus' 'minders', some were simple people, farmers and fishermen, not intellectuals, and others were family. They represented part of the earlier prophecies as to how the Messiah would be escorted, identified and known when the time was right. The Pagan or earlier Druidic way was to accept a Godhead – God (Itself) – whereas Jesus never suggested that he was God, for the Messiah was essentially a *messenger* of God.

It is interpretations of the writers of the Gospels, and later Pauline and Gentile thinking, that allied the two together. Christians have therefore been brought up to accept 'the Christ' as ultimate, the incarnation of the Godhead. This was something that Jesus never suggested, for Jewish monotheism just did not allow such a statement.

The path to the Cross to fulfil the prophecies had to be seen to be completely valid if Jesus was to be accepted as the Messiah and therefore able to usher in the New Age. Those living after the reign of Herod the Great, 37–4 B.C., accepted that 'the last times' had begun and the Messiah was imminent, so when John the Baptist, another Essene, appeared and said that the Kingdom of God was at hand, the people were obviously motivated to repent and 'save themselves' from the forthcoming sorting out of souls. Jesus, as the 'Nazarene', and of Essene spiritual training, was of 'The Line of David' and Judah – the holy line to usher in the 'Anointed Ones'. When Herod died in 4 B.C., the country erupted in religious expectation. It was a time of political turmoil and thousands were crucified by the Roman authorities in an effort to hold down their colonial empire. Crucifixion was an everyday event and by no means unusual.

I wish now to quote extensively from *The Passover Plot*, by the late Hugh Schonfield; for his expertise in unravelling the thinking and motivation of Jesus before the Crucifixion is unrivalled.

> *In approaching the historical Jesus no question of his deity arises, since before the paganism of Jewish belief in the development of Christianity no authority identified the Messiah with the Logos, the eternal Word of God, or conceived the Messiah to be an incarnation of God. The very term, The Anointed One, indicates a call to office. It was not the title of an aspect of the Godhead. We do not have to entertain at all the notion that Jesus or any other claimant to be the Messiah in Palestine at this period could suppose himself for one moment to be divine. In the early history of Christianity it can be sufficiently seen how the doctrine arose out of the impact of the Gospel on the Gentile world, and in the circumstances it was almost inevitable. There are plenty of instances still today of Christianity in many lands being coloured by the polytheistic faiths the Church has conquered and absorbed.*
> (Hugh Schonfield, *The Passover Plot.*)

We must look at Jesus as a highly intelligent, cultured, 'trained' individual with complete faith in himself and his purpose. It is on those lines that we can go forward to the point when finally, in fulfilment of the prophecies, he is nailed to the Cross. Jesus had to demonstrate by his actions and the actions of those around him that he was totally authentic.

We know now from the Dead Sea Scrolls that the Essenes had a prophetic understanding of the past to the future, and it seems that Jesus fully understood the path he had to tread as his accepted right.

> *From first to last his actions are marked by the utmost purposefulness and he speaks with an authority which made a profound impression on all who came in contact with him. He is revealed as a man who knows exactly what he is doing, and why. More than once in respect of his end he is reported to have said: 'My hour has not yet come'.*

Therefore,

Why should we not conclude, historically, that, before his baptism by John, Jesus had succeeded in producing a kind of blueprint of the Messiah's mission with the prophetic requirements organised to show a progressive programme of events having their climax at Jerusalem when he would suffer at the hands of the authorities?

Here could be the explanation of much that is mysterious in the Gospel story of Jesus.

So much of the New Testament of Jesus is pure fairyland with later added influences from the East and the Buddhic teachings. We have been led to believe, through modern dogma, in a completely different Jesus to the powerful, self-willed man of the times. Let us go back to Jesus' birth.

There was nothing peculiar about the birth of Jesus. He was not God incarnate and no Virgin Mother bore him. The Church in its ancient zeal fathered a myth and became bound to it as dogma. Since Christians largely continued to suppose that their faith stands or falls by the doctrine of the deity of Christ, the dogma goes on being sustained to the detriment of what is really significant about the person and contribution of Jesus. It is pathetic to have theologians, whether orthodox or liberal, trying to save themselves and the credit of the Church's teaching by questing for terms which will enable them to retain what they should have outgrown.

Jesus was the first child of the family, it seems with four younger brothers and possibly two younger sisters. There are many stories that Jesus travelled as a young man before his ministry to Tibet, to Britain with Joseph of Arimathea and to Egypt, but the Gospels give us no direct evidence of this. However, the writers of the Gospels, setting down the story of Jesus retrospectively, were deeply influenced by the teachings that had been coming out of India for several centuries – the teachings and sayings of the Buddha who had lived 700 years previously. Many of the 'sayings' of Jesus can be directly related to Buddhic texts, for at that time, 100 A.D., Buddhist monks had been travelling widely throughout Asia and the Middle East. It is perhaps therefore possible that Jesus' sayings were not just the thinking and influences of that latter time, but encompassed his own thinking from a period spent learning the Buddhic way – the eight-fold path to salvation and the doctrine of reincarnation so successfully eradicated from later Christian teachings. Perhaps whenever we read 'resurrection' we should re-read 'reincarnation', and then so much more of the Jesus story would make sense. The Aramaic word for 'resurrect' also translates as 'resuscitate'.

There is a theory that the 'Magi', the three wise men, astrologers, who travelled from the East were Buddhist lamas from Tibet who wished to be at the birth of Jesus because they knew he was the reincarnation of the Buddha. But this is surely a lovely fairy tale? It is suggested that the lead up to the Passover was a carefully laid plan by a highly dedicated and dramatic player, an actor who filled an expected prophetic stage with incredible charisma.

Jesus had three things to accomplish: firstly, to deliver his prophetic call to national repentance in the very heart of Jewish life where it would reach the greatest number and command the most attention; secondly, to bring himself personally to the notice of the highest Jewish authorities, who previously had only certain reports of his activities in Galilee; and thirdly, with the help of his friends, to set the stage for the revelation of himself as the Messiah and the accomplishment of his destiny.

With the help of the Oracles Jesus had deduced that he was required to suffer ignominiously at the hands of the rulers at Jerusalem. As self-confessed Messiah this stood to reason also. Under Tiberius no King of the Jews could exist who had not been approved by Caesar, and confirmed by the Roman Senate, and it was the business of the authorities in Palestine, Jewish and Roman, acting for Caesar, to apprehend anyone claiming to be a king. In the case of one who was not of the Roman nobility nor a Roman citizen he would be condemned to death, if found guilty, death by crucifixion, the barbarous punishment the Romans meted out for highway robbery, mutiny, high treason and rebellion. That Jesus was aware of this is shown by the words he used just after he had privately and under pledge of strict secrecy admitted to the twelve that he was the Messiah. 'And when he had called the people unto him with his disciples also, he said unto them, whosoever will come after me, let him deny himself, and take up his cross, and follow me. For whosoever will save his life shall lose it; but whosoever shall lose his life for my sake and the good news, the same shall save it.' He could not yet state openly that he was the Messiah.

The Jews didn't want to antagonise the Romans, and the Romans wanted to avoid insurrection, so Jesus had to play one against the other. He set up a base for himself in the house of Martha and Lazarus in Bethany, conveniently outside but near to Jerusalem. At the supper in Martha's house in Bethany we are told he was anointed by Mary with oils so precious that Judas remarked, they 'could be sold and the money given to the poor'. By this time, just a few days before the Last Supper and the arrest in the garden, Jesus already knew and had announced his forthcoming 'death' and healing and said, 'on the third day I will rise again'.

However, since he had contrived the whole scenario, he was determined to suffer as little as possible with a view to 'survival' off the Cross. The anointing with spikenard was a deliberate aromatherapy treatment of oils and spices to prepare for and lessen pain later. Jesus saw himself as the 'Anointed One' with oil (balm) and the physical use of a specially prepared ointment, 'anointment', that in turn was part of the ritual of the expression of Messiahship – the preparation of the 'Divine Body'. The triumphant entry into Jerusalem could finally set him on the path to the Cross.

The Last Supper, the Passover supper, when Jesus led his disciples to the upper room of the chosen house, is central to Christian practice because of its association with the bread and the wine; probably water for Jesus, as the Essenes did not take intoxicating liquor. The communion service was built on this aspect of the meal.

There were fourteen present at the table, not thirteen. These were the twelve disciples, Jesus himself, and the 'Beloved' disciple as owner of the house and the upper room of the supper. This has always been suggested to be John, the priest, but was possibly Joseph of Arimathea, the brother of Jesus – the advisor and 'intelligence' whom Jesus needed to fulfil his scheme, and vitally, a member of the Sanhedrin itself.

At the end of the meal, after Judas had left, Jesus raised his wine cup known as 'the cup of blessing' and subsequently the 'Holy Grail' or 'Grail Cup', and gave the blessing: 'this signifies the new covenant of my blood which is poured out for many'. At the end of the meal he departs for the Garden of Gethsemene. But what happens to the Grail Cup?

At the Passover Jesus decided to reveal himself publicly as the Messiah, which he knew would enrage the Sanhedrin and the chief priests. He had already set up his arrest in the garden and knew that he would have to be tried in secret at night in order to be brought before Pilate the next day. Timing was crucial. He had to be called early enough to be put up on the Cross and remain there for long enough for his 'death' to seem possible, i.e., consistent with the time he was on the Cross – yet not so long that he had every possible chance of survival and subsequent treatment in the specially prepared tomb by Joseph of Arimathea which was ready for him after he was taken down. The plan was that he was to be released as early as credible, at the special request of Joseph to Pilate.

Jesus was probably crucified at about midday, perhaps earlier. Even whilst on the Cross, the 'reported' sayings seem to have been borrowed from the earlier scriptures to add colour and certain fulfilment to the situation by the gospellers:

> With various incidences there is a reflection of the language of the Scriptures, especially of **Psalm xxii**, the psalm which begins: 'My God, my God, why hast thou forsaken me?' The soldiers cast lots for the robe of Jesus in fulfilment of **Psalm xxii:18**. They pierce his hands and his feet in fulfilment of **Psalm xxii:16**. The chief priests and scribes mock him and wag their heads in derision in fulfilment of **Psalm xxii:7**. They cry: 'He trusted in the Lord to deliver him: let him deliver him, if he delight in him', in fulfilment of **Psalm xxii:8**. Bystanders gave Jesus vinegar mingled with gall in fulfilment of **Psalm Lxix:21**. When he is believed to be dead they do not break his legs, as they do those of the robbers, in fulfilment of **Exodus xii:46**. Instead, his side is pierced with a lance in fulfilment of **Zacchariah xii:10**.
>
> There is the strongest consciousness here of the prophetic testimonies. We may grant that certain things happened, some of them usual, which seemed to answer to such Scriptures. But there has been invention as well to obtain a more exact correspondence and to supplement the paucity of facts.

During his time on the Cross, Jesus was offered a sponge supposedly filled with 'vinegar' to assuage his thirst. Within his plan, a short time after the Crucifixion, he had to contrive to be seen by the authorities as 'dead', so that he could be removed as soon as possible. Jesus is said to have died in the ninth hour or 3 p.m. and very soon after drinking the vinegar – so what happened?

Spiritualists and psychics are well aware of, and often trained in the practice of, 'out of body experience' – the ability for the mind and consciousness of the individual to leave the physical body and travel in a meditative state to other places or situations, usually to give what is called absent healing. It is possible to leave the body in an almost near-death state to the point where the mind, in separation, is looking back or down on the physical form from above. This sometimes happens to people unexpectedly and uncontrived in normal dream states during sleep or after an accident.

Perhaps Jesus deliberately went 'out of body' on the Cross. This would have been part of his training as an initiate of the Essene priesthood, so that at the actual nailing and through the agony, until he supposedly gave up the ghost, he could well have been 'out of body'. The author knows a woman who during the Second World War was captured in Paris by the Gestapo at the age of seventeen while running messages for the Resistance. She was interrogated and tortured. At the commencement of her torture, being strapped naked to a table in a basement and beaten with rods, she went 'out of body' and watched her feet and hands being broken and her body abused in deeply painful ways, but 'she' felt nothing. The torturers were nonplussed that she gave no reaction to their extreme physical brutality. However, she said that she knew she couldn't stay out indefinitely watching what was being done to her. Eventually, when she saw herself being thrown back into her cell she had to return to her physical body. She said that the shock of the pain on 'return' was horrific but she had survived the actual trauma of the moment of fear when the torture had started.

Perhaps Jesus slipped in and out of body during the Crucifixion until he was finally brought into the sanctuary of the prepared sepulchre for treatment. His body could then be 'claimed' at the earliest possible moment after the Crucifixion. Nevertheless, there was great surprise that he had died so quickly. But Pilate, one recalls, had 'washed his hands' of the whole affair and didn't want to be involved in what he saw as a strictly local Jewish scenario.

The Roman governor Pontius Pilate was detested, and the lordly family of Annas, which held the sacred office of the high priest in fee with gold from its well-filled coffers, was feared and resented.

So Jesus, with lots of secret help from his closest friends, not the twelve disciples, and through timing and considerable ingenuity, had completed the legacy of personal sacrifice to fulfil the prophecies and provide the Jewish people with a Messiah and a cause.

Quickly, he was whisked away into the new and specially prepared tomb or sepulchre made ready for the event by Joseph of Arimathea – rather like being rushed into casualty after an accident. All was ready to accept the seemingly life-less corpse of Jesus who needed rest and care in darkness if he was to be ready to leave and 'resurrect' by the third day, and finally to complete the Messianic promise.

In his sufferings Jesus could know that he had triumphantly passed the Messianic test, successfully carrying out the exacting stipulations of the Oracles. The tremendous task to which he had applied his mind and heart was con- cluded. But in these moments he still had something to do, to provide for the

mother he had been forced to neglect to pursue his mission: he now entrusted her to the care of his dear disciple. His last effort was to call out, 'I thirst'. In response someone standing by raised to his lips a sponge saturated with wine vinegar. Almost immediately he passed into oblivion.
(Hugh Schonfield, *The Passover Plot*.)

Holger Kersten suggests that it was not vinegar in the literal sense, but a specially prepared drug, containing a 'narcotic' such as 'myrrh' or 'incense', in accordance with Jewish custom, that was used in order to ease pain and assist Jesus in losing consciousness, as it was necessary for him to appear to be 'dead'.

The drug used in Persian and Hindu sacrifices was [and is] *'Haoma' or the soma plant (asclepias acida) known as the drink of immortality, enabling anyone familiar with the drug to appear to be dead for up to three days. The other narcotics regularly used perhaps in conjunction with soma were hemp (cannabis indica) and opium. Soma is known in the West as swallow wort.*
(Holger Kersten, *Jesus Lived in India*.)

The Essenes being healers and herbalists would have known of these magical potions and surely been part of the scheme that Jesus had devised to fool the authorities, even supposedly after being pierced in the side with a lance by the centurion, Longinus. No doubt Jesus received the maximum attention to his wounds; his shredded back from the whipping, his pricked head from the thorns and his cut side from the lance. But he was young, physically very strong and prepared by every known medical potion to overcome his ordeal, which he probably did.

'We' as Christians have been brought up to believe that Jesus died on the Cross and so we accept it as a fact, a point of blind faith. But have we ever really read the Gospels objectively and attempted to analyse the information therein? As Hugh Schonfield tells us, Jesus did not expect to have seen his disciples for the last time:

Jesus had been convinced that his Crucifixion would not be the end. Provided that he discharged faithfully the duties incumbent upon him as the Messiah in his manifestation as the Servant of the Lord, he was assured that God would exalt him in readiness for his further manifestation as ruler over the Kingdom of God. The glorification would be initiated by his resurrection. According to the synoptic Gospels, as his last trials approached, he had spoken to his disciples with confidence of his rising on the third day. He even went so far as to make an appointment to meet them afterwards in his beloved Galilee.
(Hugh Schonfield, *The Passover Plot*.)

Jesus himself clearly told us of his imminent survival:

Matthew 26:32 – *But after I am risen again, (survived), I will go before you into Galilee.*
Matthew 28:7 – *And go quickly and tell his disciples that he is risen from the dead and he goeth before you into Galilee there ye shall see him, lo I have told you.*

Mark 16:7 – *But go your way tell his disciples and Peter that he goeth before you into Galilee there shall ye see him as he said unto you.*
John 20:18 – *Mary Magdalene came and told the disciples that she had seen the Lord.*

We also have the well-known meeting of the disciples soon afterwards when Jesus had fully recovered his physical health in Galilee:

John 20:19–20 – *And when he had so said, he shewed unto them His hands and His side. Then were the disciples glad, then they saw the Lord.*

Then said Jesus to them again, 'Peace be unto you: as my Father hath sent me, even so send I you'.
John 20:24–28 – *But Thomas, one of the twelve, called Didymus, was not with them when Jesus came. The other disciples therefore said unto him, 'We have seen the Lord'. But he said unto them, 'Except I shall see in his hands the print of the nails, and put my finger into the print of the nails, and thrust my hand into his side, I will not believe'. And after eight days again his disciples were within and Thomas with them; then came Jesus, the doors being shut, and stood in the midst, and said, 'Peace be unto you'.*

Then saith he to Thomas, 'Reach higher thy finger, and behold my hands, and reach hither thy hand, and thrust it into my side: and be not faithless, but believing'.

And Thomas answered and said unto him, 'My Lord and my God'.
John 21:1 – *After these things Jesus shewed himself again to the disciples at the sea of Tiberius.*

It is at this point that the Gospels virtually end but many enigmas remain unanswered. Let us try and list them and then offer some possible explanations.

1. What happened to the disciples who were present during the path to the Cross, for many are not mentioned in the Acts of the Apostles?
2. What happened to Jesus, who had completed and fulfilled his portrayal of the Messianic prophecy, yet having survived the ordeal, disappears at the early age of about 35 years?
3. What happened to Mary the mother of Jesus?
4. What happened to Joseph of Arimathea?
5. And, most importantly, what happened to the Grail Cup of the Last Supper?
6. What about the legend of the Turin Shroud?

CHAPTER VI

Jesus Survived

To India

Can we, as Christians, think the unthinkable? Can we unlearn all the rote of faith pumped into us and our peers down many centuries of religious manipulation? Can we contemplate Christianity if Jesus survived the Crucifixion, was treated successfully and quickly in the sepulchre, and moved secretly away to recover his strength quietly elsewhere? For that is what he tells us in the Bible, 'I will see you in Galilee'.

After the Crucifixion, when Jesus had completed his chosen role of Messiahship and personal sacrifice, he had to disappear, but not before he had offered reassurance and renewed faith to the disciples, as he had already arranged prior to the Cross.

Holger Kersten tells us in *Jesus Lived in India* that five kilometres outside Damascus there is a place called Mayuam-i-isa, 'The place where Jesus lived'. Jesus is said to have travelled with Thomas Didymus, 'doubting Thomas', to visit a King Nisibis, near Edessa, whom he healed. Jesus sent Thomas to India to preach, where he subsequently went to Cochin to found the first Indian Christian Church.

We do not know the exact relationship of Thomas to Jesus, but according to *The Gospel of Thomas*, as emerged from the Dead Sea Scrolls, he had received a special and secret trusted part of Jesus' teaching.

Holger Kersten also tells us that The Acts of Thomas describe the stay of Jesus and Thomas at Taxila (Pakistan) at the court of King Gundafor, in the year 47 A.D. Then going eastwards to the borders of Kashmir, we arrive at the town of Mari or Muree, which means Mary, where there is a grave honoured way back into time, called Mai Marida Asthan, the final resting place of Mother Mary – suggested as the grave of Jesus' mother, who had accompanied him on his new travels. Again going East, we arrive at the capital of Kashmir, Srinagar. South of this city is the plain of Yus-marg, 'the meadow of Jesus', where some of the children of Israel settled after 722 B.C. and continued to live there as shepherds. It is they who have passed down the reports of Jesus settling there.

History tells us that in 721 B.C., Sargon II captured the Kingdom of Israel and killed or exiled the twelve tribes. Several of the tribes fled to Afghanistan and Kashmir and settled in the lush valleys amongst the mountains of north India. These 'lost tribes of Israel' as they are called, settled happily in a new country; a land flowing with milk and honey, like parts of Syria they had left. It is said that the name Kashmir originates from the ancient Hebrew 'Ka', meaning 'like', and 'Shiv', meaning 'Syria', – so Kashmir becomes 'like Syria'. Two distinct types live in Kashmir, the physical attributes of one being obviously Indian and the other clearly Semitic. There are also many place-names indicated in the Bible that appear in Kashmir, for instance:

Ure – Uri
Asham – Ashema
Amairah – Amairah
Achahal – Ashbal
Beithpoer – Beithpoe
Gadha – Gadha
Gilgath – Gilgotha
Keran – Keren
Harwon – Haron
Himas – Hamath
Ladakh – Laadah
Tibet – Tibhath
Leh – Lehi
Moab – Moab
Shopiam – Shopham, etc., etc.
(Aziz Kashmiri, *Christ in Kashmir*.)

Many castes and tribes are mentioned in the Bible amongst Moslems and Hindus, and many Jewish customs are echoed by the people of Kashmir, including social and eating habits, festivals and burials.

After the Crucifixion it was therefore necessary for Jesus, having fulfilled the prophecies through his supposed death, to take his teachings of love and forgiveness to the lost tribes in far-off northern India.

Jesus said, referring perhaps to the lost tribes:

Matthew 5:24 – I am not sent but unto the lost sheep of the house of Israel.
John 10:16 – And other sheep I have which are not of this fold them also must I bring and they shall hear my voice and there shall be one fold and one shepherd.
Matthew 23:37–39 (Luke 13:34–36) – O Jerusalem, Jerusalem, thou that killest the prophets and stonest them which are sent unto thee, how often would I have gathered thy children together even as a hen gathers her chickens under her wings, and ye would not. Behold your house is left unto you desolate. For I say unto you, ye shall not see me henceforth till ye shall say – Blessed is He that cometh in the name of the Lord.

Surely Jesus was telling the people of Jerusalem that he was going away, but at the time they didn't realise it, or understand.

Jesus was known in Kashmir as Yasu or Yuz Asaf, or Isa, i.e., Jesus, and his tomb, as accepted by Hindus and later Moslems, is in Khanyer Street, Srinagar.

73

Holger Kersten informs us that the Hindus say: 'He was a prince who came to Kashmir from a foreign land – his name was Yuz Asaf'. And that he was a 'Nabi'. This story of the prophet is still common knowledge.

The legend in Kashmir recalls that the same family of devout Hindu people have had charge of looking after this tomb for some 1900 years. And the Hindus say with incredulity, 'But of course your Jesus didn't die on the Cross – he died here'. This is their long-standing and accepted tradition. The Koran also specifically states that Jesus survived the Crucifixion, as does Sri Sathya Sai.

If only the Vatican library would open its shelves to modern enquiry perhaps the truth would be known. But if all the myths and rumours through time were true, then of course Rome would be seen to have duped us all along and the dogma of Christianity would be a sham and a deceit.

The Lost Disciples, Glastonbury and Celtic Wales

If Jesus went off secretly to India with Thomas Didymus, a crowd could not have accompanied him and gone unknown or undetected. Therefore we have to ask ourselves what happened to the other close allies who were so near to Jesus in the last days of his ministry, ending at the Passion.

The important lynch-pin in the Passover plot was the intelligent, rich relation and staunch supporter of Jesus in all his stratagems, namely Joseph of Arimathea – Jesus' brother and Sanhedrin official. In ancient British tradition, Joseph later travelled to Britain, when he was a merchant in the metal trade buying tin. Cornwall was the major producer of tin from the mines of Exmoor and Dartmoor and the hills of Cornwall from as early as 2000 B.C. This valuable mineral was not known to exist in the Middle East, yet it is a vital component of 'bronze', which is an amalgam of copper and tin by fusion. At the beginning of the Bronze Age, from 2000 B.C., bronze was used to produce weapons in north-west Europe. The ancient Phoenicians were the seafarers who sailed from Palestine out into the Atlantic to achieve a secure round-about journey to Cornwall, not wishing to give away their source of tin to their rivals. It is now thought that Jesus had a son, also called Jesus, in which case the suggestion that parts of Cornwall were visited by Jesus, a young lad in the company of his uncle on his buying trips, could have substance. The village of Sancreed, port of Marazion and the 'Jesus well' at Thebetherick, near Padstow, are still considered 'sacred' today.

Joseph, also known as 'James the Just', and Jesus' son (Jesus II), both of the Essene way, could well have made contact with the 'local' priesthood of the Druids who were flourishing and widespread in Britain at the time. The centre of British Druidry was in South Wales, which was also the seat of the Silurian Kingdom – the royal tribe of the Celtic west-country fulfilling the priestly monarchistic traditions of the warrior kings. The Druidic traditions, incorporating the belief in 'One God', reincarnation and the idea of self-sacrifice for the good of others and country, were so akin to the Christian teaching as to be immediately compatible. The Druids were reported, in the later Roman Annals of Caesar and in his chronicles of the British Isles, to be a blood-thirsty tribe of cannibalistic flesh eaters and ritual murderers practising human sacrifice.

This is untrue – it is perfectly normal for a conqueror to denigrate and demote his conquests into oblivion and ridicule.

The story is that Joseph and a small band of trusted companions set out from Palestine after Jesus' departure to bring the Gospels to the gentiles of north-west Europe, to France and into the British Isles. The persecutions that followed the Crucifixion were swift and disastrous, and by the time Jerusalem was finally sacked in 70 A.D., the Christian faith had already been well dispersed and offered to many peoples far afield. Undoubtedly, thousands of Christians fled Palestine and dispersed all over Europe and as far afield as Britain and Ireland. The suggestion that Patrick and Christianity didn't come to Ireland before 470 A.D. is surely false. It is believed that the later finding of Israelite and Christian treasures in the Temple of Solomon by the Knights' Templar, and their subsequent transportation for safekeeping to Rosslyn Castle in Scotland, will one day reveal many truths.

It is hardly possible that Mary, the mother of Jesus, travelled with him to Kashmir. Everything in the Bible suggests that the women all thought him to be dead. So where was his final tomb or burial place? If Jesus' body had really gone from the sepulchre on the Monday, three days after the Cross, why do we not hear of it, perhaps a hundred or three hundred years later, as a secret passed from disciple to disciple? But we *don't* hear about it because it just wasn't there. There has never been any evidence, story or myth of another burial place or tomb anywhere in Palestine or Syria since. Jesus had physically left his homeland to continue his mission elsewhere. Did he bring with him his family, his mother? Probably not. In fact, if he had taken a collection of women of different ages, they would surely have slowed him up and inadvertently revealed his presence somewhere, disclosing his survival. This therefore discounts Mary's burial at Muree in Pakistan.

The disciples had to think Jesus was dead and buried – so some of Jesus' closest followers had to travel elsewhere, away from him and in another direction, i.e., West, not East, to the land of the Druids.

Joseph therefore embarked on his pre-arranged plan to bring safely away Jesus' closest followers. The disciples, as Jesus' minders, had already dispersed to their rural pastimes as farmers and fishermen – Jesus had shown himself to them on the sea-shore and had shared a goodbye meal with them there. It was the other close helpers, no doubt some in on his deception, who went West:

Mary – the mother of Jesus;
Mary – the wife of Cleophas;
Martha and Lazarus, the brother and sister who sheltered Jesus at Bethany, and Marcella their servant;
Entropius, Salome, Clean, Saturninus – the 'blind' man restored by Jesus,
Mary Magdalene, Maximin, Martial, Trophimus and Sidonius.
(George Jowett, *The Drama of the Lost Disciples.*)

This band of people are said to have travelled across the Mediterranean to Marseilles and moved up through France to cross from Brittany into Cornwall, and so eventually, in 36 A.D., arrived at Glastonbury and travelled on into

South Wales to the area we now know as Glamorgan, where they sought asylum and sanctuary with the Silurian princes at the centre of the Celtic/Druidic Faith. The last of the Kingdom of Judah and the House of David thus aligned itself with the Celtic Kingdom of Britain. This was the beginning of an historical drama that is still unfolding itself today, between the original Celtic Church and Rome.

The Gospel, in the form of the living Jesus, had gone to teach the lost tribes of Israel in north India, and the Gospel, through the lips of the surviving band from the Passover, had travelled to the heart of the only compatible and accepting, indeed welcoming, tribe in the West. This was at the sacred 'Isle of Avalon', Britain itself. Aval, the Celtic name for apple, was the emblem of fertility, giving the whole country its ancient name. This brings us back once again to the apple as the sacred fruit of 'knowledge'; from the Garden of Eden in the heart of the Pagan world of Druidic Britain.

As we have already seen, Jesus' message of love, truth and forgiveness was totally compatible with the core of Druidic thinking and practice. It was therefore readily accepted and acknowledged by the local priests. Jesus as the 'Prince of Peace' who had willingly sacrificed himself for the benefit of the salvation of his people was himself seen to be, and was accepted as, an Arch Druid – a chosen one of God whose teachings were totally valid. Five hundred years later Celtic Columba, St. Columbcille from Ireland, was to say, 'Jesus is my Druid'.

The lost band headed by Joseph, Jesus' brother, and Mary his mother, are thus reported to have brought Christianity to Britain in the year 36 A.D., and so within the realm of Druidism began the melding of the two ways, leading to the first Christian church in Western Europe. Undoubtedly, more Christians from Palestine began to trickle through to Avalon and Cornwall, and gradually the intermarriage of faith took place. The Jesus band reportedly also started marrying into the line of the Welsh Silurian princes, forming the beginnings of another, fresher line of 'Judah' in Britain. This Celtic line later became the line of the Princes of Wales in the eleventh and twelfth centuries – the line of the famous Owen Twyddyr. For 'Judah' read 'Tudor', hence subsequently the House of Tudor – the Kings and Queens of England of the fifteenth and sixteenth centuries A.D. centring around the Princes of Wales and the powerful monarch, Henry VIII of England. This we will come back to, later.

Let us now consider the situation in 43 A.D. Rome decided to attack as it realised that the greatest threat to its western realms were harboured in Britain. Here was a remnant of Christianity, thought to have been dealt with in Palestine, but who surfaced in north-west and started to convert the local kingdoms whose warriors were famous for their courage and power. There was a danger that Gaul (France) might be threatened – a scenario of possible unrest suddenly appeared here at the north-west corner of the Roman Empire. Conquest was the only answer.

News of the conversion of the British, so many years before present history proclaims, was sufficient for the Emperor Claudius to dispatch two of his best legions with orders to destroy the British Druids and Celtic Christians, and proclaim that acceptance of the Druidic and Christian faith was a capital offence. In particular, the edict is stated to include 'any person descended from David'. Consequently, the Roman legions invaded Britain, in 43 A.D., at Chichester in order finally to wipe out the Christian faith.

The British armies were led by Guiderius, King of the Silures, and a younger brother of Arviragus, Duke of Cornwall. Prince Charles is the present Prince of Wales and Duke of Cornwall! Soon the Cymri-Keltois (Celts) of Wales, under Caradoc, joined forces. Under the direction of the Arch Druids, Caradoc was elected to be the 'Pendragon', or commander, of all the forces. He became known as a great commander under the Roman name of Caratacus. The British tribes, the Cymri Welsh, the Silurians of the West, held together by an unbreakable faith in the combined Celtic/Druidic and Christian path, were too much even for the most experienced legions of Rome. Their commander, Aulus Plautius, saw his forces decimated. However, reinforcements arrived and eventually, after nine years of constant battle, Rome won.

At one stage, in 45 A.D., Emperor Claudius even offered his daughter, Venus Julia, in marriage to Arviragus in order to gain peace. During a truce of six months Arviragus and Venus Julia married and, in a bizarre turn of events in Britain, the sister of Caractacus, Gladys, married the Roman commander Aulus Plautius. In his annals, Tacitus remarks how strange it was that a Christian, Gladys, who took the name of Pomponia, was sent for trial because of her Christian beliefs.

However, the truce fell through and Plautius was recalled to Rome as an unsuitable commander and honourably relieved of his command. Battles continued. Finally in 52 A.D., when the Emperor Vespasian himself had come to Britain to oversee the campaign, with no less than four of his greatest generals with him, did he finally succeed in beating the combined Celtic tribes at the Battle of Clune in Shropshire. Entropius reports in his Roman records that during the nine years war 32 pitched battles had been fought.

The British commanders were taken to Rome as honourable prisoners and granted special privileges during a seven year open 'captivity'. Since the leaders of the Silurians had married into the Roman aristocracy, a curious melding of blood and faith took place, for the Silurians had by this time already been converted to Christianity by Joseph of Arimathea. The centre of Celtic/Druidic faith in the area of Glamorgan was not overrun by the Romans, and the first Christian church outside the Mediterranean had been established amongst the 'gentiles' in Britain. In a bizarre way, by 52 A.D., Christianity had also secretly surfaced in Rome itself. When (St.) Paul consecrated Linus (son of Caratacus) as the first bishop of Rome in 58 A.D., the Druidic and Christian faiths finally joined together through an extraordinary course of events. Centuries later, the King of Britain, Henry VIII, was to break with Rome and re-create a new Celtic Church in the West as Anglican or Protestant. This obviously caused deep distress and questioning within the Roman Catholic Church, as the very essence of the Christian faith was seen to be divided.

CHAPTER VII

The Grail Cup of the Last Supper

The Cup

When Joseph of Arimathea and the lost disciples arrived in Britain in 36 A.D., they settled finally in Glamorgan and built the first Christian church. However, Glastonbury was supposedly Joseph's destination, then an island in the meres of west Somerset, a vast swamp stretching to the sea, intersected by small rivers and reedy channels. The buildings were made of wattle, split-hazel wands and daub clay – mud that dried into a hard mortar, holding the structure in place. Joseph's first church there, a wattle and daub rectangle, was said to have been made in this way. But it was the thirteenth century monks, seeking attention and authentication in the Norman Templar age of chivalry, that transposed Joseph from Wales to Somerset.

The questionable story of Joseph arriving finally at Weary Hill is well known in British mythology. Joseph is said to have stuck his thorn staff into the ground, which the next season burst forth into leaf and flower, a whitethorn bush – hawthorn – that has always been 'sacred'. This sacredness originates in ancient folklore that says the flowers of the whitethorn, or maybush, should never be brought into a house as it brings bad luck. This is because the musk of the new may blossom is so incredibly heady and powerful that it's said to smell like a woman menstruating; the essence of fertility and birth.

It is said that Joseph brought to Britain the Cup of the Last Supper as the most important relic of Jesus and the Crucifixion. It has been known for many centuries as the 'Holy Grail' and it is around this vessel that so many myths of knighthood and chivalry have evolved. In folklore we are led to believe that the Grail Cup is a gold chalice, studded with precious stones, diamonds, rubies, sapphires and emeralds perhaps. It is said to be an object of immense material value quite apart from its symbolism. Many cups have been put forward as authentic – several in the possession of the Catholic Church – one particularly in Spain that is carved out of one piece of agate, hollowed out to be a cup and mounted with gold and silver and gems. But this is just another Roman artefact reflecting the riches and decadence of the late empire before it crumbled from within. Then there is an early Iron Age cup of bronze, found in the marshes near Glastonbury – some say this is the Grail.

78

Within the Chalice Well at Glastonbury a 'millefleur' multi-coloured glass saucer-dish about five inches in diameter was found when the well was being cleaned out back in the 1920s, in the days of Bligh Bond. But none of these really fulfilled the legend of the Cup of the Last Supper, or the actuality of the sort of vessel Jesus might have had in front of him on the table.

A more likely story of the Cup is a fascinating and simple tale, and it unravels like this.

Jesus and the disciples had laid on the table in front of each of them a wooden platter and a small circular wooden water or wine *bowl*. The food would have been on larger platters, passed along the table and the guests would have helped themselves with their right hands, with which they would have eaten. Forks and spoons would not have been used as forks were not even invented until 1650 A.D. Wine and water would have been in earthenware jugs.

The cup Joseph brought with him was a little wooden bowl and it is said to have rested on the altar of the abbey at Glastonbury, in the area of the original church at the present west end of the ruins of that great structure. This was the cup that Jesus is said to have used to bless his disciples at the table and is the cup that supposedly caught drops of his blood when his side was pierced by the lance of Longinus, the Roman centurion at the Cross.

We are told that the cup remained at the abbey until Henry VIII of England decided to dissolve the monasteries in the 1530s. The reason for the Dissolution has always been given as the refusal of the Pope (Britain had been Roman Catholic since Saxon King Osway in 666 A.D.) to grant him a divorce from his wife. The real reason was that the Catholic Church had become so powerful in its holdings of land and wealth that its very existence was threatening the lore and power of the Celtic monarch. There was a line of knowledge of the ancient mystery tradition held within the Court of England that went back through to the beginning of time in this country – to the esoteric priests of light, the mathematicians, dowsers and diviners who had always been part of the early pre-Christian religion, particularly of course the Druidic faith. The Judeo Celtic line of Judah, through the lost disciples, had become Tudor, i.e., Henry Tudor, was being threatened by Rome.

History has seen the Roman Church in recent centuries eradicate firstly, the Cathars, and then, in collusion with the French King, the Knights' Templar, with incredible cruelty and barbarity in the name of Rome's brand of Christendom. These two organisations in turn had become so saintly and purposeful in the simplicity of their Christianity that they had seemed to threaten the materialism, power, and sheer spiritual ego of the Papacy itself. The spiritual and business grip that the Church had over Europe was such that the lesser kings and princes of the European states had to follow the party line and give way, or be swallowed up in the doctrine of divine authority. Henry would have none of this. Remembering the early Celtic Church, his Church, as monarch and leader of the faith of the nation, he summarily dismissed Catholicism and proclaimed the Church of England as it is known today in direct opposition to Rome. What he did effectively was to restore the value of the monarchy to its original Celtic power base. One of simplicity in its dogma and practices, following the original concept of the Pharaohs – as head of state and head of the spirituality of the nation. Rome still has never forgiven him!

But it is the Cup we're now interested in. The mythical media story of 1200 A.D. is that three monks set out secretly from Glastonbury prior to the sacking of the monastery for the Cistercian monastery of Strata Florida in mid-Wales, 15 miles inland from Aberystwyth and the Irish Sea. This beautiful abbey, St. Mary's Abbey, housed the Grail Cup (known as St. Mary's Dowry in the Catholic Church) safely for years until word came to Strata Florida that troops were on their way to attack the abbey and remove its 'treasures'. However, the cup was probably already in Wales from the earliest date because there is no mention of it in the treasure inventory of Glastonbury Abbey at the time of the great fire in the thirteenth century.

When later troops were threatening the Welsh churches, three monks set off, to bring the Cup safely out of Wales across the Irish Sea, with a plan to lodge it safely in the great Cistercian abbey of Mellifont in Co. Meath. But this never happened. Half-way to the coast, the monks felt they were about to be overtaken by the troops, so sought sanctuary with a Catholic family in Nanteous, the home of the Powell family. When the last monk was dying, he summoned the head of the family to his bedside and explained that he was the last Keeper of the Cup, and asked the head Powell if he and his heirs would take over the guardianship of the Cup, as the saying has been passed down, 'until the Church shall claim her own'.

For many years this precious object (diagram 47) was at Nanteous, where many hundreds of people from all over the country came to seek absolution from the Cup. There is an extensive record of miraculous healings that have taken place for people who believed in its power and have had the faith to make their way to it to pray for help. The family used to pour water through

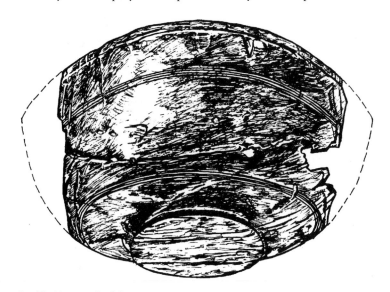

Diagram 47. *The Nanteous Grail Cup.*

this broken little bowl which was put in a special glass dish to hold it. This water was then bottled and given out to seekers to drink and pray for healing.

In more recent times, Nanteous Abbey, as it became known, passed out of ownership of the Powells and the Cup passed into the female line of the family, a lady from that family currently being the Keeper of the Cup. It is with her kindness and permission the author tells this story.

During the last century the Cup was 'lent out' to local people for curing their ailments against a pledge of money or a valuable article, perhaps a watch or wedding ring. The Cup was then taken away for about a month and the money or article left as security. Two examples of such pledges are illustrated in diagram 48:

> *23rd Jan 1882*
> *2 half-sovereigns deposited in the drawer, library table;*

and to an *Ebenezer Vaughan*:

> *for the use of his wife left £1-0-0*
> *Cup returned 5 October 1858 Cured.*

It seems the Cup was kept out quite a long time to be drunk from until a cure was effected, and the slips testify – and they are very numerous – that cures took place with great regularity. Many pieces were broken off as talismans!

The Cup is now being kept in a bank for safety as it seems several Welsh nationalistic individuals and organisations appear to think they ought to have

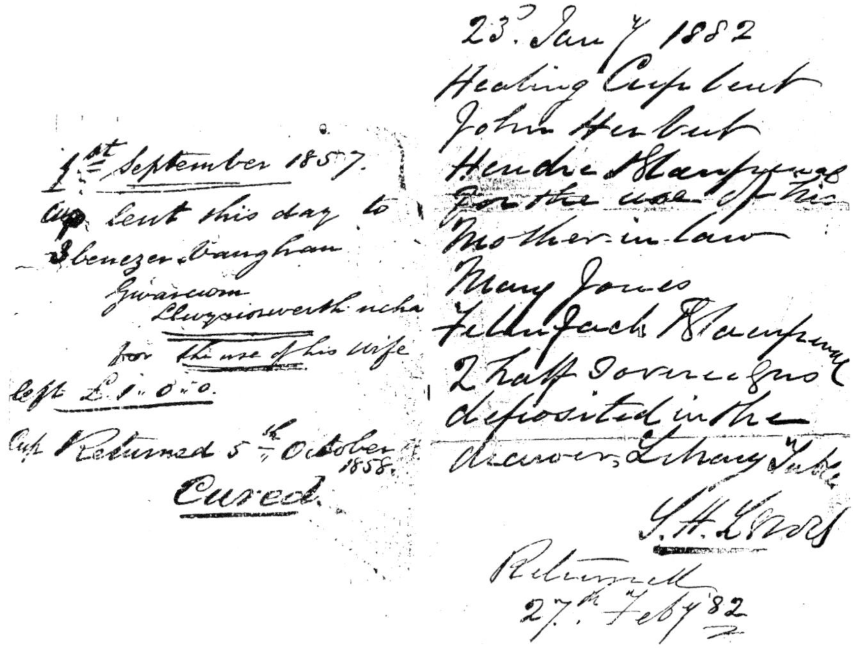

1st September 1857.
Cup lent this day to
Ebenezer Vaughan
for the use of his wife
left £1.0.0.
Cup Returned 5th October 1858.
Cured.

23rd Jany 1882
Healing Cup lent
John Herbert
for the use of his
Mother-in-law
Mary Jones
2 half Sovereigns
deposited in the
drawer, Library Table
Returned
27th Feby 82

Diagram 48. *Two pledges for the Cup* (***Private collection***).

ownership of it. Occasionally it is brought out by the guardian for the benefit of pilgrims who seek it. The author heard of it for the first time in 1984 but as always the man who disclosed its very existence was sworn to secrecy as to its whereabouts. It is up to each individual, if interested enough, to find his or her own path to the Cup and this usually takes a lot of personal detective work. A series of unusual coincidences, if there are such things, led the author to the Cup finally two years later.

My pilgrimage started in the heart of Wales at Strata Florida where a 'dowsing' of the Abbey had been requested by a client. Gradually the story of the Grail came out and it was with great trepidation that we – two of us – approached the Keeper for permission to handle and view the Cup. Also, permission to photograph the Cup was finally given, two visits and three years later, with a view to inclusion in this book (colour plate 3). So it is with thanks that I can now illustrate what remains of this little wooden wine-cup that still, even now, over two thousand years later, produces miraculous healings, cures and events.

You will see how gnarled and incomplete the Cup now is, such a simple humble little article of seemingly no sparkle or noticeable value; it is not a jewelled vessel of gold. Yet if we think back to the events of the Passover – the Last Supper – the blessing by Jesus to his disciples with the wine or water, it has a wonderful significance:

> **Matthew 25:28** – *For this is my blood of the new testament which is shed for many for the remission of sins.*

The Cup is exactly what we would expect if we bothered to think about the table of the Last Supper, and reflects the simplicity, the beauty and the humble touch of the man we call Jesus of Nazareth. How sad it is to see our present priests all togged up in their finery, in front of heavily-laden, sumptuous altars, puffed up in their egotistical male ego, pontificating to us in a way that must seem bizarre indeed to the realms of the saintly spirits that followed the path of humility and poverty in the original Celtic Church.

The Chalice

The Chalice of the Christian communion is a direct reference to the Grail Cup as it is from this vessel that Christians receive the wine or water representing the blood of Jesus. The bowl of the Chalice however had other purposes in early Christian usage, particularly amongst the astronomer priests; those highly educated mathematicians and metaphysical scientists of the early Church.

A late sixteenth century German Chalice, from Augsburg, is illustrated in black and white plate 3. The bowl of this silver-gilt Chalice Dial is shaped as a hexagon, or six-pointed star, i.e., the centre part of two conjoined triangles – the centre of the Star of David, no less. Within this bowl can clearly be seen the engravings of the paths of the zodiacal celestial bodies – you will note Aries the Ram and Taurus the Bull. So this Chalice had a clear astronomical usage. The fact that it depicts the Zodiac is also significant, since publicly the Church denigrated and dismissed anything to do with astrology as 'devilish', yet

B&W plate 3. *German Chalice Dial, c.seventeenth century A.D.* (**British Museum**).

secretly followed an initiatory teaching that specifically included many 'banned' practices – particularly dowsing and divining!

Another German Chalice Dial, late sixteenth century, is illustrated in *Pi in the Sky*, page 129, this time with a central gnomon to throw a shadow around the bowl – a Sundial.

Colour plate 4 illustrates the Ardagh Chalice, from eighth century Ireland. This beautiful Chalice has eight markers around the underside of the base of the rim for the eight-fold year: two solstices, two equinoxes and four quarter days, and the central boss has five markers between double scroll spirals for the energy of water in five-fold symmetry. In the very centre is a rock crystal to energise the 'blood' or water.

To find the true Celtic chalices of the very early churches we have to look in those sixth-century oratory structures on or off the west coast of Ireland. In this drawing (diagram 49), looking through a dry stone entrance to the east window we see the altar slab of unhewn rock. Cut into the slab is a chalice 'stoop' – totally plain, completely simple and entirely useful – living water from the living rock (diagram 50).

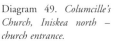

Diagram 49. *Columcille's Church, Iniskea north – church entrance.*

Diagram 50. *Columcille's Church, Iniskea north – altar and holy water 'stoop'.*

Cauldrons and Sacred Fires

Flavia Anderson suggests that way back in Greek times at, for instance, The Oracle of Delphi, the sacred and ritual fires were lit by the use of metal mirrors using the Sun's concentrated rays to ignite the kindling:

> There was a sacred fire at Delphi and another at Athens, and Plutarch in his *Life of Numa* tells how it was lit with the Sun's rays. This they usually effect by means of metallic mirrors, the concavity of which is made to follow the sides of an isosceles triangle and which converge from their circumference to a single point in the centre. When therefore placed opposite the Sun so that its rays fell upon it from all sides they are collected and concentrated at the centre, the air itself is rarefied there and light dry substances (kindling) placed there will quickly blaze.
>
> (Flavia Anderson, *The Ancient Secret*.)

Anthemius, a Greek mathematician at the court of the Emperor Justin in Byzantium, attempted the study of the effects of light. One of his experiments was to use a mirror in the shape of an oven. This is important, for if we interpret 'oven' as a source of light and therefore fire, we can relate this to the Cauldrons of mythology that are never empty – the source of sustenance from the king or chieftain of the tribe.

In Irish mythology, we know that the Dagda lives in the solar temple of Newgrange where the Winter Solstice Sun penetrates deep into the womb of matter every 21 December, lighting up and procreating the rebirth of the New Year and the seasons. In the same way, the Cauldron as the source of fire rekindles the brand or torch of the king in his hostel and tells his people that the life of the king is extant; that he lives whilst the fire blazes. When he dies the brand of fire (male) is thrown actually and symbolically into the lake to be extinguished by water (female) –'the Lady of the Lake'. As mentioned in Chapter III, the brand not only represents both light and fire, but also the silver flashing sword of the king, Excalibur – derived from the Greek Ex-Kylie-Pur which translates 'out of a cup, a fire'. So the symbolism is unique. The mystical city of 'Camelot', deriving from the ancient tongue 'Camu-lot' meaning 'bent light'. Again, we have the symbolical use of white light to produce 'fire', seemingly as if by magic.

However, there is another age-old method of producing fire – from the energy of the Sun. These rays, unseen in form, are transmuted into the seven component rays we know as the colours of the rainbow. This is the splitting of light through a form of matter. So perhaps we should start to think of the Grail – the Holy Grail as Holy Fire. Today, we all know how easy it is to start a fire with a magnifying glass or 'lens' as it is called. But to the ordinary people of past ages it was pure magic, a source of great wonder that 'the priest' could seemingly produce fire out of his hand – the catalyst of this fire being either a lens of rock crystal or glass.

Rock crystal occurs all over the planet and was used extensively as quartz in the earliest burials of the Stone Age. As we saw in Chapter IV, it has the unique property to bend light (polarised light) i.e., sunlight, through 45° thereby creating a balance between electricity and magnetism. However, this refractive property is again important here because the sublime city, 'Camelot' or 'bent light', reiterates the idea of the use of light to ignite the fires of the seasons and candles on the altars at the time of the (Christian) festivals. It also relates to the mythological celestial city of the 'crystal' heart.

Flavia Anderson asks us:

> Is it possible then that either a mirror or a crystal could be the Grail? The answer I think is that both 'Sacra' were displayed to the initiates of the Grail cults. 'Li Saint talleors d'argent' is the silver bowl shaped mirror.
>
> Wolfram [a medieval poet] expressly tells us that the Grail was a stone. He says:

'And this brotherhood so gallant doest thou know what to them I shall give
Their life and their strength and their valour – they know by a **stone** they live
And that stone is both pure and precious – Its name has thou never even heard
Men call it Lapis Exilis – by its magic the wondrous bird The Phoenix becomes ashes and yet doth such virtue flow
From the stone, that afresh it rises renewed from the ashes' glow
And the plumes that erewhile it moulted spring forth yet more fair and bright'

In the end he says:
'And this stone all men call the GRAIL.'

Therefore the Grail stone was a stone that produced fire. The *rekindling* of a fire from ancient times was considered a *resurrection*, a rebirth in itself, symbolised by the rise of the phoenix, the firebird of golden feathers.

The new king ascends to the throne and rekindles the brand or torch outside his hostel – he is the reincarnation of a previous king, in himself the ritual head of the land. The new fire is the true Shiva aspect of the Trinity.

At Tara, the capital of Iron Age Ireland, the Druid king extinguished the ritual fire at the festival of Samhain and rekindled it to start the new year of the seasons. It was his prerogative and no-one, on pain of death, preceded him, except finally Patrick as an act of Christian defiance. St. Patrick in his journeys around Ireland is even said to have made fire using the Sun's rays refracted through an icicle in winter – a miracle of course!

In Irish mythology there was a famous battle on the plains of Moytirra above Lough Arrow in Co. Sligo. Primitive people used the flint, steel and tinder to ignite fire, and these articles were carried at the waist in a pouch or pocket.

*Accordingly fire struck in this way was called 'teine-creasa', fire of the 'crois' or girdle. In the same way the Scottish sporran takes its name from the Gaelic for flint, **spor**, and means the 'flint bag'. The Firbolgs who lived in Ireland before the coming of the Milesians with the Cauldron of the Goddess Dana were probably called after the fire bags, from bolg a bag, and **pur**, the Greek which had a common origin with our word fire. In other words, they were the more primitive men who drew fire from flints in contrast to the Milesians who possessed a cauldron and crystal. In Brittany the fairies known as Korrigans, whose speciality was to haunt the megalithic stones, were believed to carry red pouches slung over their shoulders in which they kept their treasure. According to legend, a mortal who found one of these pouches discovered in it only dead leaves, hairs, sand and a pair of scissors; but when holy water had been sprinkled on this rubbish, the leaves turned to gold, the hair to pearls, and the sand to diamonds. What happened to the scissors is not recounted, but on the tombstones of Iona they are used to designate the burial place of a female and might therefore have served in Breton legend as an emblem of the Goddess. Of the other treasure one can only say that the golden leaves of Glasir, and the sand which makes glass are ingeniously represented; and as for the pearls (remembering the pearl-rimmed cauldron of Annwn) it may be this very vessel from which the Korrigans took their name, for the Gaelic for kettle or cauldron is coire.*

In the *Mabinogion*, Perdur's serpent stone had the property of producing as much gold as was desired – this surely was a rock crystal and precluded gold as 'fire'. A globe or glass filled with water is another magical article that produces fire by refraction and reflection.

The rock crystal was referred to as the fruit of the golden tree in *Virgil*. Sometimes the crystal was described as *an apple* and in fact the attribute of Diana of Nemi was an apple branch. Once again we come back to the fruit of the tree – a rosy fire could be the secret of the tree and its fruit in the Garden of Eden. The *pommel* of a sword, sometimes enclosing a rock crystal ball, used to ignite fire on the knight's travels, also derives from the word apple, 'pomme', in French, and Latin, 'pomum', meaning fruit. So not only did Adam and Eve experience the celestial fire of the Kundalini rising as a 'snake' or 'serpent' up their spines, but also gained the knowledge of producing fire with a piece of natural rock crystal. Both symbolise in parable the very essence of life – birth and rebirth; kindling and rekindling; procreation, life, death and reincarnation – The Grail itself.

The Arthurian Legend

When considering the Grail we always return to the mystery of the Arthurian legends. How the boy king claimed his rightful place before all the knights of the kingdom by successfully drawing the sword out of stone, or an anvil. An anvil represents the enduring heaviness of ego that can only be dispelled in knighthood by the search for the light or grail. This is a wonderful allegorical tale, for the sword is the sword of light that he drew out of a crystal. Thus a beam of celestial light could ignite 'fire', seemingly as if by magic out of his hand. This was indeed awe-inspiring, but of course Arthur had been initiated by the magician Merlin, a metaphysical scientist, an alchemist, a sorcerer, a weaver of spells and a worker in the light, who had custody of the boy king.

This story is the essence of the Arthurian or ancient mystery tradition in the British Isles and goes back through Druid times into the Stone Age itself, when the spear or sword of light 'shafts' into the centre of Stonehenge at the Summer Solstice sunrise to illuminate the sacred space and ignite the 'holy fires' on the central altar.

The Turin Shroud

This was supposedly the wrapping cloth of Jesus after the Crucifixion, and has been held sacred for many years by the Catholic Church but there has always been great speculation as to its authenticity. Recently, the Church allowed a thorough examination to be done by several eminent University scientific laboratories to test its date – was it 2,000 years old, was the imprint of the face of Jesus, etc. etc.? The conclusion from carbon dating techniques was that it dated from between 1250 and 1350 A.D., so it could not concern Jesus.

Lomax and Knight, in *The Hiram Key*, have recently suggested that when the Church and the French king finally persecuted the Knights' Templar, starting on that fateful day in October of *Friday 13th* 1307 A.D., they actually crucified its leader. He was Jacques de Morlay, a large man who was tortured and nailed up in a re-enactment of Jesus' Crucifixion. As the leader of the Templars he was thought to be, and projected as, the Anti-Christ personified. It was his body and image that was wrapped in the shroud 14' of linen taken from the central Temple of the Knights in Paris. So indeed, the shroud is of a crucified man but not of Jesus. That the Church itself perpetrated such an act, once again shows its hypocrisy and duplicity in passing off the shroud as the wrapping of Jesus. It was just another attempt to authenticate the Resurrection, for the tomb was empty, the shroud unwrapped and the body already gone.

CHAPTER VIII

Earth Energy Stars

The pattern of the Earth's most finely evolved material grows to crystal symmetry and the patterns of the planets around us also seemingly conform to a similar geometry. To understand the progress so far is to realise that the surface of the Earth is just another barrier within the density of matter and the passage of light. The air around us is comparatively thick due to gravity and we are held more firmly to the Earth than if we were on top of Mount Everest. Put another way, if we were descending from outer space we would come from weightlessness to the upper atmosphere where we would begin to feel the pull of the Earth's gravity and the beginnings of density. As we moved closer to the Earth, this density would increase proportionately until we approached the surface – yet all densities have a connective atomic passage through them.

We also know that all these different densities of matter have evolved with atomic form, particularly if they are crystalline/crystal form 'at rest' in the mineral kingdom, 'in growth' in the animal and vegetable kingdoms or 'in motion' in the elements of water and air. Throughout all these patterns there is a natural imprint and interlock of energy, which builds up into an 'aura' or 'grid' through which the life-force acts. This life-force of the Earth permeates everything and can be tuned into by any human being wishing to raise consciousness.

Many people living in the country have, on occasion, heard of water dowsers, strange characters considered rather 'fey' who can tell where there is water, its depth, its rate of flow and its mineral content. They do this with a forked stick, usually a hazel, or a pendulum, that leaps around in their hands at the appropriate place. These people are also called 'diviners' and they are tuning into energy, a natural flow or static body of energy of one type within the body of another; here water in earth. They are sensitive to these vibrations and therefore can define them. This is the simplest form of dowsing. All other natural substances can be located in the same way, for example, oil, gravel, copper, gold – each having its own vibrational response. This includes disease and illness, hence alternative healing practices.

The life-force 'grid' can be defined in geometric patterns within concentric circles forming into what is termed an Earth Star. These Stars are, in their

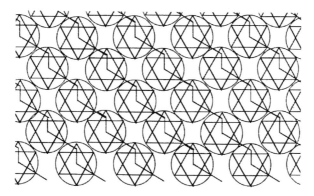

Diagram 51. *Earth Stars (plan view).*

true complete state, connected to one another and cover the surface of the Earth just like a bee's honeycomb in a basic circular/hexagonal shape. They are not just flat, as we can plot them on a map, but spherical like a complete three-dimensional rainbow half above our surface. The energy of these Stars is invisible to normal sight but can be seen with sensitive or clairvoyant sight and plotted either on the flat surface of a map or by physically walking the ground, using a pendulum or divining rods (diagrams 51 and 52).

The exact shape and dimensions of these Earth Stars are completely symmetrical. They have been re-identified and defined in size, shape and colour by the late Clive Beadon, in his work as a professional dowser. To quote his definition:

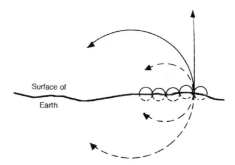

Three-dimensional Earth Stars as they occur all over our planet. An infinite number of other sizes, natural and man-made, permeate through these auric levels.

Diagram 52. *Earth Stars (side elevation).*

The surface of the Earth is covered with an interlocking pattern of energy lines. The pattern shows a six-pointed star within a circle, each unlit touching the next and linked together by the major energy line running through the centres. The basic colours of the lines of the patterns are white, red, black and blue and where damage has occurred these colours will show but they are splintered off in all directions with no coherent shape or form.

In areas away from man's activities the patterns can be traced in their balanced, repeating shapes, but where they have been damaged, fragmented lines are generated and it is near these points that disharmony occurs. To a dowser, these lines have the characteristic that they show as black and carry the apparent information of being water. It is probably the origin of the traditional black leys and black streams.

These patterns, sometimes like the acupuncture lines of the human body, are normally in balance but they can be diverted or destroyed and the resulting disharmony and uneasiness affects people in the area. Since we all have the dowsing sense, although we may not be aware of it, we can all be affected in varying degrees by such disturbances. The effect of such damage is being noted by an increasing number of interested people and there seems to be a growing correlation between their presence and inexplicable tension, unease and illness.
(Clive Beadon, *Earth Stars*.)

A distinct similarity will immediately be noted between the basic shapes of platonic geometry, the basic shapes of crystal symmetry and the pattern of the movement of the planets around the Earth. We can go further than this and suggest that the sequential pattern of planetary movement in the heavens, and as represented in the Earth Star, mirrors the pattern of movement of the protons and electrons within the atomic structure of crystals when put from rest into an activated state, and therefore in the patterns of the Solar life-force itself.

Stone Age Man, S.A.M., understood and used this auric field and its symmetry, or 'grid', to help him attune to the idea of cosmic consciousness. His intimate relationship with water (birth), earth (matter), air (atmosphere) and fire (the Sun), all interacted together to form the principle of 'One Kingdom'. S.A.M. was able to see these energies clairvoyantly and use them with the help of his intuitive dowsing ability to lay out his stone circles and landscape temples.

Diagram 53 shows the layout of a dolmen site from Carrowmore in Co. Sligo. The structure itself, with the inclusion of many tiny pieces of quartz, sets up the six-pointed Earth star pattern in symmetry, thereby creating at its centre point, the burial place; a spiral of energy rising through the ground from the underground water conjunction below. This, in principle, allows the 'soul' to leave the body (remains) and travel back into the realms we call in Christian terms 'heavenly' – or back to 'God'. These simple little metaphysical Stone Age burials, situated at places designated to be very sacred, involved ancient practices carried forward through time into the Bronze Age and Iron Age, and thus into the layout of our Celtic churches and later large cathedrals.

This principle was extended by S.A.M. out into the landscape to cover large areas of countryside, again to produce a 'landscape temple' – a sacred area covering often many hundreds of yards or acres in size, depending on the suitability and conformation of the tribal area; even eventually from country to country.

In Co. Sligo, is the enigmatic megalithic site on the Bricklieve Hills above Lough Arrow. The passage cairns, as they are called, cover a large area of convoluted hillsides spanning a mile in diameter. At first sight, the cairns are seemingly placed at haphazard points on the hilltops. But with the use of the pendulum, the layout becomes clear and forms into the beautiful six-pointed star pattern we are now so familiar with.

The centre of the Star at Carrowkeel is not obvious, just a small cave going straight down into the earth, now filled-in to within ten feet of the surface with slippage, turf and heather. Furthermore, it could seem that these cairns were laid

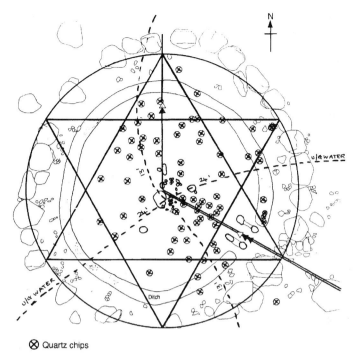

⊗ Quartz chips

Diagram 53. *Carrowmore Dolmen excavation.*

out in accordance with the planetary bodies with the cave as the Sun centre, then Mercury, Venus, Earth, Moon, Mars, Jupiter and Saturn respectively, revolving around the centre point; even Jupiter and Saturn seen seemingly in conjunction at four places (diagram 54).

S.A.M. has thus shown us his wider vision, his planetary connection from as early as 4000 B.C. Where, we need to ask ourselves, did this knowledge come from? Surely an earlier civilisation long past, but remembered through inner mythology. The layout of later Christian structures is inherited from this knowledge.

There was a time, and at certain places, when these Earth Stars and the connective grid were in balance on the surface of the Earth, but gradually as evolution built them up, man has disrupted and depleted them. Now, with man polluting and manipulating the crust and aura of the Earth, there are few places left where the Stars are still complete, unbroken and in balance. Where these energy lines are not in symmetry, but fractured and broken, then all sorts of unpleasantness can result. This continuous spherical cover on the surface of the Earth is the first layer of the Earth's aura and can be likened to the area immediately on and above the surface of the skin of our bodies; the pranic level. If we have a boil or scar it ruptures the surface of our skin and the energy all around becomes unbalanced, e.g., we feel heat from our tumour telling us of an area of disruption within a zone, or 'grid', of nerves and tissue. If perhaps you can envisage one pore of your skin as one Earth Star of the Earth's crust, you will begin to get the idea. The Stars on the surface, close to the density

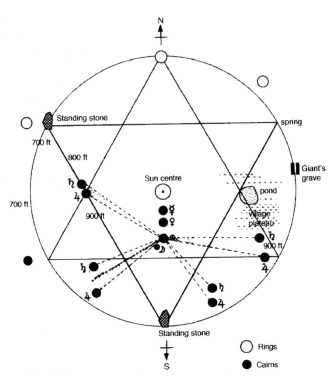

Diagram 54. *The Carrowkeel Star planetary conjuncts.*

or body of the Earth, can be compared to the level where all negativity and fear is trapped close in gravity.

Where an Earth Star is out of balance internally, the energy pattern can be realigned by the use of selected crystals and hard stones – set in a certain pattern within a copper spiral. These have been called **Spirals of Tranquility** by their creator (see Appendix D). The copper rings encircle and energise these chips, which, because of their atomic and chemical structure interacting with each other, create a natural energy force-field that is strong enough to permeate through the whole atmospheric Star, forming a vortex to bring it back into its true symmetrical form. No substance other than crystals has the inherent atomic symmetry or balance to enable this.

As these Earth Stars have been more and more disrupted by man during the passing centuries, so the original use that the Earth Stars were put to in the alignment and construction of ancient sites or energy centres, such as our early churches and great cathedrals, has become occulted. There was a time before the discovery and use of smelted metal where there were large areas with a balanced energy 'grid' in operation. S.A.M. built his structures on special points and conjunctions, within these circles, and always erected his standing stones and dolmens in a particular place. He worked either by instinct or information from the use of the pendulum, conforming in a selected way to the energy of the Earth Star, the Sun, Moon and the planets.

The early Christian constructions followed these patterns where possible. See, for example, details of the Rock of Cashel, Salisbury Cathedral and other great churches in Chapter XII.

It was the gradual influx of the warring immigrants spreading out from the centre of the European land-mass to the corners of the known world, with their new weapons of iron, that destroyed and disrupted the ancient sacred places. This destruction has continued and even today unaware farmers, planning officers and property developers remove or refashion the depleted switched-off remaining examples of these structures within the once integrated vibrant 'grid'. The Earth Star force-field followed the natural path of the energy imprint of the whole cosmic structure and was as real to S.A.M. and the early Christian monks as our modern electricity grid is to us, covering, but now marring, our countryside.

The Earth Star fits concisely within a circle forming a pair of ascending and descending equilateral conjoined triangles similar to the schematic Saturn/Jupiter conjunctions and the structure of the crystal atom. Energy must have both input and output points – these are clearly marked at the south-east and north-west points of their path, through the centre of the structure. Note the inner hexagonal shape produced by the conjoined triangles (diagram 55 and colour plate 5).

As well as the internal structure lines that permeate the Earth Star, there is a formation of concentric circles of colour that spread out from a central cross to

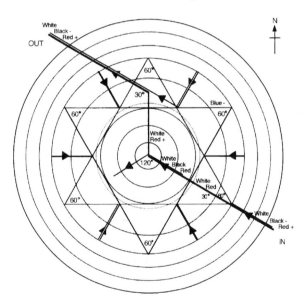

Note central hexagon showing + -, ✡
rhomboid (◊) showing + - and equilateral triangles
ascending and descending conjoined, showing
input energy and output energy positions.
Input lines of red, white and black act as the cable
that activates the structure.

Diagram 55. *Earth Star – basic 'diviners' Star pattern* (**Clive Beadon**).

the perimeter. These gradations, from grey/black at the lower level, to the white/ gold light, have been defined and annotated by the late Clive Beadon as follows. He called them 'Tranquillities':

1. Grey
2. Grey–Black
3. Black
4. Black–White
5. White
6. Violet–White
7. Violet
8. Violet–Blue
9. Blue
10. Blue–Green
11. Green
12. Green–Yellow
13. Yellow
14. Yellow–Red
15. Red
16. Red–Grey (triangular perimeter)
17. Violet
18. Violet–Blue
19. Blue
20. Blue–Green
21. Green
22. Green–Yellow
23. White—Silver
24. White—Gold

However, Earth energies continue to circle to 32 and higher energies (consciousness) from 32–64.

CHAPTER IX

Early Celtic Monks and their Churches

Bell, Book and Candle

When the first monks arrived at the furthest extremities of the known world in north-west Europe, they settled in with the rural communities easily, as their new religion was compatible with the old Druidic way.

The Druids had taken over the Stone Age structures and the Christian monks soon started to build their little oratories within the Druidic circles, using the same principles of natural energy transfer to enhance their buildings. Since the earlier structures had deliberately been built over the conjunction of underground water-courses to actuate the power points, so the little churches followed these same principles (diagram 56).

The earliest churches surviving in western Europe are on the west coast of Ireland, built sometime from the fourth to seventh centuries A.D. by the Celtic monks or 'Culdees' as they were called. 'Culdee' means 'worshipper of God'. This period was known in north-west Europe as the Dark Ages, a time spanning several centuries after the Romans had left and their empire fallen from military power into chaos. As the Imperial military might cracked from within, so the Cross of Christianity was taken up, ironically after many millions had been per-secuted and killed before the national conversion. As the sword was laid down, having failed to eradicate and destroy the new religion, Rome, glad to find an alternative to the now useless sword, took up the Cross enthu-siastically. The poacher had effectively become the gamekeeper and the Caesars of old were replaced by the Popes in

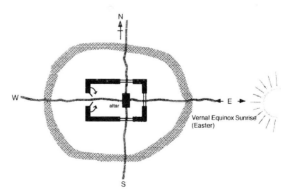

Diagram 56. *Early Celtic Christian church on 'riser' in ring fort – altar at conjunction over underground water courses.*

the realisation that if the people following 'The Way' were so imbued with the 'Light of God' and seemed to have a special spiritual love able to transcend all forms of brutality and terror, then it – 'The Way' – must have something incredible within its foundations. So the Cross was accepted by its latest converts and the minds of the population began to be taken over by spiritual manipulation and the exercise of a new form of power; the control of the emotions and the mind. Gradually a power base was built up whereby it was deemed necessary to make the Celtic Christians on the farthest seaboards fall into line and toe the new Papal edicts.

The monks in Ireland had travelled originally through the Mediterranean and up the western seaboards of Spain, Portugal and France, perhaps through England and Glastonbury, to seek refuge and peace on the little promontories and peninsulas of western Ireland and Scotland. Here they built their tiny oratories, seemingly in permanent grace and tranquillity, till the coming of the Vikings at the beginning of the ninth century.

These monks were known for their ability to travel simply, seeking sanctuary and food from the tribal Irish, and carrying only 'bell, book and candle'. The bells of the early monks had been picked up *en route* from the farmers and shepherds of the Iberian peninsula. These were the cow bells of ancient manufacture that still ring 'clink clonk' around the sunny hills of Portugal today. The one illustrated (diagram 57) is said to be St. Patrick's bell, although how he got it from Portugal if he were a slave in Wales is problematical. A similar bell (black and white plate 4) was bought by the author in 1982 from a remote village junk shop near Evora in Portugal. Note the similarity in shape, size and the lap

Diagram 57. *Patrick's Bell and Shrine (**National Museum of Ireland**).*

joints – the old way of wrapping a joint into itself. Also note the three-fold tree of life embossed on the metal. Both bells are bronze and dipped in brass. The Portuguese example has a wooden clapper suspended on a leather thong and makes a really lovely, deep, resonant clonking sound.

Anyone familiar with the west of Ireland will know of the many beautiful little stone churches on the mainland and on some of the remotest islands imaginable, only reached in small boats, 'curraghs', at seasonal times of calm. These are places of relentless storm and isolation in winter when the Atlantic rages and the gales whip in with incredible force, often completely covering up the smaller islands with spray. To have lived in a tiny community as a celibate monk must have been very difficult and demanding; constant toil for four months of the year, from November until April, to keep the community established and alive.

B&W plate 4. Cow Bell – Portugal, c.seventeenth century A.D. (*Private collection*).

It is generally thought that these monks spent their whole time labouring and in prayer and meditation. Some people even think they were great gamesters and gamblers, ridiculously citing the beautiful little calculator made out of wood in the National Museum of Ireland as a monks' 'gaming board', but in reality a 'peg' calculator (diagram 58).

See how the Vesica Pisces squares the circles of the outer and inner diameters and is clearly marked by the two different sized heads of the monks – neatly tonsured accordingly (diagram 59). The pegging of the holes ($7 \times 7 = 49$ holes) represents the 'magic square' of Venus. It provides a seven-fold calculator or a weekly and moonthly calendar, and within itself a 3, 4, 5, 6, 7 calculator used with neat little bone pins.

The Annual Festivals

The monks were highly trained in mathematics and metaphysics, healing, solar, lunar and celestial observation and calculation. They positioned their oratories to enable them to calculate the phases of the Sun, Moon and the stars, and to annotate and record the movements of the spherical bodies in order to plot the past, present and future to produce their ephemeris.

 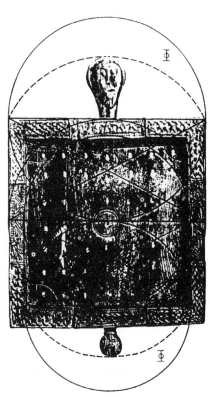

Diagram 58. *Irish monks' 'board game' – peg calcula-tor (**National Museum of Ireland**).*

Diagram 59. *Irish monks' peg calculator and the Vesica Pisces.*

We have mentioned the solar and lunar movements but now let us look at how the monks recognised the early Christian festivals, marked by the movements of the heavenly bodies, and renamed them accordingly. That many of these festivals were subsequently taken into the Christian calendar helps us to realise and enjoy their true significance. These festivals marked their eight-fold wheel of the year and were celebrated season by season – quarter by quarter – year in, year out.

The stages of the year were far more than just a succession of events to do with watching the Sun or Moon so that crops could be planted and grown at the right time. As the sequence of these events took place time after time and year after year man realised there was a deeper significance behind the rhythms of the natural progressions, both on the surface of the Earth and in his own inner being as he grew from youth to old age, birth to death.

As we know, four of these distinct annual moments, the mid-points of the seasons, mark the most intense times, whilst the other four, the cusps of the seasons, mark the least intense moments when one season changes over into the next succeeding one. The four mid-points occur at the solstices and equi-noxes and are well known by the position of the Sun – the fixed times of the solar calendar every year. The four cusps, known as the fire festivals or quarter days, are not so marked, being more fluid or movable in their placing in the calendar. In fact, all eight are 'fire' festivals in respect of being part of the *solar* year. The fixed solstices and equinoxes represent the dominant 'masculine' aspects, and the cusps or quarters the more impressionable 'feminine' aspects. The four phases of the Moon, which are the basis of our weekly and moonthly calendar are effectively a solar cycle in miniature.

In order to recognise and celebrate the changeover points, the priests of old thus made the quarter days coincide with the nearest lunar festivals at the time of the full Moon. This meant that the quarter days were movable within a margin of a fortnight, either side of the hypothetical quarter point. It also had the practical advantage of directly linking the solar cycle with the lunar cycle, and in this sense one could consider the quarter days to be lunar festivals.

The feminine and masculine always work together in life and thus the twelve-fold lunar cycle operates in partnership with the eight-fold solar cycle; the solar cycle with its four solstices and equinoxes complemented by the four quarters. Each cycle in itself has its more masculine and more feminine aspects working together – the full Moons of the lunar cycle rising alternately in the 'male' (positive) and 'female' (negative) zodiacal signs. The lunar festivals were thus used to prepare the person for the solar festivals – the feminine phase being the receptive part that prepares the way for the spiritual impulses to come into the womb of matter, and the masculine phase being the outgoing, expressive part which puts into action that which has been received.

Thus the disciple initiate offers the Grail Cup of his heart and soul to receive the light of the spirit; the cup is filled to overflowing. He then goes forth as a son of 'God' to give that consecrated Grail to the rest of life. In other words, when our souls are born into this world, incarnate as physical bodies, we do not suddenly see and understand truth. It is always there but we have to find it. We can liken this to the Sun, which although always present, is sometimes hidden (occulted) from sight behind the shadows – that it has gone away is simply an illusion. Consequently, we spend lifetime after lifetime seeking the greater mysteries in the depths of our own evolving consciousness. With the unfolding sense of awe at the immensity of our purpose in seeking the 'absolute', comes an understanding of the infinite order and balance in the natural world – that each and every vegetable, animal and human being is 'of God' too. The human being was in essence a microcosm of the greater universe. Ultimately, self-knowledge – 'know thyself' as carved on the Oracles at Delphi – was the only true path whereby he could reconnect with his divine origins, seeing the cycles of development in nature similarly at work in human life.

This cannot be grasped suddenly but has to be acquired through following a path of initiation from one point of knowledge or awareness, then acceptance, to the next. The mysteries therefore came to be known as 'the path', 'the journey', or in modern terms 'seeing the light'. The people who chose, and today still choose, to put themselves voluntarily on this path to 'enlightenment' do so from a deep inner sense of the workings of the life-force as a manifestation of the power and love of God; the power of supreme balance. Sooner or later on

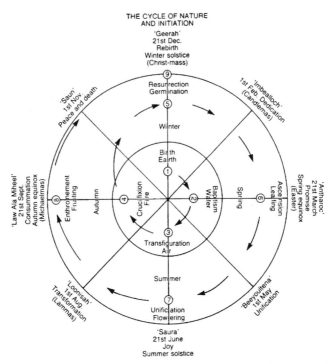

THE CYCLE OF NATURE
AND INITIATION

'Geerah'
21st Dec.
Rebirth
Winter solstice
(Christ-mass)

Resurrection
Germination
⑤

Winter

'Saun'
1st Nov.
Peace and death

'Imbealloch'
1st Feb. Dedication
(Candlemas)

Birth
Earth
①

'Law Ala Miheel'
21st Sept.
Consummation
Autumn equinox
(Michaelmas)

Enthronement
Fruiting
⑧

Autumn

Crucifixion
Fire
④

Baptism
Water
②

Spring

Ascension
Leading
⑨

'Antharoc'
21st March
Promise
Spring equinox
(Easter)

Transfiguration
Air
③

Summer

'Loonisah'
1st Aug.
Transformation
(Lammas)

Unification
Flowering
⑦

'Beeyoultena'
1st May
Unification

'Saura'
21st June
Joy
Summer solstice

Diagram 60. *Druidic/Christian calendar.*

this journey the individual will encounter a 'mystery school' of occult knowledge and, if they have prepared themselves sufficiently, may recognise with a sense of great humility that they belong to 'the White Brother/Sisterhood'. This is not a club or a gathering but an esoteric community of 'light', linked by soul consciousness from one being to another at the higher level of vibration, working towards the ultimate purpose of the progression of the Earth in its cosmic journey. The interaction between the powers of God and good (God) working through each individual or group soul allows many strange and wonderful events to happen in everyday life, thus holding the powers of darkness, ignorance and fear at bay.

The Druids were the priests of the later Bronze Age and Iron Age, holding the knowledge of these mysteries, learnt from their predecessors of the Neolithic period, and continuing the old established celebrations. These celebrations or 'Festivals' are still known today and, as we can see (diagram 60), have been named and dated to mark the change-over from one season to the next:

1. We start with the **Festival of the Dead** or Death, or the Festival of Peace originally on 1 November each year, known to the early Irish as Samhain, pronounced 'Saun'. This **winter quarter day** is now celebrated as Halloween on 31 October, All Saints' Day on 1 November and All Souls' Day on 3 November.
2. Next is the great **Festival of Rebirth** at the **Winter Solstice** on 21 December; the Irish Geerah, now widely celebrated three days later as the 'Christ-mass' on 25 December.

100

3. Then the **Festival of Dedication** or the **spring quarter day** of 1 February called Imbloc, pronounced 'Im-be-all-ock', known as Candlemas, St. Bride's or St. Bridget's Day.
4. The **Festival of Promise** occurs on 21 March at the **Spring Equinox**, called Antharoc and now celebrated as Lady Day, and shortly afterwards at the first full moon – as Easter. It is linked to the Jewish Passover.
5. The **Festival of Unification** is 1 May – the **summer quarter day** called Beltaine, pronounced 'Beeyoul-tena', celebrated as Corpus Christi or Ascension Day.
6. The **Festival of Joy**, the great mid-season outpouring of the Sun on 21 June is the **Summer Solstice**, known as and pronounced 'Saura'. Midsummer Day is three days later.
7. The **Festival of Transformation** is the end of summer, 1 August, called Lugnasadh, pronounced 'Loonisah' (Lug's Day). The **autumn quarter day** is celebrated as Lammastide.
8. The **Festival of Consummation** on 22 September is the **Autumn Equinox**, called 'Law Ala Miheel', now celebrated as St. Michael's Day or Michaelmas, on 29 September each year.

The symbol of the Celtic Sun Cross within a circle $\oplus$ universally denotes the Earth, specifically the four seasons, and can be seen as representing the divine breath of God creating life at each stage of evolution. In nature we see how these patterns or laws are worked out in evolving life-forms. Peter Dawkins, in *The Cycles of Initiation*, helps us to understand the natural life-cycle from the planting of the seed to the harvesting of the fruit.

Firstly, late autumn is a period when the seeds are sown in the earth and at Christmas time they have reached a point where they can be germinated. Then, the life-force goes into the seeds in the ground and brings about a quickening or germination and they begin to sprout underground. During the last part of the winter the seeds slowly grow up towards the surface of the ground but are still in the dense element of earth.

When we come to the start of spring, these germinated seeds, hidden in the ground, begin to pop up and appear in the open air and sunlight. Then spring has truly begun. During spring, the plants grow more and more and start to leaf. Some of the early plants even begin to flower, but generally they are going through their leafing experience.

We then come to the end of spring, to the Beltaine Festival, when there is another outpouring of energy that quickens the whole of plant life so that they form flower buds and begin to flower. Some will have flowered earlier but this calendar demonstrates the general law or pattern, i.e., nature begins to flower and the flowering continues apace throughout the summer.

When we reach the autumn we get the fruiting. The flower withers having served its purpose of creating the condition to enable the fruit to grow from that flower. The flower has become fertilised and it conceives and gives birth to a 'child' – the fruit. The fruit then grows and ripens until eventually there comes the harvesting of that fruit, followed by, in the case of corn, the drying of the harvested wheat during the last part of the autumn and then the threshing

– the recovery of the seed. The seed is either resown or taken to make bread. All that is not needed is burnt and returned to the ground as humus. So another cycle begins, this pattern going on and on.

It is interesting to note that during the present Piscean Age, the earth sign of Virgo is its polar opposite. If we remember the Vesica Pisces, which represents the duality of the fish, this polarity symbolises humanity integrating the fluidity of water with the fixed element of earth – or put another way, the age when spirituality (a Christ) is conveyed through the realms of matter to life forms here on Earth. Again, we can see the parallels with the mystical concept of alchemy and the symbolism of transformation. Pisces is ruled by Jupiter, the planet of expansion, religion and higher levels of consciousness. So we have been under its influence since the birth of Jesus – born at the point in the zodiacal cycle when Aries and Pisces merge. The Pisces-Virgo polarity is also closely linked with the sowing and reaping of the harvest. This can be likened to the reaping the harvest of karmic debts since humanity was awakened to a Christ on Earth.

Christmas is the great Christian annual festival celebrating, we are told, the birth of Jesus, but there is no historical reference to this Christian 'fact'. Indeed, many astrologers calculate that Jesus was born in August, October or 15 September – and anyway he certainly wasn't a Pisces. Christmas day, 25 December, celebrates the solar festival of 21/22 December, marked by the Winter Solstice, the shortest day of the year. At this point in the calendar, the Sun seems to sit still on the horizon for three days before it starts to travel back along the horizon as the days begin to lengthen towards summer and the whole of nature starts to rejuvenate again. The word solstice literally means 'the Sun stands still'. At this time it is at the point furthest south from the equator, before starting its journey back; in the northern hemisphere towards summer and giving the southern hemisphere its winter. Note too that we celebrate Midsummer Day three days later than the Festival of Joy or Summer Solstice, the longest day. That the birth of Jesus is marked in our Christian calendar three days after the Festival of Rebirth is especially significant. This metaphysical priest stated at his Crucifixion: 'I will rise again in three days'.

Ireland's Secret Language

For Irish people, the great Cairn of Newgrange, the centre of the ancient Stone Age tribal culture, is aligned to the Winter Solstice sunrise. The festival is revered and celebrated with true Pagan and Druidic zeal alongside the present Christian ways. Newgrange was/is the home of the god Dagda whose son is Ogma, and it is Ogma, the aspect of the Sun that is a great Pagan deity who resides in the great 'burgh'. From Palaeolithic through Stone Age and Bronze Age, and into the times of the Culdees, 'Ogma' became the language of the Sun itself – so from this great Pagan deity we have the origin of the sacred and secret language of all times and all tongues on Earth. Later it was called, and still is in Ireland, 'Ogham' or 'Ogam', pronounced 'OM' in ancient Irish.

The history of Ogham as a language, as reported by philologists, is that it is an engraved commemorative sign language used by the Celts of the third-fifth centuries A.D. and is inscribed on the hard edge of small standing stones that commemorate chieftains and tribal boundaries. It is a language of 25 symbols that were given alphabetical values by the early Christian monks and used as the secret written language between themselves.

There is a misinterpretation of the wondrous source of all language going back into the mists of time and to the beginnings of phonetics – the picking up of resonant sound as a means of communication. In the beginning, wo-man formulated words to express an idea or an artefact.

Let us again consider Newgrange and the engraving of the triple spiral deep within the recesses of the cruciform chamber of the Cairn. Remember this is the 'burgh' or 'hostel' of Ogma and 'he' *is* the Sun. The rays of the Sun beam into the cairn as a shaft of light like the crusader's sword or the knight's lance penetrating the darkness to enlighten and fertilise the very earth itself. 'OM' is the sound in Eastern mythology, particularly Hindu mythology, that goes back to 3000 B.C. at the time of Krishna (Christ), and the start of the 'Vedas', the holy books of Hindu culture. 'OM' is the primeval sound of the universe – the creative sound of all that ever was and is and will be – the very breath of God itself. It consists of three connecting circles or spirals. The first, Vishnu, is the holder of reality that keeps matter on its path. The second is Shiva, the destroyer – not the negative force of death and annihilation, but the fire that burns away the evil dross of the past and that aspect of the present that is useless. It thereby allows procreation and new birth – reincarnation – a new beginning to occur. The third aspect is Brahma, the creator of all. The Shiva energy was the expectation of the Jewish people in 5 B.C. as it is for us now in the supposed advent of our New Age – great expectations indeed.

Many people practising meditation are very familiar with the inner mantra of 'OM', and chant it to expand consciousness and open the 'third eye' (pineal) and the crown or 'Cave of Brahma' (pituitary). The cranium is the cairn of the human body and the third eye the entrance into the sacred space of our personal inner mythology. The creative 'OM' lies sleeping within, awaiting activation, so that we may once more embark on our journey back into the God-head that is ourselves, which we have never left. The early monks deeply involved with the mystical meditative life surely experienced this beauty, and were also able to access what *Jung* termed 'the collective unconscious'.

Returning to Chapter I and the hunter following an animal along an unseen underground water track, remember the five side-bands of energy that come to the surface parallel to the centre line. Now let us look at the human body, wo-man, and realise that we too have a centre line from the base of our body, the base chakra in the pelvis, up through the navel, sternum, Adam's apple(!), nose and brow, to the fontanel. Note that we also have five *meridians* running through us too, either side of this centre line which terminate at our five fingers and five toes, as annotated by Chinese acupuncturists and Shiatsu practitioners. This principle is exactly the same in our body as water is in the earth, for truly there is no separation (diagram 61).

As the hunter followed the centre line of the animal track, so he felt the side-bands with his fingers and toes – he literally dowsed them using his whole body

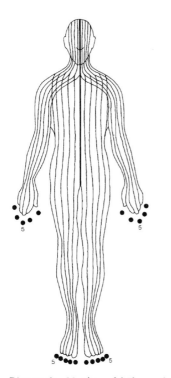

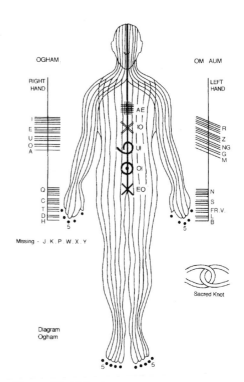

Diagram 61. *Meridians of the human body.* Diagram 62. *'Ogham'.*

Diagram 63. *Standing Stone with DNA Sun Cross and 'Ogham'* **(National Museum of Ireland).**

as the pendulum, sensing the variations of intensity outwards. Gradually, as he became familiar with this subtle energy, so he started to express it with his hands; one to five fingers left and right hands, across the centre line of his body (diagram 62). To sensitise and open his fingertips to exterior vibrations he parted his psychically raised Kundalini energy in the crown chakra through the open side chakras of his head (colour plate 6), and sent this energy down to and through the hands to his fingertips. Gradually sounds were articulated and became the 'ughs', ahs' and 'oos' of language as an expression of this unseen vibrational resonance – and so 'Ogham', the silent, secret language that became divine and sacred, was born over millennia and can be seen depicted in the early standing stones (diagram 63).

While the monks took a vow of silence, sometimes as a penance or punishment and sometimes at the direction of the abbot, this didn't mean that they couldn't communicate, because it was easy to 'talk' in 'Ogham' – just as those people who are deaf and dumb do today on the television each night, fully comprehending their sign language.

'Ogham' was 'the Word', the creative breath of the interaction of Sun with water in earth, through air – the very essence of God's gift to us: 'In the beginning was the Word and the Word was God'.

Poem: Words

Let me dig into your crown
Really listen to what you say
Dig deep into the whirl of mind
Flashing from thought to thought
Through the nine eternal
Words.
Behind our thoughtless expressions
Hidden in the depths of wordlessness
Lies divinity – sleeping
Trying to be released, surfaced
Into sunlight – golden meanings
Full of quantum flashing crystal
Thoughts.

Sacred Oratories

The earliest little churches are known today as oratories, literally small chapels, built of dry stone by the overlay method, called 'corbelling', to keep the water out. They are generally shaped like an inverted boat, although some of the cruder ones were oblong and thatched. Perhaps the most famous and beautiful oratory is Gallarus, which is sited near Slea Head on the Dingle Peninsula in Co. Kerry, Ireland. It is one of a local group of oratories. Others are known as Brendan, Kilmalkadar, Kiltentain and Reask, and also include the famous group of very early hermetic structures a little further south on the barren outcrop of the soaring island cliffs of Skellig Michael (diagram 64 and colour plate 7).

The Gallarus Oratory is built in a small stone walled enclosure at a site carefully chosen by the monastic community to incorporate a good underground water conformation. This was so that the building

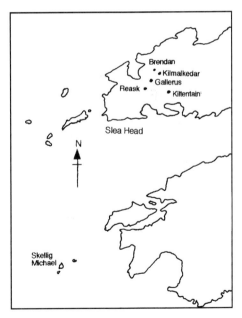

Diagram 64. *Western Co. Kerry showing Dingle Peninsular, Skelligs and Oratories (*James W. Mavor*).*

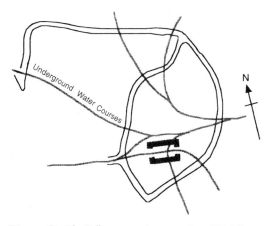

Diagram 65. *The Gallarus monastic community, c.550 A.D.*

would comply with the essential requirement of having a cross-flow of water under the altar – a conjunction and therefore an east-west flow along the body of the nave, i.e., through the east window and out at the entrance or west door (diagram 65). This flow thus energised the whole building and particularly the altar spiral that manifested from the conjunction, from day to night, positive to negative; thereby sanctifying the bread and the water – the blood of Mother Earth.

The altars were dry-stone tables in the centre of which was carved out a cup or stoop for the water. Being *in* the stone itself, this water was energised by the conjunction beneath. The water was literally altered or *altared*. Looking back to the story of the marriage of Cana in Galilee when Jesus turned the water into wine, perhaps this was just allegorical and he sanctified or energised the water so that it became 'holy' water in this true sense.

James Mavor explains the orientation and elevation of the Gallarus Oratory looking to the eastern horizon (diagrams 66 and 67) as follows:

Gallarus is oriented on its longitudinal axis, 278.8° true or 8.8° north of true west. From the west entrance it is possible to see the eastern horizon at an angle

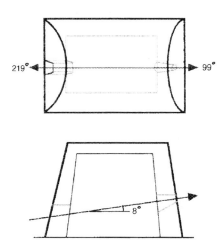

Diagram 66. *The Gallarus Oratory – orientation and elevation to eastern horizon (**James W. Mavor**).*

Diagram 67. *The Gallarus Oratory – the east window looking to the equinox sunrise.*

of 8° above the horizontal, i.e., to the rising Sun at the vernal equinox – 21/22
March each year on the elevation of the landscape horizon.
(James W. Mavor, *Gallarus Oratory and the Dingle Peninsular.*)

The Easter Sun at the equinox is a magical time of the year; the real beginning of spring when the Sun crosses the equator from the southern hemisphere back into the northern hemisphere – a time of erratic weather, spring gales and, storms, and always glorious rainbows. But it is the first full Moon after the Easter Sun, varying its arrival by up to a fortnight each year, that determines the date of Easter. The word Easter comes from the Anglo-Saxon word 'Eostre', meaning 'Goddess of Spring'.

We have already noted that in the Stone Age, S.A.M. was aligning his structures to celestial configurations, notably the back stone of Newgrange, engraved around 3000 B.C. showing the constellation of Draco the Dragon. Also, in *The Orion Mystery*, Robert Bauval and Adrian Gilbert show us how the three pyramids at Giza, in Egypt, built in 2445 B.C., are laid out on the ground to conform to the three main stars of Orion's belt. The astronomers and astrologers of ancient times were deeply interested in both precession – the movement of Earth's cycle around the Zodiac – and of the tilt of our axis, telling us of the millennium mysteries so vital to the continuing stability of Planet Earth. The latter was vital information because of the ancient mythological knowledge of the last great catastrophe at the end of the Ice Age, in about 9000 B.C., when the planet experienced vast upheavals due to polar shift. This concept is also discussed in Graham Hancock's book, *Fingerprint of the Gods*.

It is therefore apparent that the early monks, mathematicians, astronomers, healers, mystics and metaphysicists were keenly aware of their 'position'. What better place to site an observatory than on such extremities, looking out over the sea to the endless flat horizon, along which the Sun set at a different point every evening. What a perfect observatory they had at a latitude of between 50–55° north.

The stars had a longer timetable and were another aspect to plot and consider in calculating the evolution of the planet. Between 600–1200 A.D., two of the eleven brightest stars in the sky, Altair and Betelgeuse, set within 0.3° azimuth of each other. From 800–1200 A.D. they were gradually joined by Procyon, another very bright star, slightly to the north. In 1200 A.D. all three stars set at precisely the same point on the horizon. This incredible event of a triple conjunction in the sky must have been calculated years before, and generation after generation of monks must have anticipated and looked forward to it with great expectation. Such a trinity is a rare event and probably drew ancient memories of the Jesus story of the triple conjunction of the planets over Bethlehem (Mars, Jupiter and Saturn) that came together in 7 B.C. as the three astrologers from the East travelled to the birth of Jesus.

The triple conjunction of stars at Gallarus was a unique event and there is convincing evidence of astronomical intent to align the structure both to the equinox sunrise and bright western stars. This point is along the oratory axis,

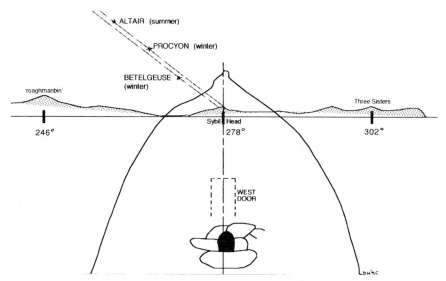

Diagram 68. *The Gallarus Oratory – looking west to horizon, showing three bright stars setting at the summit of Sybil Head* **(James W. Mavor)**.

with a precision of plus or minus 0.5°, at the summit of the coastal hill of Sybil Head. Here, three first magnitude stars were in conjunction at the same point. Thus, this oratory was deliberately built with deep inner knowledge to fulfil a landscape and sky architectural temple plan in its orientation and position – a design of great brilliance and beauty, telling of the genius of these early Christian monks (diagram 68).

Round Towers and Tenth Century Churches

As the monks travelled from the Middle East and along the Mediterranean, up through Portugal and Spain, so they came in contact with the minarets of the new religion of Africa – the followers of Mohammed, the Moslems. The practice of chanting prayers by the hour from these soaring towers seemed very similar in practice to the monks' hours of Christian worship. The round towers of Ireland, built from about 950 A.D., are historically said to have been refuges against the attacks of the Vikings – the principle being that the fleeing monks climbed their ladders into the high doorways and pulled them in after them, thus escaping the raiders. This is a delightfully fanciful idea!

The towers were actually replacements for the old standing stones, built on the same principle over water conjunctions that activated the whole ecosystem. The height and type of stones in the towers attracted the Sun's energy like a huge stone antennae or a TV aerial (diagram 69). Electro-magnetic energy was directed into the ecosystem, as was the case with the old stones of the circles, as we saw in diagram 10. The towers had the same function in a more modern way.

Historians have suggested that the entrance doorways to the towers were built high up, at differing heights – there was no regular building pattern – to act as

108

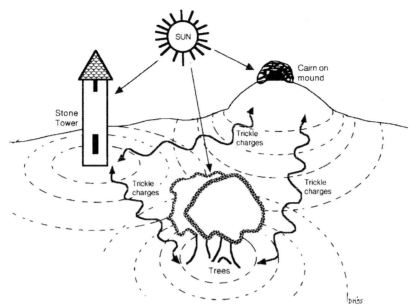

Diagram 69. *Stone antennae over underground water flows balancing the ecosystem* (**Prof. Philip S. Callahan**).

TABLE 2 **Oratory Alignments** (James W. Mavor, *Gallarus Oratory and the Dingle Peninsular*)

1. **Gallarus** (Oratory)	278.8°	1°	Procyon Altair Star Betelgeuse (set)
	98.8°	8°	Equinox Sunrise
2. **Reask** (Oratory)	281°	1°	Procyon Altair Star Betelgeuse (set)
	101°	4.7°	Lateevemore Summit Spica (rise) (500–900 A.D.)
3. **St. Brendan** (Oratory)	279°	1°	Procyon Altair Star Betelgeuse (set)
	99.7°	1°	Equinox Sunrise
4. **Kilmalkadar** (Church)	264.7°	0°	Spica (set) (500–900 A.D.)
	84.7°	12.5°	Aldabaran (rise) (600–1200 A.D.)
5. **Skellig Michael** (Large Oratory)	62°	0°	Regulus (rise) (800–900 A.D.)>
6. **Skellig Michael** (Small Oratory)	79.5°	0.5°	Procyon Altair Star (rise) Betelgeuse

a safety measure. However, they have failed to note that below the doorway the tower was filled with rubble. Seemingly, for some unknown reason, this could not have been for stability, as it was above the ground. If analysed, the rubble would be found to be highly para-magnetic, i.e., positive in force, as it was an essential part of this 'dry cell battery'. The height of both the doorway and tower was determined at any site by the requirements of the place, i.e., the amount of electro-magnetic force necessary at that point. The monks used this sophisticated method of balancing the local agricultural system and were able to grow wonderful gardens and crops around their towers as a result. At present, the remains of 67 towers have been recorded and another 23 are accepted sites. In general, they had a height of approximately 90 feet, with a base of diameter 16 feet, tapering at the top to 13 feet, on 4 feet foundations.

The towers were used for 'sighting' the Sun, Moon and stars, and usually had 'slit' windows on the highest level, under the little conical roof oriented north-south-east-west. Messages in 'Ogham' could be flashed with mirrors of polished metal, usually silver, from tower to tower over long distances if there was sight. This is the principle of the heliograph; the 'paten' (of a chalice) was the instrument used.

Philip Callahan tells us:

The round towers of Ireland are placed on the ground to match the night sky constellations. Of the four obvious alignments, Draco is the most perfect. Cassiopeia forms two Ws — one west to east and one north to south. Ursa Major (the Big Dipper) is slightly misplaced. Camelopardalis is also close to perfect. The ecclesiastical centre of southern Ireland, Clonmacnoise, is the pole star. The ecclesiastical centre of northern Ireland, Armagh, is the ecliptic pole. The round tower at Meelick is located as the star of Thuban, and Devenish round tower ... is located at the star Eta Draconis. Both were used to align the great pyramid. I am certain that a round tower base could be found at the ruins of the abbey at Keenaghail, completing Draco on the ground. There is a series of round towers along the southern coast of Ireland that make a series of bright stars (first and second magnitude at the southern horizon of the Irish Sky).
(Prof. Philip S. Callahan, *Ancient Mysteries, Modern Visions*.)

This engaging theory, illustrated by diagrams 70 and 71, suggests an incredible understanding of the whole country of Ireland as one vast landscape temple. How the monks laid out this vast concept at a time when the country was wooded and full of swamps and undrained land, and when communication was extremely difficult in practical terms, is really quite extraordinary. Their understanding also shows a level of cosmology, wideness and depth of human consciousness that even today is difficult for us to comprehend. The fixing of the stars to the land was designed to make a real and positive statement of the principle of 'no separation' with Planet Earth itself. Who planned the layout, who was the master-mind behind the concept, who surveyed the work and how? And how long did the whole project take from start to finish? Since this was clearly a great religious work-programme, is it written up anywhere in some dusty leather tome, hidden in a forgotten archive? We may also ask, who were the bishops of Clonmacnoise over this time, and who gave them the ideas to get started? Surely these unnamed and now faceless monks were re-incarnations of the earlier priesthood of the Stone and Bronze Ages.

While the churches of the tenth–twelfth centuries A.D. developed and became larger and more sophisticated as the Church expanded its influence and wealth, the basic principles of the occult use of metaphysics can be seen to continue to flourish and expand in church architecture.

In about the tenth century a transept was added to the shape of a church, but only where the necessary under-ground water-flows were found in the right conforma-tion. The round towers were also sited near the church, one only at each centre, also over a conjunction. This was to feed energy and power along the water courses into the body of the church itself, so that in vibration, the sacred space of the building became alive – from the entrance at the west door through the east window.

Another water line, or con-junction, was necessary at the west end of the nave to place the baptismal font on. Here, the baby brought into the doorway has its first sacred experience. Having been con-ceived in and born out of water from its mother's

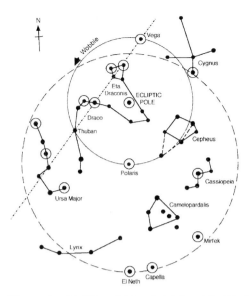

Diagram 70. *The Winter Solstice celestial sky, c.950 A.D.* (**Prof. Philip S. Callahan**).

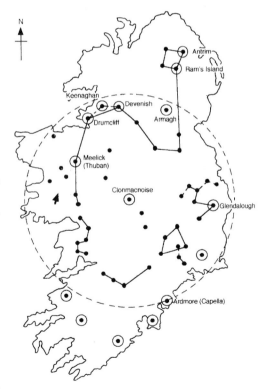

Diagram 71. *The round towers of Ireland in relation to the Winter Solstice celestial sky, c.950 A.D.* (**Prof. Philip S. Callahan**).

111

womb, it is now marked with the sign of the cross, the Celtic Sun Cross, not the Crucifix, on its third eye and crown chakra at baptism – a water birth into water faith. Once baptised, the child may, if it died shortly after, be buried in the sacred precincts of the church itself. The church thus claimed another soul 'for God' and dues were aptly paid by the spiritually uplifted parents. Had the child not been baptised, it could not be buried in holy ground and was shamefully buried secretly at night in a children's graveyard outside the church, probably somewhere remote in the woods or the hillsides. The Church had no compassion or forgiveness when it was not going to get its financial dues, as would apply if, for instance, a child was stillborn. Worse still was a child born of an incestuous relationship. The gathering of money has always taken precedence in the Church, and the lifelong business of favours; from birth, confirmation and marriage, until death, is still seen reflected today in the lifestyle of the top echelons of the clergy.

After baptism, a person could worship in the nave of the church and only cross the transept on his or her way to the altar rail to kneel in supplication, sub-mission and reverence before the priest, to receive a blessing and the spiritual food of the 'blood' and the 'flesh'. Beyond the altar rail was sacrosanct, the domain of the priest, the initiate, as only he was aware of the siting of the altar over the spiral of underground water conjunction. Here, he stood in front of the altar and gave his blessings at the end of the service.

The church in its layout had fulfilled the necessary shape and conformation to project a complete chakra system in plan and elevation onto the Earth. The west door represents the entrance or base chakra, the nave the stomach, and the transept the solar plexus and heart chakra – the two wings being the out-stretched arms of the 'figure', so to speak. The choir is obviously the throat chakra, the altar rail the brow and the altar itself, the crown (diagram 72). The whole body of the church is therefore energised and made alive by its architecture. The power of the priest was as an initiated, anointed and ordained member of the elite spiritual power-bro-kers of the land, answering to no-one except first, his bishop, then the Pope and therefore God himself.

Note that the cross shape of the diagram is

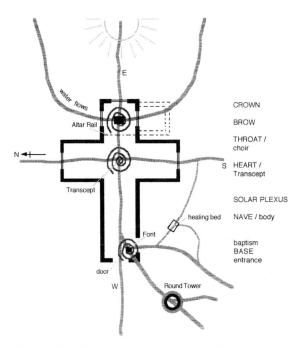

Diagram 72. *Celtic Church and round tower, c.1000 A.D.*

similar to that of the illustration of 'Christ and the Triple Spiral' on the cover of the book, as well as the Hermaphrodite of Paphos (diagram 26 and Appendix A).

Within the enclosure of the church, there was often a healing bed or slab of rock, situated over another conjunction of underground water. This would be known as a place of healing – where a wo-man might receive help from pain in various parts of the body; internal organs, haemorrhaging, women's menstrual problems, mental problems etc., etc. The efficacy of the 'bed' depended on the vibration of the energy beneath, and therefore the 'colour' that emanated through to the surface. If, for instance, the energy was blue, it would have a healing effect on the throat chakra; if green, the heart; yellow, the solar plexus and digestion, and so on. Simple really, if you can dowse, as they, the priesthood, were trained dowsers and seers. Anyone unordained who had such an ability was removed and killed as a witch on the orders of the bishop, but of course tortured first and made to confess to hideous, fabricated lies to justify the murder.

By 1200 A.D., Rome was growing more and more powerful, and sadly, the practices of the mystic Celtic monks of the West, the inheritors of the ancient knowledge, with their own metaphysics as dowsers and diviners, were soon to be curtailed. The ancient culture of the Celtic Church was to be reshaped and brought under the yoke of the dogma of the Popes exerting absolute Christian power. By now Rome had set itself up as the only arbitrator of the 'Word', deliberately obliterating any opposition by ridicule and murder.

Cross Slabs or 'Grave Stones', Glencolumcille, Co. Donegal

In the Celtic West there are many standing stones from the Christian era that are supposedly marking graves. Sometimes they do, yet they are also placed at

Diagram 73. *Celtic Cross slabs, Co. Donegal, c.sixth century A.D.* (**Michael Herity**).

dialling points. These points mark significant sightings for the Earth–Moon and Sun positions at eclipses, sometimes at solstices and equinoxes, but also at the eighteen year Sun–Moon rise.

Michael Herity illustrates the slabs in *Gleanncholmcille*, so we can see how the monks used the symbol of the Earth as the lowest engraving, wo-man being of and on the Earth. Next, in the middle of the three engravings, the Moon is depicted. Note how the Moon, with its difficult though predictable rise and set, is shown as a wiggle, and the top engraving depicts the Sun as the 'God' of the sky and of the earth (diagram 73).

The Sun is usually carved on the top of a standing stone, as a Celtic or Sun Cross, which also depicts the DNA rising through the seventh chakra or crown, or a maze, depicting the brain. We also saw the Sun Cross in diagram 63, inscribed with 'Ogham'. This is true Celtic Pagan practice from earlier Druidic ways – memorials to the Earth, Sun and Moon and not the Crucifixion Cross as the main point of worship.

CHAPTER X

Iona, Inishmurray, Inishbofin and the Vikings

Background

From about 500–800 A.D. the early Christian churches had developed in Britain and Ireland in comparative peace. But in 793 A.D., the first of a catastrophic series of events occurred on the east coast of Britain that was to change the history of the Western world. In 793 A.D. the Vikings struck.

What is perhaps surprising, historically, is that they had not attacked Britain before this date. However, this new-found source of precious objects, silver and gold, and a ready supply of slaves, women and children from along the north eastern seaboard meant that the first incursions were swiftly followed by further raids of growing intensity, further afield. The Vikings then established a forward base in the Orkney Islands from which it was easy to expand their raids down the west coast of Scotland and on into Ireland.

There were three great Christian centres on the western seaboard at that time – the most famous being on the island of Iona, the Island of the Dove. The next was on the island of Inishmurray, 'Innish Muiredaig' in south Donegal Bay and the third, on Inishbofin, 'Inis BoFinne' – the Island of the White Heifer, off the coast of Co. Mayo. There were many other smaller monastic communities at the time, but served by so few monks that their capture, slaughter and devastation was scarcely recorded.

Iona

Iona was special. The monastic settlement had been founded by Columcille, an Irishman who had set out, in 563 A.D., from the place of his name, Gleanncholmcille, in south-west Donegal, after he had had a serious disagreement with the then King of Tara and had been banished. Columcille settled in Iona, said to be of the oldest recorded rocks on the planet – although surely he was not to know this at the time, nor necessarily that it had any special significance. From this island, Columba, as he later became known, converted the Scots to Christianity, and by 800 A.D. the community numbered over 150 monks. The place had become a living shrine and was no doubt graced with many valuable artefacts and accoutrements. Regrettably, that was exactly what the Vikings were seeking.

The Annals of Ulster record that the year 806 A.D. was one:

> *. . . in which a great plague broke out in Ireland. The community of Iona slain by heathens that is, to the number of sixty-eight.*

The Annals of the Four Masters also tell us:

> *Columcille was plundered by the Ciaill and great numbers of the laity and clergy were killed by them, namely sixty-eight.*

To this day, the strand on which the Iona community were slaughtered is known as the Bay of the Martyrs.

There were three kinds of martyrdom experienced by the early Church at that time. White martyrdom meant pilgrimage to Rome; green martyrdom was to become a hermit monk living in silence with nature and following the true Druidic traditions of old; and thirdly, red martyrdom was the letting of one's blood for the Faith. For the Vikings, imposing red martyrdom was common practice as any monks who didn't bow down to Viking authority, and offer up their settlements and treasures, were promptly murdered. The favourite method of murder was known as 'the eagles' wings'. The unfortunate was split down the chest along the ribcage with a battle-axe, turned on his chest to the ground, and his ribcage and arms pulled outwards and backwards so that the splayed ribs looked like the reddened feathers of a large bird. This incredible cruelty had its effect on the sparse communities and each settlement lived in constant fear of attack at any moment. The swift raiding boats would suddenly appear over the horizon, run up the beach and attack with deadly swiftness. The defenseless islands and seaboard communities had no chance of survival and were duly devastated, one by one.

The layout of the Earth Stars of Iona is interesting as basically four Stars cover the island with a major energy or Earth Star line branching north, near the actual centre of the island, in the hills, at Eithne's Fold (diagram 74). This is the true metaphysical centre of the island, and it is interesting to note that Eithne is a name in Ireland of the Goddess or 'angelic force' of the ancient world. Maybe there is some Stone Age structure there, or its remains, to mark the spot.

The Hill of the Angels is important, as every early community had a place from where they could 'dial' or plot the rising and setting Sun, Moon and stars. Once again, a convenient roughly central place or hill had to be chosen. This became known as the Hill of the Angels, whereas it should be known as the Hill of the 'Angles' – the dialling hill for the monks to prepare and annotate their moonthly and annual calendar (diagram 75). However, we have seen that the principle of the chakra system of the human body was also incorporated into the structure and layout of the early Christian buildings; in the nave, transept, choir and altar of the church. Similarly, it was also usual for the landscape temples to be laid out reflecting the chakras of the body, to bring the energy and worship of the natural kingdom into a true relationship with the monks themselves. Places of meditation, retreat and healing were set up on convenient outcrops to enable this.

Just such a chakra system was chosen from the landing place on the island, the 'Port of the Community', representing the base chakra. Note the comparison to

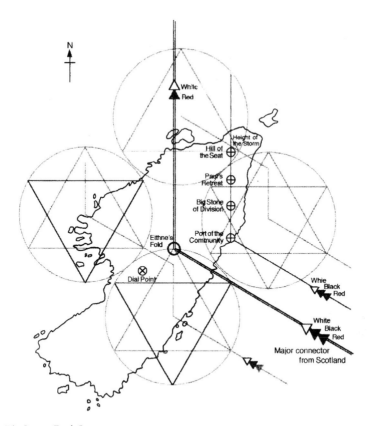

Diagram 74. *Iona – Earth Stars.*

Diagram 75. *Iona – dial point, 'Hill of the Angels'.*

117

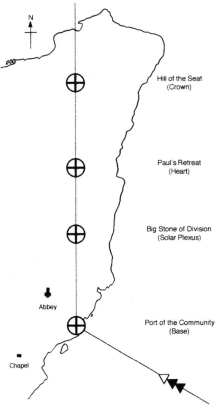

Diagram 76. *Iona – the chakra system.*

entering the nave of the church through the west door (diagram 76), illustrating the chakra system of Iona, and showing the line from the Port up to the Big Stone of Division (solar plexus chakra), on to Paul's Retreat (heart or throat chakra) and finally to the Hill of the Seat (crown chakra).

Iona is still today recognised as a very sacred and holy space, and is visited by thousands of pilgrims each year; people of many spiritual persuasions, not by any means all Christians.

Inishmurray

The island of Inishmurray (Muiredaig) lies six miles off the coast of Sligo in south Donegal Bay. The settlement there suggests a history that goes back to the Neolithic period. The Christian settlement is said to have been founded by Abbot Molaise Laisnen, son of Delgan. It was he who supposedly banished Columcille, or later Columba, to Iona after the battle of Cuil Dreimhe in north Sligo, which took place in about 561 A.D. This settlement had been founded, in about 520 A.D., from its parent monastery on the mainland at Skreen, on the coast to the south. The first Viking raid is said to have occurred in 802 A.D., but was probably just before the turn of the century, at the same time as the raid on Iona.

The beauty of Inishmurray is that the monastic remains are in such excellent condition with nearly all the original walls standing. The cashel walls were restored at the end of the last century and were probably originally built as a defence against the Vikings in the later ninth century. These walls enclose about a third of an acre and contain a number of buildings: 'The Church of the Men', 'The Church of Fire', 'Molaise's house', 'Wake of the Virgin' and the 'Lenten Retreat'. There are three outdoor altars built over water conjunctions, one in particular with a beautiful small standing stone with a Celtic Sun Cross at its head – as we have already seen, the real DNA cross of the rising energy from the conjunction below (diagram 77).

The main Earth Star energy line that crosses Ireland, all the way through from the east coast at St. Patrick's Island to Newgrange, and on to this little island, goes through the cashel with the energy split in the beehive cell to the chapel beside it, and on out to its centre in Donegal Bay. The beehive cell is used as a capacitor and accelerator of the spiral, since it is again sited over a water line, just as the cairns had been sited and used for a similar purpose way back in the Stone Age, 3,500 years before.

The triangulation of the Earth Stars around the island show a build-up of two other fields – a small Star around the cashel centring on the beehive cell and a larger Star annotated on the map with the enigmatic note, 'Site of Altar'. This clearly tells us that those early monks knew about the Earth Stars and were able to plot them – how else could they have sited their altar at such a point? (diagrams 78 and 79).

Around the perimeter of the island of Inishmurray are

Diagram 77. *Innishmurray – altar and DNA Standing Stone Sun Cross.*

various 'Stations of the Cross', probably laid out from the cashel to mark the dialling points of the phases of the Moon and Sun. Fourteen stations represent

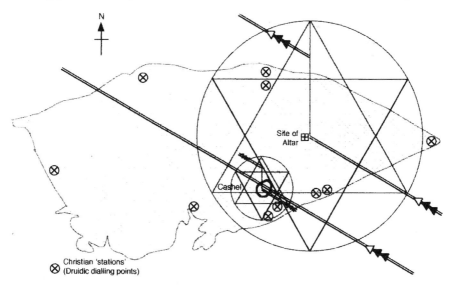

Diagram 78. *Innishmurray – Earth Star layout.*

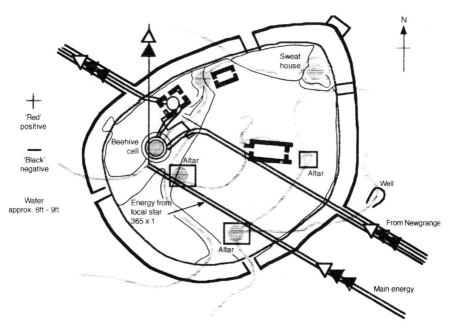

N

+
'Red'
positive

—
'Black'
negative

Water
approx. 6ft - 9ft

'Red' positive

Beehive
cell

Altar

Energy from
local star
365 x 1

Altar

Sweat
house

Altar

Well

From Newgrange

Main energy

Diagram 79. *Innishmurray – the cashel.*

half a moonth: two seven-day periods or a seven-day positive, seven-day negative natural solar energy switch.

There is an interesting local story about the round beach stones on the altars – some of them are carved with the Celtic Sun Cross, i.e., spherically in three dimensions. These are known as the 'cursing stones'. The theory is that if you wish ill on anyone you turn the stones whilst sending out your chosen malediction! To do this, since the altars are sited over water conjunctions, the negative energy of a curse would only be valid if the stones were turned anti-clockwise. How sad it is that we concentrate on the negative, whereas if we wanted to send out healing and positive thoughts or even – dare it be mentioned – love, then no doubt this would happen if the stones were turned clockwise!

This island has been uninhabited since the last families were rehoused on the mainland in the 1930s, like so many of the remote communities of the Western Isles. In 1928, the new Irish Free State was unable to cope with the responsibility of looking after such individual tribal communities. Inishmurray had its own king in those days. There were no helicopters and communication was extremely difficult, to say the least. The islands never had electricity so the earth energies there are still pure and unpolluted. The bird sanctuaries now established along the coast on such islands perform very valuable resting places for the migratory birds – just as they served the early monks until the wild, cruel Norsemen destroyed the last vestiges of the early Celtic and Druidic Church that had survived, regardless of the gradual Romanisation of Saxon Britain after the Synod of Whitby in 664 A.D.

It was this synod that directed Bishop Colman (an Irishman), to leave Lindisfarne and return to Iona, but he decided to move on to Inishbofin with his English (Saxon) monks to found a large monastery there in 668 A.D. However, the English monks and the Irish monks were not able to live in harmony – the English seemingly being diligent and constantly hard-working, whereas the Irish monks wanted to visit the mainland and their homes in winter, leaving the unpleasantness of the hard, cold toil to their foreign fellows. Bishop Colman settled the dispute by founding an alternative monastery on the mainland and the Irish monks left amicably to live at Mayo Abbey.

Bishop Colman is said to have brought with him some of the treasures of Lindisfarne, notably the Shrine of Aidan. These shrines, judging by the remaining examples in the Irish National Museum, were made with silver and gilt overlaid on wooden boxes containing the bones of the relevant 'Saint'. The outside was usually mounted and set with cabochon rock crystals to energise the contents. The later raiding Vikings were obviously attracted by these sumptuous shrines as they represented 'good plunder'.

Inishbofin

Currently, the Ordnance Survey maps of Inishbofin show little of the remains of a large Christian community, so it is difficult to produce a metaphysical reading of any site there. One wonders, perhaps, if this information is correct, because in the sea nearby is tiny Caher Island, renowned today as a very sacred place. It is remote, difficult to land on and still has the remains of a seventh century church and surrounding cashel wall. There are also about a dozen beautiful examples of early cross engraved standing stones showing its importance as a refuge and burial ground of eminent people.

Irish people revere this little island beyond any other in the West, and every year make hazardous pilgrimages to it in the local traditional light sea canoes called 'curraghs'. The island was also known, although uninhabited for many years, as a source of excellent poteen.

These three little islands have been included because they represent the last outposts of early Celtic/Druidic Christianity extant before the Viking conquest and never really to be re-established again. After the Vikings had finally been defeated, in 998 A.D., by Brian Boru at the Battle of Clontarf, the Normans came into Ireland and a new phase of Christianity and Christian building began. The simplicity and magic of the Celtic Church had finally been blown away into the realms of our inner mythological folk memory. Yet living in the west of Ireland today, it is still possible to intuit a deep spark of Celtic spirituality flowing through the pathos of the music, poetry and art, not least in the hillsides of what was once the edge of the known world.

CHAPTER XI

The Tara Brooch

The most famous of all Irish artefacts is the beautiful early Christian equinoctial ring calculator, mistakenly called a 'penannular *brooch*'. The Tara Brooch (colour plate 8) was found in the mid-nineteenth century at Bettystown on the seashore of Co. Meath and ended up in the hands of a jeweller in Dublin who copied it and exhibited facsimiles at the Great Exhibition in London in 1851.

The official description of this 'brooch', from the National Museum of Ireland, is as follows:

Made of cast silver-gilt with gold filigree, amber and polychrome glass orna-ments. Diameter of ring 8.7 cm, maximum width of terminal plate 4.55 cm, length of pin 32 cm, weight 224.36 gms.

This is a comparatively small example alongside some of the enormous ones in the museum, and although it is just small enough to wear in a plaid shawl thrown across the shoulders, it is really quite impractical. It has therefore been called a 'brooch' for want of any understanding of its purpose. You will note it even has a carrying strap of plaited silver-gilt wire from its side. The National Museum states that it was given the name 'Tara Brooch' by the jewellers and seemingly no-one in modern times has seen its close connection to the royal site or its inherent geometry.

However, in Egyptian history we read of Akhnaton, the Pharaoh, who killed his father and married his mother, Queen Ti, by whom he had a daughter. The modern name Tara is derived from Teamur – 'Tea-Mur', the wall of the Queen of Egypt. Wall can be translated as 'earthen bank' in Irish.

In the following verse, translated from the poem *Temark II* from the *Dun Senchas*, Book of Leinster version, we read:

Breaga Tea – the teeming home
Is famed because Ti was a noble dame.
The funeral mound under which is the great one of the standards –
The burying ground which was never rifled -
The daughter of Pharaoh with tale of warriors
Tephi the bright who used cross, the hill -
Slope framed a stronghold (handy the labourer)
WITH HER STAFF AND WITH HER BROOCH SHE TRACED IT.

To understand the use of the calculator (for that is exactly what it is), we must unravel the basic geometry of the piece, step-by-step (diagram 80, 1–9). Peter Dawkins explains the geometry of the Tara Brooch as follows:

Let's take the geometry step-by-step. In the first diagram you will find the basic geometry of the six-pointed star, drawn as the first circle and then the six other circles drawn round it which divide the circle into six. Then from one of the

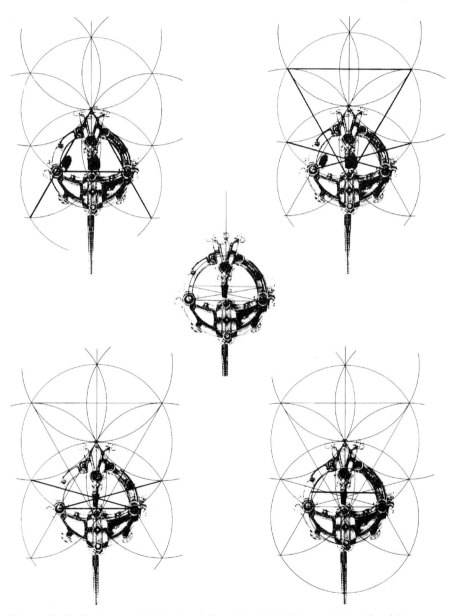

Diagram 80. *(1–9) Geometry of the Tara Brooch* (**Peter Dawkins**). *(Diagram 1, 2, 3a, 3b and 4)*

123

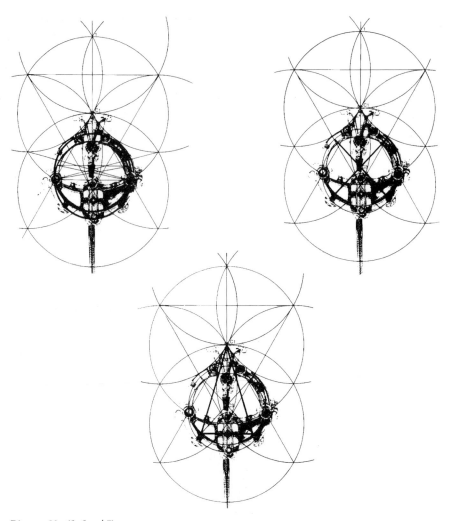

Diagram 80. *(5, 6 and 7)*

arms of that star the first triangle can be drawn as shown. This is the fundamental of all geometry. In the second diagram you can see added in the big triangle that forms one half of the great six-pointed star that fills the initial circle. I have also drawn in two other lines that derive directly from the bigger star figure, which we will need in finding out the centre of the circle.

Diagrams 3(a) and 3(b) will show you how the centre of the circle 4 is found. It is in the mid-point of the base of the smaller triangle whose apex is the centre of circle 1. Diagram 4 gives you the next horizontal line needed for finding the centre of circle 3. Diagram 5 completes the geometric lines to give you the centre of circle 3 and I have shown both circles 4 and 3 drawn on this.

These two circles, circles 3 and 4, are slightly different sizes and they are offset by that small amount that you can see. This is a critical offset and

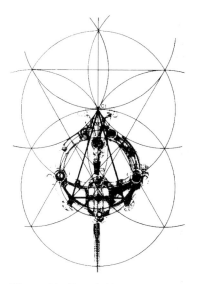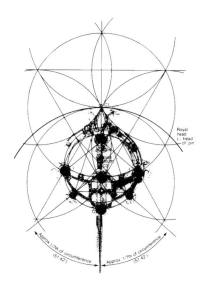

Diagram 80. *(8a and 8b)*

allows the geometers to derive some amazing geometric solutions. I have not come across this before until I looked at the Tara Brooch and it is really quite wonderful It eventually gives us a way to divide a circle up into sevenths.

Diagram 6 begins to show how the next figure of importance is found, namely the 33° triangle; diagram 7 goes on to show you this triangle drawn out. The angle of the apex is the 33° one and this is highly significant. Again, it is not normally very easy to find a geometric way to draw a 33° triangle, but here it is. Magnificent!

Diagram 8 shows the whole lot, including the way that the 1/7s of the circle are found and clearly this was one of the functions of the brooch, because if you know where the centre of circle 4 is, which is easier to find on the brooch once you know its whereabouts, then the two smaller bosses on the outer circle of the brooch will give you the sitings for dividing the circles into sevenths (including the main axis). The 33° is delineated by the other two small bosses that fall on the two lines of the 33° triangle; and so the owner of the brooch, knowing where circle 1 is at the top of the pin, would soon be able to construct his 33° triangle from the centre of 1 down to the two smaller bosses. The designers of the brooch have in this way occulted the actual geometry that gives rise to that triangle. As you can see, it is very clever indeed.

You can see that in places the geometric lines do not pass exactly through the centres of the circles. This is probably because of the age of the brooch and the way the photography has been made of it, but at least it is near enough to show you that its geometry is really intended and that the design of the brooch is derived from it.

In diagram 8(a) you can also see how the centre of the crown chakra of the 'king' is found. The centre of it is not found exactly by the two lines drawn in. On diagram 8(b) these two lines are as if marking the centre of this crown

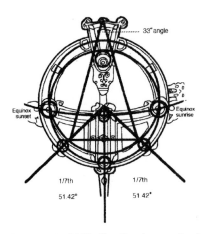

Equinox sunset

Equinox sunrise

1/7th   1/7th

51.42°   51 42°

Diagram 80. *(9) The Tara Brooch geometric calculator simplified concise geometry*

chakra. *In actual fact, when you look at the photograph of the brooch this is not quite so. However, this is the best geometric arrangement that gets anywhere near marking this crown chakra. Surely it was meant because it gave rise to a little triangle which delineated the eyes and the brow and the top of the head of the man, and this is a very important triangle indeed. The horizontal base of that triangle goes right through the bridge of the nose. As the whole face is a summary of the whole body of man himself – that is to say, it shows the whole law in the face, just as the whole body shows the whole law of God – so the bridge of the nose actually marks the heart centre in terms of the face. By 'bridge' is meant the point just a little below the eyes. The two eyes of the face of the man lie just above this triangle base and the apex of the triangle delineates the actual brain, of which the two hemispheres are showing beautifully as the two spirals (or as shown in other traditions, as two rams horns). The mouth and nostrils lie lower down below the base of this small triangle, as you can see, and the mouth, again, has been found already by one of the geometric lines that helped us find the centre of circle 3.*

From the head of this illuminated man the crown rises up beautifully with the golden disc marking the crown chakra itself and (diagram 9) the great crown resembling a very big version of a pharaoh's crown, or a bishop's mitre. The arc of the top of this huge crown is formed as being on the arc of a fifth circle whose centre is right down at the bottom of the brooch, and in this way they have joined root with the crown in a rather amazing way – or perhaps I should say, sacral with crown, because if we count the bosses going up the brooch we find the lower boss could represent the sacral chakra. The next boss (which is diamond shaped) could represent the solar plexus. The next boss represents the heart and this is associated with the centre of circle 4). The next boss (i.e., the centre of circle 3) is not marked by a boss but lies on the pin of the brooch, mid-way between the heart boss and the mouth of the face on the head of the pin. This centre, I think, marks the throat chakra. It is strange how it is occulted but perhaps this has great significance. The next chakra is marked by the centre point between the eyes on the face of the head of the pin, which, of course, is marked by the final boss above the head.

The two big bosses on the left- and right hand side of the brooch indicate the left and right arms and hands, and from those hands rises up the rainbow or arc which is the Ark of the Covenant. The complete arc, or arch, is actually a whole circle and so the circle carries down below the hands, and in this case

126

down the sacral chakra, or what would appear to be the sacral chakra, which is cabbalistically the principle called Yesod, or Foundation, the place where all things are generated or procreated. I think the root chakra must be intended by the actual ground itself into which the pin of the brooch is stuck – because in this brooch is the whole temple complete and beautifully drawn.

The Tara Brooch is complicated geometry but it is very wonderful. Every geometric figure had a particular meaning. What is so marvellous is that the whole thing begins from the basis of the six-pointed star which is the greater universe, then the brooch itself is one part of that universe, i.e., at one point of the six-pointed star like a planet revolving around its Sun. Then, furthermore, out of the brooch itself comes the head of the king or illuminated man with his great crown upon his head and this is, of course, as it should be, the head of the so-called pin of the brooch itself. It is a fabulous head, especially as the geometry defines the features of that beautiful head and the carvings on the face itself delineates different energies of that face. The face is a great key because the face reveals divinity – it is the 'countenance of the Lord'. Yet it is also (and quite rightly so) this head of man which controls the directions that the brooch can give. The arm of the pin is the axis/spine of that man and this is what can be swung in different directions; or indeed, actually spiked into the ground and the arc of the brooch swung around to coincide with the arc of the horizon and of the rising stars. From this, sitings can be made and the geometry drawn out on the ground ready for the building of temples and the working of the energies.

(Peter Dawkins, The Gatekeeper Trust, researched for Michael Poynder, *Pi in the Sky*.)

After all these hundreds of years, since the Tara 'Brooch' was discarded on the shore at Bettystown, probably by some fleeing Viking robber, its secrets are unfurled again.

From this geometry several other possibilities arise. What, for instance, is the meaning of the two interlocking circles occulted within its frame and why should the pin or spike travel around its frame? Here are shown the movements of Planet Earth from one Great Age to the next (diagrams 81 and 82).

As the Earth turns around its pole it is, at the same time, spiralling through space around its central solar Father, the Sun, and once again, we can depict this duality of the Earth/Sun/Earth centres (diagram 83).

The dimensions of the Earth in relation to the Moon have always held a fascination, and as previously

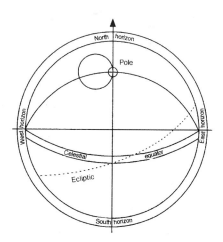

Diagram 81. *The principle of the spherical geometric calculator, e.g., the Tara Brooch and later the astrolobe of the twelfth century A.D.*

127

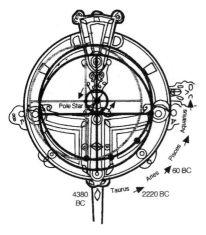

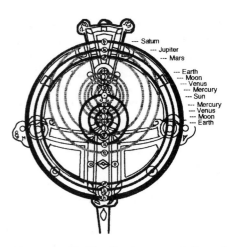

Diagram 82. *The Tara Brooch zodiacal calculator – central Zodiac showing the circuit of the Earth's celestial pole of the ecliptic, thereby giving dates of the ages between each Zodiac sign.*

Diagram 83. *The Tara Brooch – concentric Sun and Earth centred solar system.*

mentioned, we are told that the Great Pyramid – Pi-Ra-Mid – has these proportions built into it. This is beautifully shown on the Tara Brooch in the proportional relationship between the main frame and the pin-head, since half the frame represents the radius (Ra-Di [Day]-Us) of the Earth to half the pin-head representing the radius of the Moon (diagram 84).

It is fascinating to realise that the sum total of the radius of Earth and Moon, 3,960 miles and 1,080 miles, equals 5,040 which, when broken down, gives the simple multiplication of $1 \times 2 \times 3 \times 4 \times 5 \times 6 \times 7 = 5,040$ – the fulfilment of light – and this also gives us the pyramid angle of $51.51°$, the division of the circle into one-sevenths.

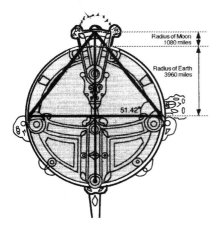

Diagram 84. *The Tara Brooch – Earth and Moon proportions.*

For what reason is it, do you think, that the British Isles have always been held very sacred in all mythology, as the islands of Hyperborea? The Pyramid angle of $51.51°$ gives us the clue – for we subtend that angle here at our latitude from the centre of the Earth. Here is also the magical point of the Sun's arc (ark) at the Summer Solstice mid-day point over our islands. For it is the arc of the summer Sun that gives us the Ark of the Covenant or the arc of the Golden Mean proportion – the most sacred proportion of all geometry (diagram 85).

Once again, if we now plot the arc of the Sun and Moon around the frame of

128

the Tara Brooch we can easily use it as a clock from the solstice summer and winter points and the Moon's more complicated but similar paths, its rise and set points. So far the Tara Brooch has given us predictable information, just as a hand-held calculator, but why is it that no-one has ever thought to relate it to Tara, the great kingly site itself?

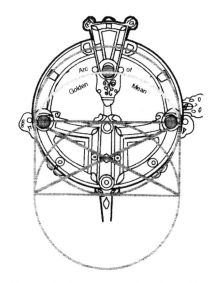

Diagram 85. *The Tara Brooch – Golden Mean proportion.*

The energies of Tara flow across the map and three different size Earth Stars conjoin there. Now superimpose the brooch over the site and you will see how the arc of the top of the pin exactly conforms to the arc of that Earth Star and how the point of the pin reaches to the Star centre by Rath Maeve in the south. These well-known structures fall beautifully into place within the geometry of the frame (diagram 86). Here you can clearly see how the frame and rotating pin can follow the arc of the Sun around the knobs and bosses to dial the time of the day, the season and year.

If the actual purpose of the brooch as a temple calculator seems remarkable, there is more to come. Now reverse the brooch and place the pin-head at the southern point with the pin pointing due north. Here the 'Hall of Tara' fits into the crescent of the lower part of the frame and the brooch is also seen to fit exactly the other way up, i.e., south to north (diagram 87). But surely that is impossible! But is it? Apparently from early records, certainly in South America's Inca/Mexican/Aztec civilisations, it is suggested that around 700 A.D. the Earth's magnetic field turned completely on its axis and magnetic north became south. Perhaps this incredible instrument shows this too.

We have plotted the Sun and Moon rising and setting points for Tara in 2000 B.C. If we now transpose those points onto the Tara Brooch around the arc of the ecliptic for the different seasons of the year, it is easy to see

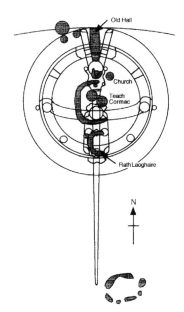

Diagram 86. *The Tara Brooch over Tara, Co. Meath (north/south).*

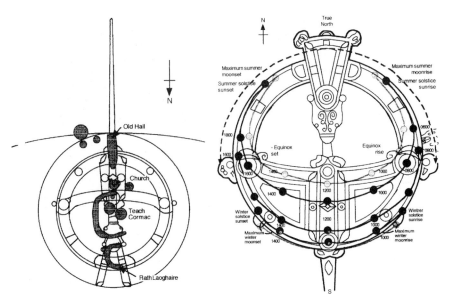

Diagram 87. *The Tara Brooch over Tara, Co. Meath (south/north).*

Diagram 88. *The Tara Brooch – Sun/Moon calculator or clock.*

that the brooch performs as an accurate clock for the months of the year, and also from day to day and hour to hour (diagram 88). Note how the Summer Solstice Sun at twelve noon gives us the arc of the Golden Mean.

There are many calculators similar to the Tara Brooch but generally not as important. It is the royal 'brooch' and comparable to an 18 carat gold Rolex Oyster watch beside a standard watch; some are virtually unengraved and look coarse in comparison, annotated by the archaeologists as 'provincial'.

Now we can begin to notice other artefacts from other countries to see if we can find a thread of similar geometry to substantiate the 'template' of the Tara Brooch. First let us go back to the 'tomb' of the Sun King himself, Tutankhamun of Egypt. Here we see the royal pectoral pendant of the winged scarab, representing the Sun and topped by the Moon disc (diagram 89). Superimpose a Tara template over this piece and draw on the geometry using the same format and descriptions (diagram 90).

The Sun centre is the scarab and the arc of its travels around the brooch is clearly shown from equinox to equinox, at left and right, where red carnelians are set. These two stones also represent the rising Sun in the east and the setting Sun in the west. The Moon disc is engraved firstly with three figures, a direct reference to the Trinity of the triple spiral and secondly, on the crown chakra of the Christ figure.

Irish history reports the journeying of Egyptians around north-west Europe, and the marriage of Queen Ti into the ancient Irish princely Druidic line perhaps confirms the sacred knowledge of Egyptology – conveyed by this geometric lore – melding with that of early Christianity.

One of the most beautiful illustrations in the eighth century Irish illuminated manuscript called *The Book of Kells* is the picture of 'The Arrest of Christ in the Garden of Gethsemene' (colour plate 9). However, if we look at this picture closely we can see that the arc or the arch above Jesus' head and the supporting side pillars project a squaring of the circle and the Golden Mean proportion (diagram 91). By now we could expect something like this, hidden from ordinary eyes yet drawn in a sacred metaphysical book. All the clues are there for us enlightened twentieth-century people now to decipher.

Diagram 89. *Tutankhamun's pendant* (**Cairo Museum, Egypt**).

Jesus said, 'I am the Light of the World', and it is in the garden that the light is arrested and shortly supposedly to be put out at the Crucifixion. When the light of a higher initiate (of the Essene order) is nailed to the Cross of matter, the temple is rent asunder at the grossness of the very act, but magnified out of all proportion because Jesus did not die!

The position of Jesus' arms is notable. If we draw a triangle from the arms, we get a basic geometric 45°, 45°, 90° triangle upside-down, the base running through his eyes and ending at the centre of the two side crosses (diagram 92). See the rising snakes of the Kundalini at the base of the side pillars. The very centre of the Tara Brooch fits over Jesus' third eye – his eyes stare out through the eyes of the two eagles' heads and his mouth is in the centre of the central 'boss' or jewel. The two side jewels of the

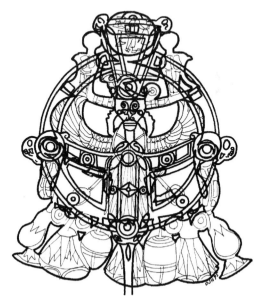

Diagram 90. *Tutankhamun's pendant with Tara Brooch superimposed.*

131

Diagram 91. *'The Arrest of Christ' – squaring the circle and the Golden Mean.*

Diagram 92. *'The Arrest of Christ' and the Tara Brooch calculator.*

brooch of red enamel, again representing the rising and setting Sun, are over the centres of the two side crosses.

The early Celtic Church held the ancient mysteries in their secret initiations, teaching the priests the geometry of the Sun, Moon and Planet Earth as part of

Diagram 93. *'The Arrest of Christ' and the Tara Brooch (45° triangle).*

'The Way' – expressed in artefacts and sacred structures. 'The Way' was the wonderfully clear, clean understanding of nature's energetic vibrations weaving through every aspect of our lives, day to night, but while hidden were continued through the teaching of a pure, positive Paganism – the duality of Pan and the Christ as 'One'.

Now turn the picture upsidedown and superimpose a picture of the Tara Brooch over the illustration (diagram 93), and we see to our utter amazement how Jesus is depicted as the brooch itself, a solar, lunar and celestial calendar; prophet, diviner and metaphysician – positively breath taking. So we ask ourselves who drew this, who knew this, who ordered it and why? Surely it was to

allow future generations to understand the sheer power of the metaphysical 'Word' as the very breath
of God itself; something inherent
deep within ourselves. For God is
not external and remote, but within
us all – for we *are* God, everyone
of us, whatever colour or creed.

Within the two pillars of the
Royal Arch of the Golden Mean, as
depicted so clearly in the Christian
illumination of 'The Arrest of
Christ', we can superimpose the
Masonic symbol (diagram 94).
Together, 'the Square' of the mason
and 'the Compass' of the geometer
make up the symbol of Freemasonry.
In *The Hiram Key,* by Lomax and
Knight, we learn that the two pillars
represent the pillars of Solomon's
Temple and the jointed arch the
coupling of the higher self above
the sacred entrance to the Holy of
Holies. This illustration shows that the Celtic Church had this knowledge
which was later incorporated into the Masonic tradition.

Diagram 94. *'The Arrest of Christ' and the Masonic geometric emblem.*

CHAPTER XII

Strata Florida Abbey and Some Great Churches

Strata Florida

About fifteen miles inland from Aberystwyth on the Welsh coast is the village of Pontrhydfendigaid – a small community at the western end of a remarkable hill valley river system that contains Neolithic cairns and standing stones from about 3000 B.C., and the beautiful abbey ruins of Strata Florida or St. Mary's Abbey, built by the Cistercians in 1166 A.D.

Back in 1985, I was asked by some friends who have a remote home in these hills if I would do a small survey of the Neolithic cairns that lie in the fields above Strata Florida. These are in the region of Blaen-Glasffrwd and the surrounding valley.

Having studied the layout and structure of Irish cairns, cist burials and stone circles, it was immediately interesting to note that again these structures were built to conform to the underground water lines and the Earth Star patterns. The chambers are of the two-to-one rectangular shape that is familiarly the oblong of the Golden Mean proportion, and it is significant that the cairn topping contains a lot of white quartz blocks. Quartz, as already described, is used as an activator of the whole structure. Not only were the quartz blocks deliberately included by the builders, but once again many of the blocks are fashioned in the lozenge shapes that are also found incorporated in the cairns of Co. Sligo at Carrowkeel, shaped, thus, ◇. This shape is the lozenge of the conjoined triangles, of a six-pointed star pattern ✡. These quartz lozenges were used to bend (refract) energy into the structure and to build up the spiral from the underground water conjunction beneath the cairn. The spiral was activated by the inherent metaphysical forces to emit ULF waves, as in the round towers of Ireland (see Appendix C).

There is a great natural Earth Star thrown up by the geological and underground water conformation centring at the cairns of Blaen-Glasffrwd (diagram 95) that takes in the surface rivers of the area. This Star contains the important Cistercian monastery at Strata Florida and the tiny settlement known as Ty'n y-cwm (diagram 96).

The whole of Planet Earth is sacred because of its divine concept, which is born out in the conformation of the landscape. It's hard to imagine anything

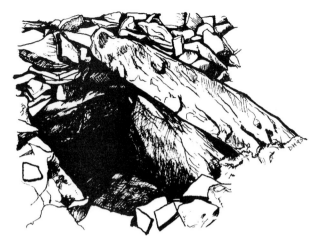

Diagram 95. *Blaen-Glasffrwd – Stone Age chamber.*

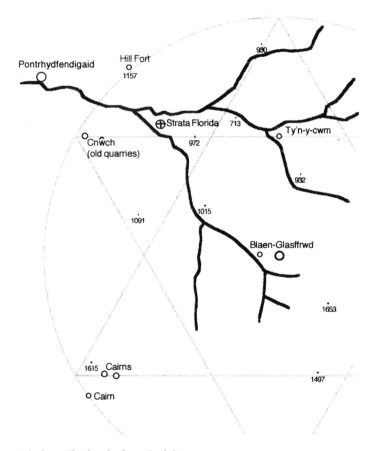

Pontrhydfendigaid

Hill Fort
o
1157

930

Strata Florida · 713

Cnŵch
(old quarries)

972

Ty'n-y-cwm

932

1091

1015

Blaen-Glasffrwd
o O

1653

1615 Cairns
O O

1497

o Cairn

Diagram 96. *Strata Florida – landscape Earth Star.*

135

special, figurative or angelic in concrete or even on a flat plain of farmland. But in hilly or mountainous country where there are rivers and valleys, it is much easier to understand how the comparison of the chakra system of the human body and the meridian lines are reflected in the shape of that landscape. The obvious comparison is where there is a river system, representing the flow of blood in running water, sprinkling from a fountain-head high in the crest of a valley hillside, the crown chakra, and following the river down its course and tributaries until finally it joins the sea in an estuary, or a lake, representing the base chakra. If the surrounding hills and rivers are in such form to represent the general shape of a body, or something resembling a human body, then it is possible to envisage a figurative angelic form. This may sound absurd to the inexperienced, yet to understand the joy of the landscape through such a concept lifts the human spirit into a realm certainly realised by the people of earlier times. It was certainly known in early Celtic monastic times, when, through humble worship, the monks were able to 'see' and feel the idea of God as very real for them in the unspoilt land they tilled so diligently.

The realm of angelic or divine revelation of the 'spirit of the land' is something reported very widely in non-Christian countries throughout the world, often by seemingly Pagan, illiterate or tribal peoples. Yet only now in our growing enlightened age do we begin to see how the early missionaries, in Christian zeal, often eradicated native customs that today we long to re-enact and experience again. We can do so in our own special places where the landscape is still mainly natural and unspoilt. Such a place is in the Strata Florida valley in Wales.

If we plot the six-pointed Earth Star north/south, pivoting on the Ty'n-y-cwm point, we can draw out a figure of the landscape temple using Blaen-Glasffrwd as the solar plexus chakra, Ty'n-y-cwm as the throat chakra and the rising hills behind as the crown chakra, up to its peak at Craig-ty-crin, and with both arms spread out to include Strata Florida in the west (diagram 97).

If we now pivot the landscape figure east-west on the throat chakra of Ty'n-y-cwm, we see that the root chakra is now the village of Pontrhydfendigaid. What was the solar plexus chakra of Blaen-Glasffrwd now becomes the solar plexus chakra at Strata Florida, the crown becomes the high hilltop above Ty'n-y-cwm, with the north arm at Craig-ty-crin and the south hand the cairn at Blaen-Glasffrwd (diagram 98).

This shows in an extraordinary way how the landscape figure fits into the north-south and east-west modes. The form of the figure is enlivened by the flow of the rivers through the body and down the arms, as water is the life-blood of the area. This creates a natural form of great grace and beauty that can be realised by walking along the rivers, through the valleys and up the hillsides.

We have already mentioned the great abbey of Strata Florida as the resting place of the Grail Cup of the Last Supper after it had been brought there from Glamorgan, possibly Llantwit Church. The Cup rested at the abbey for a long time, brought by the monks through the valleys of South Wales to seek sanctuary. So Strata Florida is deeply significant in the mythical and romantic history of Christianity.

136

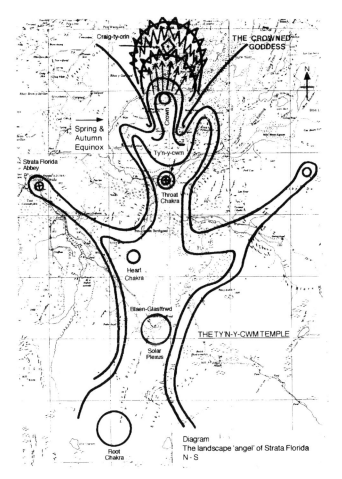

Diagram 97. *Strata Florida – the landscape 'Angel' (north/south).*

We have also seen that the Cistercians held and practised the ancient secrets of sacred geometry, which they incorporated in the construction of their churches.

Diagram 99 illustrates the underground water conformation of the abbey, showing a classic pattern of water being used to give the layout of the walls and the internal positioning of the nave, transept and altar. See how the water courses up through the nave and branches at the centre of the transept to give the position of the side altars and how the main water line splits at the altar into four lines leaving the central east window 'open' to the Easter sunrise.

The position of a water point in the centre of the transept must be unique. It may well have been the original position of the ancient altar before the enlarged abbey was built, sited over running water to energise it (diagram 100).

Perhaps the most striking aspect of the abbey is the beautiful arched entrance doorway, now open to the sky. Since the ruins now have no side or end east wall, or confining window, it is possible to look through the open archway, with its

137

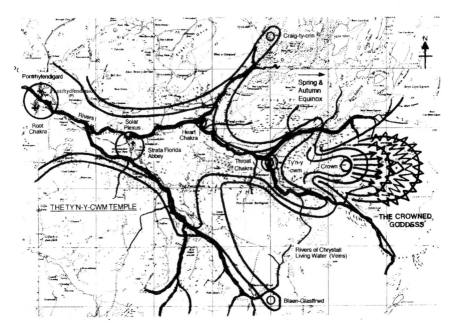

Diagram 98. *Strata Florida – the landscape 'Angel' (east/west).*

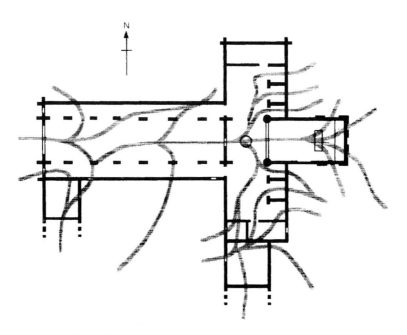

Diagram 99. *Strata Florida Abbey – underground water lines.*

Diagram 100. *Strata Florida Abbey – living water stream.*

five arcs sweeping above you as you enter to worship, directly to the horizon of the eastern prospect. It is easy to visualise the rising Sun at Easter coming up over the slope of the hillside to beam through a glorious stained glass window, illuminating the altar with its sparkling light. Then as we pass the door we notice spiral scrolls on both the right and the left which give us a clue to the geometry of the doorway itself.

Taking the point of the rising Sun on the eastern horizon as a centre, we can draw a circle that exactly fits the circumference of the fifth arc or arch above us. Then if we take the point of where the altar once stood as another centre, we can draw a further circle that cuts through the sunrise point. This gives us the Golden Mean proportion – the basis of Sun geometry and life itself, vitalising the body of the 'Sun Christ', 'wo-man' – the energy that worshippers who came into this sacred space acknowledged as their 'Christhood' during the festivals of the year (diagram 101).

Taking another look at the main entrance we note that there are seven 'lines' on the arches leading us into the centre of that sunrise. Connecting these lines to the equinox sunrise point gives us the seven rays of light representing the mystery of the rainbow – the seven chakras of the body and the 'Coat of Many Colours', i.e., the aura of the illumined wo-man (diagram 102). Surely, here is a secret of the building of early medieval sacred structures that has a line of knowledge going straight back again to the Stone Age priests.

We must ask ourselves if today this same knowledge is still held in the recesses of the mind of the Christian Church and if so why are we not told about it in our modern worship?

139

Diagram 101. *Strata Florida Abbey – Easter Sunrise (Golden Mean).*

Diagram 102. *Strata Florida Abbey – Easter Sunrise (the seven Golden Rays).*

140

Melifont Abbey, Co. Meath

When the Cup of the Last Supper was to be moved from Strata Florida Abbey in Wales, for safety, the monks were to bring it across the Irish Sea to Melifont Abbey. Melifont was another of the great Cistercian monasteries founded in twelfth-century Ireland, in 1157 A.D. It followed the classic pattern in determining its outline structure in accordance with the chosen underground water conformation, in order to give it good 'sacred' energy for its church and offices, and good flowing water for its administrative buildings such as the 'lavabo', kitchens and latrines.

The underground water lines follow the requirement of a straight flow through the nave with a cross flow to mark out the transept, through to the main conjunction at the east window for the positioning of the high altar. Melifont was destroyed along with so many other magnificent buildings by that wrecker and despoiler, Oliver Cromwell, in his puritanical zeal. But we still have all the clues we need from the water-flows to understand the layout of the abbey (diagram 103).

The chapter house is very interesting, consisting of two vaulted ceilings above an oblong chamber. The first ceiling has a plain unadorned point to it, but the second ceiling, over the centre of the further area, has a lovely central

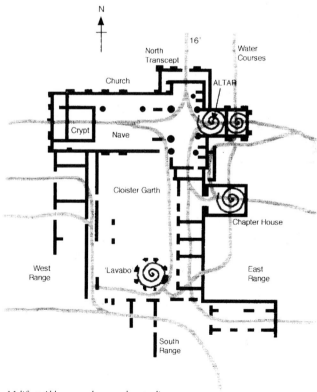

Diagram 103. *Melifont Abbey – underground water lines.*

rosette marking its position exactly over the centre of the spiral set up by the underground blind spring or spiral 'riser'. It was here, no doubt, that the Abbot sat when pontificating on the day-to-day running of his establishment. The lavabo, although a ruin, is a lovely piece of architecture, consisting of an octagonal arched balconied building of fine proportions. The south and west 'range' were the monks living quarters. The underground water in this great abbey flows from east to west and exits into the river at the west side, just beyond the walls of the building.

The abbey ruins are under the auspices of the Office of Public Works and a small entrance fee is required, but it is well worth a visit to see the lavabo, if nothing else.

The Rock of Cashel

The Rock of Cashel was the seat of the early Irish princes and later the Bishops of Munster. The Earth Star layout, superimposed over the plan of the original little church, shows that the altar, now no longer there, was sited over the centre of the Star that incorporates the later cathedral (diagram 104). The extension to the original little church, built in the seventh century, would have been added later.

Dowsing the Rock of Cashel reveals that the underground water lines are dry fissures, but still determine the original pattern of the layout of the great cathedral. The round tower (see Appendix C), was built before the cathedral and is therefore the only building on site, together with the original little church, which was placed over major conjunctions that you will note also connect up with the later structure (diagram 105).

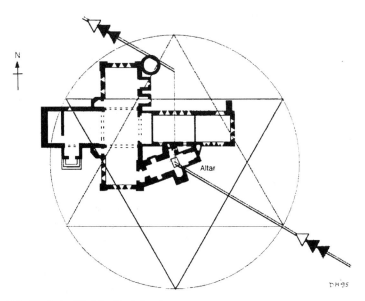

Diagram 104. *The Rock of Cashel – Earth Star layout.*

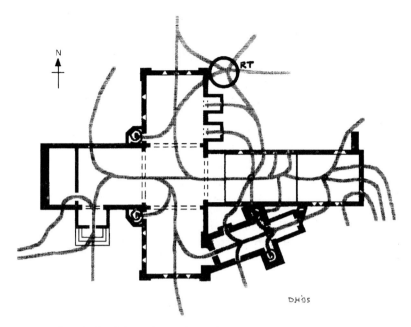

Diagram 105. *The Rock of Cashel – underground water lines.*

St. David's Cathedral

This is the great cathedral of Wales, built, we are told, on the spot of the original monastery, in Dyfed, founded by St. David in the sixth century. This puts it in line historically with the little oratories off the west coast of Ireland. David is said to have died on 1 March, 589 A.D. His name in Welsh is 'Tyddewi', later changed to 'Tudor', the House of Tudor or, as previously explained, the House of Judah and the Princes of Wales – of the original Israelite royal house and birth line through the Essenes.

The early church and monastic community settled in the valley of the river Alun which flows into the sea, passing by the now west door of the church about 50 yards below. The original little structure is on the site of the present building because the largest and strongest water conjunction is at what would have been, before the church was extended to its present proportions, the east window, now the pulpit (diagram 106). It is possible that the east window was arched or had bowed courtyards to the east to take in a second strong underground water spiral because now, with the building enlarged, high above this spring is the glorious nave roof 'pendant'. This 'pendant', incidentally, with its incurved sides, follows the ground plan in miniature of the sides of the Great Pyramid in Egypt. The point of the nave roof 'pendant' is also above the centre of a natural Earth Star (diagram 107), hence the great Sun Cross above the centre point of the cathedral, suspended as if by magic in the upper part of the building.

143

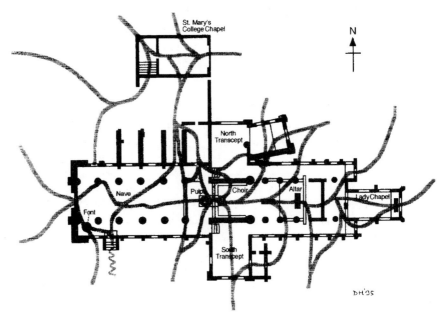

Diagram 106. *St. David's Cathedral – underground water lines.*

There is a similar nave 'pendant' in Salisbury Cathedral, also sited in the roof above a major underground spring. Surely this is an indication that the late medieval builders, when reconstructing St. David's in 999 A.D. and 1080 A.D., after the ravages of the Viking raids, understood the geometry and symmetry

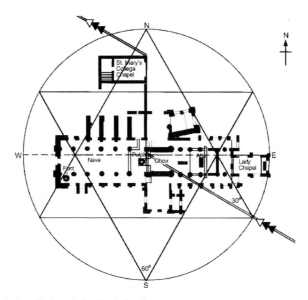

Diagram 107. *St. David's Cathedral – Earth Star layout.*

that the Earth Stars and cross-flows set up in the building, and therefore wished to mark the spot accordingly. The floor over the spring is paved with black and white chequerboard tiling, again an indication of knowledge of positive-negative polarity, and still there for us to see today.

St Andrew's Cathedral

Commonly known as Wells Cathedral, this has been included because it is the church that the current Archbishop of Canterbury was elevated from, and a church where the author attended for a time as a boy whilst at Millfield School.

There is always some point of special interest in the layout of any of the great early churches. St. Andrews, in Somerset, does not disappoint us as the water table and spring flows are numerous and vibrant. The layout is again classic, with the required flows up the nave to the present site of the altar, but now moved down by the current clergy to be more in touch with the congregation. At least the altar in its new place has been sited over a good conjunction so that it fulfils its role as a point of vibrant energy to enliven the sacrament (diagram 108). The other altars, if still used, are also correctly placed, as is the font.

It is interesting to dowse the water energy line running south from the main doorway, because this now follows a flow directly down the centre of the tea-rooms – a pleasant healing place to partake of a 'cuppa tea'. But the exciting difference of Wells is in the staircase leading to the chapter house and its

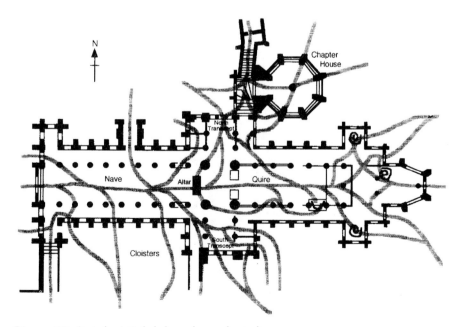

Diagram 108. *St. Andrew's Cathedral – underground water lines.*

145

stairs climbing over the roadway to the administrative buildings of the cathedral. This shows how the little zigzag of the water line is actually demarcated by the steps and their twists up and over – a meaningful touch of a master diviner and stone mason builder working together.

Salisbury Cathedral

Every year more than 500,000 visitors come to Salisbury, from all over the world. The cathedral is one of the most beautiful buildings in Europe, enshrining 700 years of English history. But it is not just a museum of the past: since its foundation in 1220 A.D., 'the worship of God has been offered every day' – so says the guide book.

This beautiful Norman cathedral, built at the flowering of great sacred architecture by the 'Freemasons' of the period, incorporates the knowledge of the ancient Stone Age priesthood handed down through five millennia.

The layout of Salisbury Cathedral follows the basic requirements of all sacred structures, the necessary cross-conformation of underground water flows to allow the correct placement of the nave and font, transept, choir and the altar (diagram 109). Any other flows or spirals were to be incorporated later, as necessary, since of secondary importance were the cloisters, library, chapter house, treasury, etc. Note the due west-east flow directly from the west main entrance through to the altar and east window. There are three major cross-flows or spring lines. The centre of the cathedral, that is, the centre of the transept, under the soaring 404 feet high spire, is over another cross-flow that produces

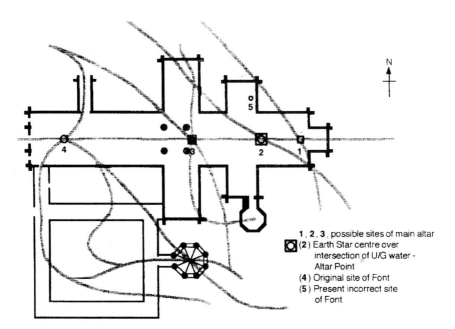

1 , 2 , 3 , possible sites of main altar
(2) Earth Star centre over intersection of U/G water - Altar Point
(4) Original site of Font
(5) Present incorrect site of Font

Diagram 109. *Salisbury Cathedral – underground water lines.*

146

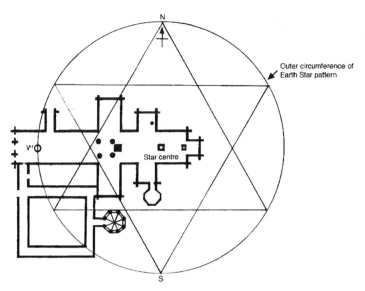

Diagram 110. *Salisbury Cathedral – Earth Star layout.*

a wonderful spiral right up the spire – after all, spires are no different in principle to the huge standing stones of old.

Salisbury Cathedral gives us an example of the centre of the Earth Star pattern being used at the original high altar (diagram 110). This shows the original altar, on the old plans called 'altare antericum magnum principale', at the only correct placing of the main altar. Any other position, and there's only one alternative, directly to the east, is incorrect. This is a magnificent building but unfortunately the current authorities seem to have no knowledge of its original layout, since the 'altar antericum' is now several feet out of place. Furthermore, the current position of the font in the transept is incorrect and in an extraordinary position that bears no relation to its proper function at the entrance to the nave; the living water at its traditional position providing the baptismal 'power' point (diagram 111).

When the original altar was built, a dowsing of the plans reveals that a rock crystal was buried at the spot under the site. This crystal produced and strengthened the confirmation of the Earth Star that has a radius embracing the site of the old position of the font

Diagram 111. *Priest baptising child at font with 'living water'.*

in the nave by the front door. The deliberate placing of quartz or rock crystal at the centre of the Earth Star pattern and also under the altar is deeply significant because, to quote Clive Beadon:

When quartz is put in the foundations of the church under the altar and where the altar is at the centre of an Earth Star pattern, when the priest gives a blessing in front of the altar the vibrations of the Star pattern change. With his right hand raised towards the congregation, palm facing, if he is wearing a gold ring or there is an amethyst in the ring or in his staff, he immediately changes the vibrations or colours of the Star lines. All colours disappear to be replaced by an outflowing wave of violet energy from the priest's hands. If he now gives the blessing all those in front of him will be encompassed by a violet wave of energy.
(Clive Beadon, *Earth Stars*.)

If, as he should be, this priest is also the bishop, and initiated into the aura and the chakra system of the body, he will enhance this wave of energy greatly, as the vibration of the crown chakra is 'amethyst' or violet. This is the reason why bishops, as the higher initiates of the Christian mysteries, traditionally wore and wear violet and have amethysts set in their rings – yet one wonders if any of them today know about this metaphysical practice?

Early Christian 'Interlacing' or Celtic Knotwork

The beautiful interlaced Celtic scrolling drawn by the early monks in the precious illuminated manuscripts such as *The Book of Kells* and on the carved stonework in the early churches has always fascinated us latter-day observers. This artwork was highly developed by the early stonemasons, and scholars have always speculated about its origins, which are obscure. No earlier tradition has the same disciplined, structured and precise interweaving.

Nine different patterns of stonework interlacing are shown from the tenth-twelfth centuries in Ireland. This work was used regularly on the panels and pillars of the early churches as a form of decoration, and we simply accept it without question as clever, fascinating, skilful and pretty. But does it mean anything? Where does it originate from and what is the message it conveys?

The author not being a musician has a little difficulty here but suggests that the interlacing, shown in diagram 112:

(a) represents a '2–3' or '3–2' pattern = a 5th;
(b) represents a '3–4' or '4–3' pattern = a 4th;
(c) represents a '4–5' or '5–4' pattern = major 3rd;
(d) represents a '5–6' or '6–5' pattern = major 6th.

These engravings follow the patterns that depict the wavelengths or resonance of, shall we say, a 'sonic dimension' of music. This can be illustrated by a laboratory computer print-out showing these patterns actually resonating. The comparisons are obvious and pictorially clear (diagrams 113 and 114).

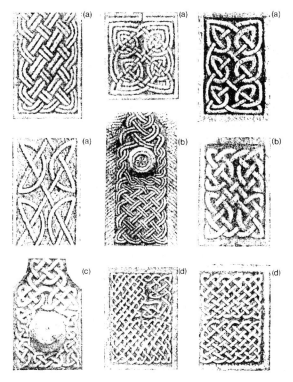

Diagram 112. *Early Christian interlacing or 'knotwork'.*

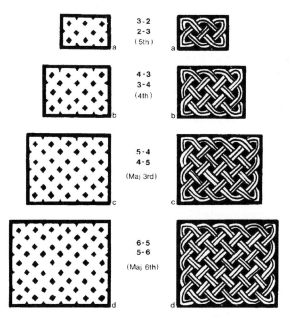

3 - 2 2 - 3 (5th)	
4 - 3 3 - 4 (4th)	
5 - 4 4 - 5 (Maj 3rd)	
6 - 5 5 - 6 (Maj 6th)	

Diagram 113. *'Knotwork/Dotwork' (**Olivia Dewhurst-Maddock**).*

149

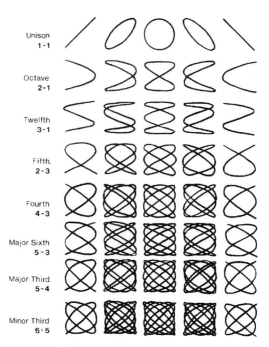

Diagram 114. *Musical resonances computer print-out (**Olivia Dewhurst- Maddock**).*

So, the engravings depict the resonance or vibration of sound as heard in the early churches. This sound can only have come from the ringing of the church bells, cast deliberately to produce the necessary notes or tones, or from the chants, both giving out mystical messages into the community and the landscape.

The only craft remaining today having any work remotely mirroring these sounds is seen in the patterns on such unlikely articles as sweaters – the traditional knitting of the famous thick natural wool sweaters from the west of Ireland, notably the Aran Islands off the coast of Galway. This surely must reflect an inbuilt musical tradition inherent in the hearts and hands of the Aran Islanders whose music was confined to the fiddle, bagpipes, tin whistle, flute and drum.

Even the painted decoration on the Cyprus water vessel, the sacred universal grail, illustrated in diagram 3 (Chapter I), shows another pattern of verticals and lozenges that are often seen on Aran sweaters, again showing a comparison to the patterns of underground water as picked up by a dowser or water diviner.

Surely, the ancient people hid their special knowledge of 'God', by reflecting it in their buildings and their crafts, and as a way of teaching the ignorant later people of today about their enlightened knowledge – universal truths that we no longer recognise. No wonder anthropologists and researchers go to remote places to find out how 'simple', 'uneducated' people live and think!

CHAPTER XIII

Ghosts, Karma and Reincarnation

Ghosts, Poltergeists and Earth Energy 'Ley' Lines

At home – in our own houses – sometimes we cannot understand why we feel uncomfortable or ill, angry, stressed, even fearful and lacking energy or the will to do anything. This is also the case at work when occasionally everything seems to go wrong and we have disagreements and rows.

Over many years' study, I have frequently found that the problem is due to underground water-flows (a conjunction or underground spring) beneath the building(s), setting up unnatural vibrations that disrupt our physical, emotional and even mental metabolism. When these water lines are disrupted, due to buildings being placed over the flow lines, a negative force is set up that travels unseen through the atmosphere – through walls and the air around us. If we inadvertently put our beds over these lines, we place our bodies, in the hope of relaxation and sleep, into such negative force fields or fields of 'dis-ease'. Our bodies then take on the corresponding vibration as a negative disruption that manifests physically as illness in many forms which, depending on the quality of the line, can affect our many different nerves, organs and functions; M.E. and M.S. may result. For example, suppose there is a green vibration going through the favourite chair or the head of the table where an old man or woman customarily sits, so a heart attack and angina is possible there. A violet line will produce constant headaches and possibly dizziness as the brain is affected. In a damp house on a blue line, throat and chest complaints will be usual. Time and time again when the doctors have failed to understand the reasons for a person's illness, I have found the cause to be directly related to the subtle household environment.

We are a water planet and unless we live in a desert country we are almost bound to have underground water-flows in our vicinity. In ancient times, the local priest or dowser was always called in to check the site before building commenced. As we've seen, this was particularly important with the layout of churches as it was considered vital to get the flow of unseen energy in tune with the structure. The Chinese call this the 'Dragon Energy' or 'Feng Shui' and place great importance on it for the future health of the occupants, using today the same ancient principles in the building of factories and offices as well as residences. Western Druidic practices are completely synonymous with this.

151

However, during more recent centuries in north-west Europe, few buildings have been constructed to these principles. It is quite usual for people to complain about 'presence's' or 'fairy lines' in their homes that we call 'ghosts'. Often we hear of houses that no-one will live in because they have a history of pain or fear and illness attached to them. Thousands and thousands of people have seen ghosts down the centuries so the phenomenon is not unusual, yet ghosts are still thought to be the hallucinations of disturbed people and not accepted by the medical or scientific community.

Where a house is built disrupting the energy of water lines, or when it is placed in the path of a magnetic 'ley' line or over an underground fissure, a negative energy is set up in the house that really does have a subtle effect on one, several or all of the occupants. The quality of the vibration or resonance can be annotated by a dowser using a pendulum and a colour wheel, and the resultant colour picked up will be compatible with the colours of the human chakras, forming an association accordingly.

In sleep we relax into another realm of consciousness and our subtle body or aura is then vulnerable outside the daytime operation of the rational mind. Supposing the underlying energy flowing through the bed of a happily married couple, in their new house, is red and blue. Then the red base chakra, the evacuatory and sexual system and the seat of anger, would be activated together with the throat chakra, the blue vibration of communication. In such a scenario one would expect sexual problems, bladder problems, menstrual problems and a shouting match to top it off. If the couple, not realising the underlying reasons for their subsequent unhappiness, continued to sleep in the same bed all their lives, then the negative aspects of the relationship could develop into untold misery and even hate; yet the original relationship might well have had every chance of success. Finally, by the time one or both die, possibly in that very bed, the soul consciousness of either or both of them could have become locked into the energy line to such a degree that at death the soul has become a part of that energy and cannot 'leave' with the bodily remains at subsequent burial.

Looking at an example of underground water lines through a village (diagram 115), the house at 'A' is clear with no problems. The water line going through 'B' is a blue line and if it flows beneath a bed it will produce throat and communication

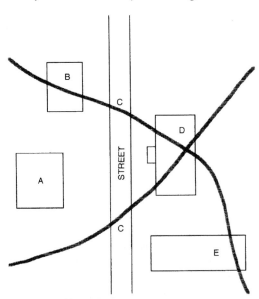

Diagram 115. *Underground water lines through a village.*

152

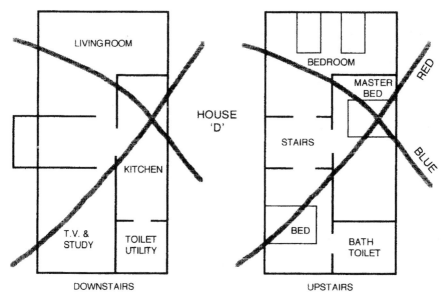

LIVING ROOM

HOUSE
'D'

KITCHEN

T.V. &
STUDY

TOILET
UTILITY

DOWNSTAIRS

BEDROOM

MASTER
BED

RED

STAIRS

BLUE

BED

BATH
TOILET

UPSTAIRS

Diagram 116. *Underground water lines through house 'D'.*

problems. Where the two flows cross the village road there are likely to be accidents or dogs and cats run over. House 'D' has two lines, one blue and one red, forming a conjunction or blind spring under it. This is a major disruption to the whole house and particularly to the couple in the master bedroom who will have a difficult relationship (diagram 116). Both, or one or other of them, might 'stay on' to haunt the house after death.

The soul within the subtle aura of the individual is now on the water line, or within the Earth Star energy field, which fluctuates its vibrations in accordance with the phases of the Moon and the water-flows due to rainfall. Sometimes non-psychic people entering the house, or living there later, are caught unawares by the fleeting vision of a figure drifting across a room or through a wall on one of these lines. This is because the individual's energy is momentarily in the same phase as the ghost's, so 'it' comes into sight. The exploration of ghosts is a fascinating subject. However, ghosts are nearly always sad, unhappy, lost or searching souls left behind on a line, longing to receive the love they lacked in life to enable them to 'move on', or 'pass through the door', into the higher realms of consciousness – to return to God or go back to the Sun from where all life emanates through the solar rays.

Increasingly in our modern open society we are learning of widespread devious sexual behaviour within 'the family' or groups. When a couple practice unnatural, bestial, sadistic or evil sexual activity over a water line, 'ley' line or conjunction, that powerful controlling energy builds up on and within the vibration of the line(s). When child abuse (within a family) is practised over a water line, pain and inner uncertainty of that debased innocence or manipulated pubescence occurs; change results in the release of another's sexual energy that builds up into a vortex of fear. When masturbation is practised either by adults or children fantasising over others with a controlling, absent minded, sexual force, that energy similarly builds up over the lines and conjunctions.

The activity of poltergeists has always attracted attention and alarm and their origins have never really been explained satisfactorily. A poltergeist is usually a very disruptive type of ghost and often active when children are going through puberty – the energy of pubescent change is in itself powerful. At the change from innocence to the beginnings of adulthood there is a strong sexual emanation in the subtle realms which may be actuated on the water lines, often to the detriment of the family. It is not strange therefore that occasionally these explosive negative forces create chaotic releases of seemingly evil energy that is uncontrollable and frightening. This is the cause of things getting moved about, plates and ornaments flying around, articles broken, doors opening and closing and slamming unaccountably, footsteps in the attic and the manifestation of horrid gargoyle faces and twisted bodies peering through walls. Our churches are adorned with gargoyle waterspouts on roof corners to show this and by putting these material images in stone on sacred buildings, we anchor and annul them, through recognition.

Where there is a disruptive line through a house of a woman with lower back problems and subsequent menstrual problems, again a poltergeist may attach to her and her family. Sometimes these energies even travel with a family when it goes on holiday and in Ireland that entity is called a 'taker'. Articles such as food, drink and clothes disappear only to reappear much later, incomprehensibly in good condition.

On the one hand, we are not allowed by the Church to believe in ghosts, who consider them an aspect of devilry. However, the exorcism of such manifestations in the form of unhappy ghosts still floating around could, in theory, only be completed by a celibate priest. He was one who had never known sexual activity so was above these evil forces. He could 'see' ghosts clairvoyantly and release them naturally into the ether without fear. Prayer by itself cannot do this, but unconditional love can – the greatest of all healing forces available to us, whatever our religion.

On a practical level, this same release, harmonising and reforming of symmetry within the home or work environment can be achieved by placing a **Spiral of Tranquility** in the house. Similarly, ghosts and poltergeists in houses can also be easily helped to 'move on' by the placement of one of these devices, as described in Appendix D.

We have seen that over long periods of time, from the Stone Age onwards, Earth Stars marked lines of higher consciousness within the landscape itself. These lines have usually been marked with Megalithic sites such as stone circles, standing stones and ring forts. 'Ley' lines are usually from fractured Earth Stars. Where a house is inadvertently built over such a line there are always psychic disruptions, ghosts, fairies, illness and odd events to contend with. If, as is usual, there is also an underground water line through the house, this will

154

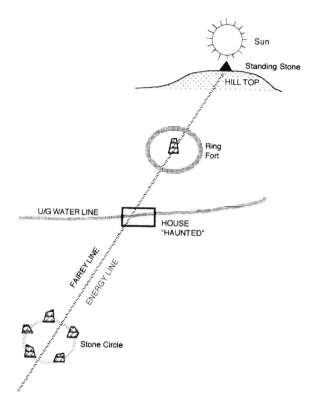

Diagram 117. *'Fairy' or magnetic energy line through haunted house – psychic phenomena.*

further aggravate the environment causing illness and emotional and mental pain (diagram 117).

It has been mentioned that in past times it was customary for the local dowser to be called in. He would plot the path of the line into the house and hammer an iron stake into the ground 'upstream' of the building, to polarise the energy down into the earth. This is only partially effective as it will only affect the underground water-flows, not the Earth Star lines. Also, today we have all sorts of new-fangled devices in our houses, supposedly to make life easier and more simple, yet the disruptive energy field around a television is over 20 feet, a microwave over 60 feet and a computer 50 feet; all working against the subtle human aura and causing the underground water vibes to go completely bananas! Sometimes we need to realise we are not so clever after all. The long-term disruption from these modern devices has not yet been assessed. Consequently, we wonder what the ghosts of tomorrow; ourselves and future generations will be like.

As we have mentioned, exorcism, presumably by a priest, is carried out on the premise that the ghost is generally an aspect of evil. This is not wholly true. Ghosts are an aspect of the holographic human aura that is activated by another living brain, at the same time emanating at the same vibration or voltage, in compatible circumstances, to the water lines or 'ley' lines. Most ghosts are therefore a manifestation of a negative vibrational energy from the past, and if that energy can be altered to become positive or is balanced, then the ghost has an opportunity to leave or 'move on'. Since modern Christianity has so little understanding of ghosts, usually the priest simply calling on the name of Jesus has little effect and the ghost remains in its unhappy, negative state. Also, if the priest is a negative thinker and secretly leads an unpriestly life, there is obviously little chance of success. However, if the priest is clairvoyant and can establish a personal psychic attunement to the ghost, then with Christian or objective love and understanding it may be released compassionately and has the opportunity to reconcile the reason behind its 'haunting', often at the same time freeing others disturbed by its vibration. This is an important aspect of the true 'healing ministry'.

Where a so-called 'witch' in medieval times was caught in the practice of the 'black' arts, in order to peg the negativity associated with her activities permanently into the ground, an iron stake or an oak shaft was traditionally driven through her heart and she was buried in unconsecrated ground. However, a 'white' witch, seeking light and positive forces, worked for ultimate good and harmony within nature. Sadly, many of the uninitiated were unable to distinguish between these practices and many compassionate and loving souls were randomly put to death.

Within the offices of the Christian church, a child that is still-born cannot be baptised. The unfortunate therefore has to be buried 'outside the church', hence the many children's graveyards in Ireland – not all are famine graves. To bear a still-born child has always, in poor cultures, been considered a deep disgrace, so the burial was carried out secretly after dark and the spot was marked with a simple unmarked stone. However, it has been found that often a children's graveyard was chosen inside an old stone circle or ring fort, so that in fact the child was actually buried in a far more holy, sanctified and special place than if it was interred in the usual cemetery.

The other burial that took place even more secretly was the burial of the product of an incestuous family relationship, when the child was deliberately killed at birth to dispense with the evidence. This was the case in monasteries and nunneries in medieval times. The author knows of an old monastery next to a nunnery in southern Spain that was recently restored as an hotel. During refurbishment, old adjoining walls were knocked down to reveal the many skeletons of babies that had been bricked up. No doubt some of these children became ghosts to haunt their sinful, priestly parents!

Karma and Reincarnation

These are both subjects carefully programmed out of Christian teaching, but still widely accepted as aspects of Eastern religions. Indeed, many people in the West are now also fully convinced they have experienced lifetime after lifetime until they finally release their soul consciousness from the 'Wheel of Karma' – the essence of acceptance of responsibility for ourselves and the Christ or 'God' within.

Christian dogma has taught us that God is external; some vengeful aspect of the heavens waiting to punish us for any transgression, to the extent that Christians in general have been brought up to accept that they are sinful, fallen and that life is meant to be a penance and a valley of tears. This is a totally opposite premise to the early Celtic Christian teachings where clairvoyance and healing were paramount to a life of simplicity and discipline – the discipline of *love*, not duty – and joy in everything. This doctrine, practised by the Druids and early Celtic Christians led to an understanding that life could be a path of service to all beings and nature; since we humans are only an aspect of the whole plan and not the plan itself. This encompassed the knowledge that wo-man does not have dominion over all and that everything has consciousness and probably a soul – how could 'it' not, if God made it? It is totally illogical to consider mankind in any way superior to any other aspect of the 'One King-dom'. In fact, it is that very superiority down the centuries that has caused, in many ways, so much misery and pain, not only to ourselves but also to nature and the animals.

Recently, in India in the Sathya Sai Ashram, a young Indian girl of about 17 years old and exquisitely beautiful, arrived with her badly crippled son to seek healing and love. A group of Europeans, deeply touched by this pathetic scenario, asked if the child could be healed and the girl helped, but Sathya Sai declined. Full of Western emotional pity they entreated him but he still refused, saying, 'let me show you the karma of the mother'. The inner television screens of the group, i.e., pictures in the mind, were activated and they saw a judge in India in the sixteenth century, cruel and rapacious, telling his chief jailer to lock up and maltreat this or that individual – the jailer then carried out all the unpleasant and cruel tortures he wished, to fulfil his maliciousness. They were then shown the judge as the mother in this lifetime, now the parent, having to take responsibility for the jailer who was her son, with all the twisted limbs, broken bones and lacking parts that he in turn had abused and caused in others. This is karma – 'an eye for an eye and a tooth for a tooth' and 'the vengeance of the Lord' – for surely we get back, bad or good, that which we do to others.

The concept of karma, or the law of cause and effect, has been programmed out of the Church; yet at this very time the Church is suffering untold degradation and shame for the gross sexual and manipulatory cruelty it has perpetrated on its congregations and individuals, particularly children, down the centuries. The horrors of child abuse in any dimension by a man or woman in spiritual trust demands our condemnation and utter disgust, and is not easily forgiven. This is the karma of the Church that has been built up over centuries but is now, at last, coming out into the open. The Church in its present form cannot survive. There are too many changes going on simultaneously – we have to ask ourselves what Jesus would have taught us or said about it all?

Whenever there is turmoil and gross negativity, we know that out of it can come a rebirth and renewal of a fresh vibrant spirituality. It is this that Christians now pray for – that a New Age of enlightenment will come after the present hierarchy has been dismantled.

Without reincarnation, the principle of the realm of the soul, incarnate on Earth to progress, transform and learn more about God – God as the soul itself – Christianity becomes hollow. There was a time when reincarnation was also recognised by the Church. Again, it was dismissed so that the Church could be projected as the sole means by which the individual could communicate with God, enabling it to retain ultimate control and power and keep the populace apart from the inner mysteries or magic of ourselves as an inherent aspect of God – able to access the divine spark within, on a personal level.

So many people have experienced vivid dreams, visions, dejà vú and incomprehensible experiences in other lives and bodies that the doctrine of reincarnation is not now so strange or unacceptable. Even the near-death experiences of many highlight life after death after life – lifetime after lifetime. It is almost becoming fashionable as a social topic of conversation, but many of those stories are lurid and coloured by emotional veils. Not everyone could have been some historical, romantic figure, such as Joan of Arc, Jane Seymour or perhaps Einstein, let alone the many people who claim some special relationship to Jesus himself. We have also been lepers and murderers, thieves and idiots; perhaps our conscious minds kindly programme these out to save us all the pain once more.

Again in the Indian Ashram, a couple of American visitors mentioned to my spiritual teacher that they thought he was getting a little 'fat', a little paunchy, and they asked him if he was taking enough exercise. 'I'll tell you confidentially', he replied, 'I'm pregnant' – long pause and a huge twinkle in his eyes – 'with my next incarnation'! Another long pause – 'And so are you'. Can we, you or I, accept we are now pregnant with our next lifetime? Personally, I think it's the most wonderful and reassuring idea I've ever heard, because it not only means 'I' can take responsibility for myself in this lifetime, day by day, year by year, but by conscious effort, may be able to influence in some way my return next time around. I might even be able to work towards some goal to be achieved next time – to be born to serve in some way special to my own unique self at soul level. It's a strange but beautiful thought, and allows us to see ourselves and our fellow human beings in a different light!

During the writing of *Pi in the Sky,* I went through a period of great introspection; a time of deep questioning and doubt, poverty and loneliness, to the extent that one day, at the very blackest time, reassurance became necessary. While I was meditating in the cairn at Carrowkeel one cold November day, feeling really low and depleted and lacking both the will and energy to continue with my researches, I decided to ask for reassurance – for some sign to be given in the near future so that I might know if I was totally egotistical and just deluding myself, but that hopefully the work was both valid and valuable for others.

In my meditation, I found myself standing outside the cairn as an old man with white straggling hair, thin, gaunt and wearing a long homespun smock-like garment. I was barefooted and wearing a pendulum on a string at my neck. Below me on the hillside were 30 or 40 men, women and children looking up the hill at me saying, 'Please don't leave us, you've come home to look after us'. The time was about 3000 B.C. and the countryside quite different from today. I realised that I was the Stone Age priest of that mountain area during that time, and that this lifetime was a recapitulation of then, with the purpose of bringing back into the present age the knowledge of the Neolithic period from within myself. Subsequently, I have shown many people around that area. Often people who are clairvoyant say to me, 'Do you know you have a guide, an old grey-haired man who walks with you?'. To which I reply, 'yes'. Yet I know that guide is myself from the past – I walk with my own 'guide', i.e., 'myself'; the hologram of myself, my ghost, my previous lifetime. Some-times people even ask me, 'Do you realise that man is you?'. I have recreated my own hologram in a time-space continuum through intent.

The point of the story is that if we make a commitment to work in the light, not at all necessarily a Christian light, then we recreate a previous lifetime where we have been specially trained to follow in the future – a future lifetime of service. I did not come to this point of realisation until I was 47 years old, when one day in meditation I 'met' a wonderful Greek mathematician. My surprise was such that I asked him why I hadn't met him before and had had to wait 47 years, to which he replied, 'I've been waiting 47 years for you to ask!'. Again the lesson is intent. If our intentions are in the correct mode, energy or vision, then surely we are given the task we are designed to fulfil in each lifetime. Once this is consciously recognised, and confirmed meditatively, then we receive a surprising amount of reassurance and help. Suddenly life becomes so very beautiful and worthwhile – no longer the previous charade of empty emotional religiosity.

If we look around at our fellow human beings with this inner feeling of know-ing instinctively the rights and wrong of 'life', it is not difficult to see those people of good intent performing decent, useful lives for the benefit of others. Similarly, we become aware of those people just coasting through life seeking happiness at a purely materialistic selfish level, and those actively involved in the manipulation and control of their fellows to whatever extent suits them. The worst aspect of wo-man's nature manifests as the out and out criminal con-man or deceiver. Whoever we are, we are building our karma day by day, like the sower who reaps the harvest of his seed, to be repaid with golden light or dreadful pain – and we are pregnant now with our next lifetime whilst we are doing it. Surely this is a glorious or dreadful thought!? It just depends on how we perform as human beings and face up to the tests we are challenged with and the responsibilities we take for ourselves.

Whilst in the Ashram in 1990, I was given the pleasure of a personal one-to-one interview with Sathya Sai, who enquired as usual, 'What do you want?', a question he often asks, to which the reply is often, 'Your love please'. I was how-ever speechless at the question because everything I had thought I wanted became suddenly totally unnecessary. He looked up at me and said, 'You want peace don't you?', something I had been asking for inwardly and secretly for years. 'I', he said, 'what is this I-I-I, who is I – no good! WANT – want, everybody wants – wants love, wants money, wants sex, want, want, want – *Peace* – how much peace you like – tell me, you may have it – how much you like?'.

By this time I was in bits and completely out of my mind. A week of confusion and inner questioning followed until one day, in meditation, a little voice in my ear said, 'Peace let me show you peace – *P*erfected *E*go *A*cknowledges *C*hrist *E*verywhere – PEACE!'. What a gift, and just what I needed – the nut of a word that we all use, all the time, without the least idea of its depth. Of course 'Christ' refers to the universal, omnipresent, omnipotent, cosmic Christ, and not the Jesus Christ expressed fundamentally and exclusively to Christianity. For Christ is everywhere in everything, of everything and there is nothing that isn't 'Christ'. 'It' is the great creative force of Planet Earth emanating through the Sun's rays to give us life and the wonderful dance of creation – 'Dance, dance wherever you may be, I am the Lord of the Dance says he', goes the Shaker hymn.

Christ, Peace, Love and Reincarnation all work together in time and space through our lifetime – lifetime after lifetime, until we reconcile ourselves to the principle of unconditional love and give up the bondage of karma and the ego. We do not have to be Christian, Catholic or anything else to reach an understanding of this basic principle of life, but perhaps we have to suffer many lifetimes to begin to understand it, often through great personal pain or grief, as we come to terms with ourselves and the waterless desert of the ego.

Today, in these troubled times, many of today's mystical teachers remind us of the relevance of Jesus and his way of love and forgiveness. For example, Sathya Sai says:

There is only one religion, the religion of love.
There is only one caste, the caste of humanity.
There is only one language, the language of the heart.
I have not come to found a new religion,
But to rebuild the ancient pathways to God.

CHAPTER XIV

Return to the Garden

To begin to understand that Christianity has lost its magic is to begin to understand something that we have lost within ourselves. We in the West had a vibrant inner mythology and understanding of ritual magic as a national heritage stretching back into the ancient mists of the Stone Age. When the first Christians began to trickle into Celtic Britain soon after the Crucifixion, escaping the Roman crack-down on seemingly disruptive elements within their Palestinian colonial territory, they were met with genuine understanding. The followers of Jesus, particularly the Bethany group, were of the royal house of David and the Essenes – initiates in the esoteric arts with a way of life, a discipline, that was closely compatible with the Druidic way. This involved healing, divination, a belief in reincarnation and prophecy, and the natural clairvoyance and clairaudience that goes with such a way of life.

Paramount in the Essene and Druidic tradition was a reverence and understanding of wo-man's responsibility for all the Kingdom of 'the One' – or 'God' – a personal inner responsibility as well as an external acceptance of the right of all things to exist and live as part of God's creative will in peace. Therefore, to take the life of any living creature was accepting a situation involving karmic responsibility – an act against the lore, not 'the law' of the Prophets.

The early Buddhic teaching, having a similar philosophy, had permeated into the Middle East from the missionary monks travelling out of Tibet and northern India. Many of the ideas, sayings and parables of early Christianity are infiltrated with this teaching. The correspondences between the Buddhist tales and the Gospel narrative in terms of content, significance and syntactic characteristics are so striking that Hans Haas closed his study with the following words, referring to the widow's mite:

> *This is not to be understood as a biographical anecdote worked up from one of Jesus' poetic teachings, as a transformed parable, but fundamentally as a legend which penetrated the realm of early Christianity from outside – and we have reason to believe from Buddhism – which was viewed in good faith as being a simple event in the Master's life and was handed down by the Christian community until Luke recorded it in writing and this was taken from his life of Jesus into the long complete second Gospel.*
(cited by Elmar Gruben and Holger Kersten, *The Original Jesus.*)

To quote further from Gruben and Kersten who explain the correspondences as follows:

> Here we have selected only a few borrowings in predominantly narrative passages of the New Testament. In his much-praised study, Rudolf Seydel discovered no fewer than 51 correspondences, analysing them in depth. The theologian Van den Bergh Van Eysinga thought that the following eleven correspondences were particularly convincing and six additional ones worthy of consideration:
>
> 1. the story of Simeon.
> 2. the twelve-year-old Jesus in the temple
> 3. Jesus' hesitation about being baptised (according to **Matthew and the Epistle to the Hebrews**)
> 4. the temptation
> 5. Mary's beatitude
> 6 the widow's mite
> 7. Jesus walking on the water
> 8. the Samaritan woman at the well
> 9. 'out of his belly shall flow rivers of living water' **(John 7:38)**
> 10. the parable of the talents **(Matthew 25:14–30; Luke 19:12–27)**
> 11. the world on fire in the **Second Epistle of Peter (3:8–11)**
>
> The lesser parallels he suggests are:
>
> 12. the Annunciation **(Luke 1:29–33)**
> 13. the selection of the disciples **(John 1:35–43)**
> 14. the statement about Nathaniel
> 15. the parable of the prodigal son **(Luke 15:11–32)**
> 16. the man born blind
> 17. the transfiguration **(Matthew 17:1–13; Mark 9:2–13; Luke 9:28–36)**.
>
> Must one therefore – even when viewing this material very sceptically assume that a large number of biographical elements, of parables and narratives from the life of Jesus, are fantasy? Borrowings were certainly also eagerly made from sources other than the wealth of surviving Buddhist texts. The Hellenistic legacy is demonstrated in the eclecticism of the evangelists, who drew freely on a wide range of writings and other ethnic traditions. The references to Jewish holy books, particularly the prophets, are also – viewed from the perspective of Christianity – borrowings, needed for portrayal of Jesus as the Messiah. It becomes apparent too that the representatives of the Jesus movement responsible for setting down the Gospels were primarily interested in reforming Judaism rather than establishing a new, autonomous religion. However, the fragments of various traditions were not disjointedly strung together in order to expand Jesus' life as if it were a novel. Instead this was a difficult, scholarly process deploying textual patterns from the multi-structured cultural web of these traditions.

If we can now consider the idea, outrageous though it may be to Christians even today, that the Passover Plot was real and that Jesus deliberately set up the whole scenario of the Crucifixion and his subsequent survival to deceive, we have to ask, 'why?'. Why go to so much personal trouble? Why then, having been successful in the deception, go through the pain and the sedated dying process, subsequently to travel far away incognito into the vastness of Kashmir?

It was obvious to Jesus that the only way he could get his Messianic message across to the people of Roman Palestine was to appear to be an authentic, willing sacrifice in fulfilment of the earlier prophecies. If the message of unconditional love and forgiveness – offered from the Christ within – the kernel in the nut of his message was not acceptable, and he was just seen by the authorities as a rabble rouser, then he knew that to give the oppressed people under the yoke of Rome any hope of salvation in the New Age, he had to be seen to have given up his very life for the principles he preached. The agony of indecision, experienced finally in the garden of Gethsemene, demonstrates the anxiety and perplexity that he subsequently overcomes.

But, and it's a very big but, he also knew that there was another world beyond the confines of the small Roman colony he had been born into – a world of wonder and magic as presented by the Buddhists. Perhaps he had even experienced their teachings in northern India before the beginning of his ministry at the age of thirty. Obviously in the so-called 'lost years of Jesus' we do not see him working for 20 years over the carpentry bench in his father's workshop. If the miracles in the Gospels are to be believed, his initiations were profound in the disciplines of meditation and the healing arts. Certainly, all the so-called recorded healings performed by Jesus have been duplicated many thousands of times over in our current lifetime and before, particularly in India. This fact alone, for those who have experienced these miracles at first hand through their spiritual teachers, as I have, helps me and my friends at least to understand, authenticate and appreciate Jesus much more fully. Indeed, it is now widely accepted that Jesus did not die on the Cross, but was taken down, recovered in the sepulchre and travelled extensively afterwards.

That Jesus chose to travel to Kashmir is a reasonable hypothesis if we remember that there were many strands of the lost tribes living there. Perhaps some of them had travelled to the East during Jesus' life and met him. Perhaps three of them were the Magi, the astrologers or the three wise men of the Biblical birth story, i.e., prominent members of the far-off Jewish community of Essene traditions who had knowledge of the advent of a special Essene birth. The birth of the/a Messiah who would not only bring hope and renewed faith to his people 'at home', but also into the far-off realms of the tribes long dispersed by the earlier wars and conquests. Another explanation is that the 'Three Kings' were the stars of Orion's belt, seen over Jerusalem in 5 B.C. and the 'Star of Bethlehem' was the rise of Sirius in the East.

Think how history would have changed if Jesus had chosen Joseph of Arimathea to go to Kashmir and he himself had decided to come to Britain instead? The fury of Rome, knowing no bounds at the early Christianisation of Britain by the lost disciples, would have been even more diabolical if Jesus had set up a new throne in England. But such a possibility was unthinkable because he would then be seen in the Western world to have survived and his cover blown. If you still think Jesus resurrected into an auric form after the Crucifixion and after a period of contact with his friends in Galilee, floating around in the astral realm, seemingly manifesting himself over a period of perhaps some weeks or months, then for whatever reason to 'ascend into Heaven', you might perhaps rethink the Bible story.

Jesus had to go far away where the influence and presence of Rome was minimal, if at all. Kashmir is remote enough even today, but 2,000 years ago it must have been almost unapproachable. It was easy for him to travel the caravan route anonymously amongst the traders and travellers, and it must have been easy to carry on his ministry amongst his own people freely and openly where his neighbours did not have to think he died, and improbably 'resurrected'.

When we say in Christian prayer, 'And on the third day he rose again from the dead' etc., we should say logically, 'And on the third day he rose again after being seemingly dead'. Referring to the 'resurrection of the body and life everlasting', if we transpose 'resurrection' to 'the resuscitation or reincarnation of the body and life everlasting', suddenly the story of Jesus becomes alive and plausible. It is often said that Jesus, as a higher being, chose his parents and sacrificed himself willingly – this was his own karmic choice as an initiate. If in fact he did not sacrifice himself willingly to 'die' on the Cross, then the idea that 'we' choose our parents, even as initiates, reincarnated for the purpose of sacrifice, is suspect. If Jesus didn't, how could we normal mortals do so? Or was his birth just a normal birth anyway?

So many people in the West today, in this our 'last times', have come to accept and experience reincarnation that the subject is now commonplace amongst all classes and creeds. Eastern religions are fully conversant with and practice such belief in the family environment. Often a child will report events that only the parents or grand-parents could possibly know about concerning relationships and nuances of experience on such a level as to be totally private, yet confirmed to be valid past-life experience. The life everlasting is, in these terms, the passage of the soul from one lifetime to the next until 'it' ultimately meets the totality of the 'Creative Force' or 'Divine Intelligence' – the cosmic Christ on a deep inner experiential level. Then the spirit of the physical being, in that final lifetime, merges with the essence of itself and becomes timeless again – a 'back to source once and for all experience', breaking free of the 'Wheel of Rebirth'.

'Catholic', as we understand it today means Rome – but traditionally it referred to the whole Christian Church, with all its many factions and tribal splits. Originally it meant 'universal', signifying the all encompassing and life-enhancing 'One-ness'.

If a Christian firmly believes in the 'second coming' and the Pope and the Archbishop of Canterbury believe in the 'second coming', then they, and you, must believe in reincarnation! However, if Jesus did not die on the Cross and the whole scenario was a brilliant deception, then there is no 'second coming' as we might expect; because anyway it would be Jesus' umpteenth reincarnation from his last death place out of Kashmir and his tomb in Srinagar. If he now reincarnated in this New Age, after a lapse of 2,000 years, and we accept that the planetary consciousness is due to change radically in 2012 A.D., then Jesus in his new form will be extant amongst us now and reincarnated already. Or, if he reincarnates this year in 1997 he will be only fifteen in 2012 A.D.! It's possible but unlikely. Maybe Jesus has already reincarnated and walks amongst 'us' today, unknown and unrecognised, or is 'he' or 'she' now someone of international status as a man or woman of peace – who knows?

But to get back to the Garden – the Garden of Gethsemene – the garden of all our hearts. It is the place of inner peace, contemplation, meditation and security; a place of aloneness and introspection, a place we wake up in every morning, every sunrise and return to every sunset. One day or night we won't wake up again and that's when the Garden changes in this lifetime. All so often in life we flounder around in the Garden unsure, lost, full of self-pity, afraid; just as Jesus did when he said at that moment of inner truth, finally having to face the knowledge of the path he had set up and the trials he was, willing or otherwise, to go through with:

Matthew 26:39 – *Oh my Father if it be possible let this cup pass from me nevertheless not as I will but as thou wilt.*

If we as Christians, or any other religion, can honestly repeat that saying every morning then we can fulfil our human-beingness to life; any form of life on Earth. If we can give way to everything we are and aspire to and release our ego into the hands of the Divine – the Cosmic Christ ideal– then 'thy service' does become perfect freedom. But to make that break demands all the sacrifice of Jesus – the Jesus, the Christ, that is latent in us all. When we crucify ourselves daily in the exercise of the thirsty, waterless desert of our ego, we perpetuate our lifetime – lifetime after lifetime – until finally we become aware of and surrender to our true purpose. Then we give way totally to the absolute and no longer have to return to the Garden. We can go on just as Jesus did to resurrect 'the next day' – the next three days after the weekend and start another day, another lifetime, afresh, offering ourselves as a living sacrifice to life not death, through the power of unconditional love. Finally, we get the message that there is no Garden, no key, no doorway, no magical formula or prayer that releases the soul back into the hands of some external 'God' – 'He' who is out there, up there, around that elusive corner. The Jesus truth is the ultimate flash of reason that illuminates our vision and transforms us, telling us that 'it' is all here now, this very second, if we can grasp the seemingly incomprehensible spiritual truth that we – 'I' – am, are, already 'it'. That 'I' am God, in God, with God, breathing God in and out, thinking God, saying God, laughing God, praying God – because there IS nothing else.

In meditation one early morning I was given this little vignette to help me understand 'the Garden':

Poem: The Garden
If you will let me into your garden open the gate
I will help you do the weeding
Bend your knee to me
Allow me to help you
Accept that I am here
All the time
There are so many flowers

165

Waiting to bloom – to
Bloom in your heart with me
Let me be your gardener
Let me hoe your fields
Let me hold your hand
On the pathways
I am so near you that
You don't see me
Look, look around
See that rose there?
That's me
See into that dewdrop
Its a spring and a well
In the depths of its me'ness
I am in the spider's web
And the trees
In the croak of the frog
And the hum of the bees
There is nowhere that I am not
Except you deny me
Then you cannot see me
In my invisibility
I am in you
I am you
You are my garden
Open the gate and
Let me in to your heart

And now what?
Back in 1924, D.H. Lawrence, a man of mystical vision in many ways, said:

To me it is important to remember that when Rome collapsed, when the great Roman Empire fell into smoking ruins and bears roamed in the streets of Lyons and wolves howled in the deserted streets of Rome and Europe really was a dark ruin, then, it was not in castles or manors or cottages that life remained vivid. Then those whose souls were still alive withdrew together and gradually built monasteries and these monasteries and convents, little communities of quiet labour and courage, isolated, helpless, and yet never overcome in a world flooded with devastation, these alone kept the human spirit from disintegration, from going quite dark, in the Dark Ages. These men made the Church, which made Europe, inspiring the martial faith of the Middle Ages.

The flood of barbarism rose and covered Europe from end to end. But, bless your life, there was Noah in his ark with the animals. There was young Christianity. There were the lonely fortified monasteries, like little arks floating and keeping the adventure afloat. There is no break in the great adventure in consciousness. Throughout the howlingest deluge, some few brave souls are steering the ark under the rainbow. If I had lived in the year 400, pray God,

166

I should have been a true and passionate Christian. The Adventurer. But now I live in 1924 and the Christian venture is done. The adventure is gone out of Christianity. We must start on a new venture towards God.

Anyone who reads the papers today or watches television regularly will be amazed at the amount of political, social and sexual comment we have to put up with from the bishops – Catholic and Anglican. It seems that there is no subject on which they are not expert. This is depressing because they are usually just as misguided as the politicians and generally base their prognosis on their own pet path to salvation or biblical reference. This book has aimed to expose the myth of 2,000 years of manipulation of vast numbers of people by a comparatively few, deeply dangerous, egotistical men who in their grandiose self-glorification have called themselves 'the hierarchy', as if to set themselves on the right hand of that external God.

The Christian Church over the past 1,500 years has shown itself to be one of the best organised, most ruthless and cruel self-perpetuating myths in the history of the world. Its doctrine is probably founded on fallacies. One – that Jesus died on the Cross; two – that he resurrected not resuscitated from the dead; and three – that he ascended mysteriously, at some later undisclosed date, into heaven. On the basis of these three ideas we have been brain-washed into the acceptance in spiritual terms that we are all unworthy, sinful and bound for damnation unless we toe the party line. Then, depending on our obsequiousness or our pocket we might buy redemption. Of course, first we have to be accepted into the organisation like any newcomer; at baptism, then going up the ladder to confirmation, then marriage and finally, even when we die, at our funeral. At each stage of life we pay our dues; money for the privilege of being acknowledged by members of this vast business.

Furthermore, to embarrass us as to our sinfulness, the people who run this organisation always wear black, the colour of negativity and death, yet when in their house of business they change to white and put on all sorts of finery to remind us of their wealth and status far above us mere mortals. Maybe the Saints commune for our benefit or theirs – certainly the forgiveness of sins is more acceptable, though let us not dwell on the sin aspect, which is so often applied to suit the forgiver i.e., the Church. Behind the scenes, now exposed by the advent of total global communication, we know that the Church is corrupt financially, socially and sexually to the point that we wonder how it can possibly still survive and be in any way trusted or respected. As Lawrence said of the Roman Empire:

The flood of barbarism rose and covered Europe from end to end . . . Christianity as it was founded by Rome has run its course.

As has Rome and Canterbury, and the current way is no longer valid.

But there is an answer and there is still just hope. Out of every downward spiral in the human syndrome, when we reach rock bottom as individuals or tribal groups, sooner or later we have to drag ourselves up out of the mire. At the moment we are still on the way down because the eternal male, sexual, ego – that dreadful dominant force that has subjugated the Goddess, the female

Virgin, for 3,000 years – is suddenly realising its inherent weakness, its paucity, its own myth and is having to take steps to enter the Garden again.

It is in the Garden that birth takes place. Here is the realm of birth, death and rebirth – of both the heavenly spiritual realms and the human physical realm. The place where we meet Jesus and where the Goddess reigns, where through the lunar waters of the womb, air meets matter and is transformed through fire, the eternal Sun. Then, mere men have to give way and away. For when the Goddess decides to move, to take steps to weed the Garden, mere men, born of the Goddess, born out of the Goddess, suckled, cared for, loved and educated by the Goddess, take heed.

For the Goddess is not just the Virgin, Mary the bride, Bridget or the old crone, but Mother Earth herself – Gaia – and she is now speaking through the New Age. So today, the whole planet has an air of expectancy that something may be about to happen – change – leading to scientific, social and spiritual freedom. Out of the religious turmoil, ideas and individuals are being thrown up to challenge the existing structures. Beacons of light are emerging of a radical new vision; transforming thoughts, practices and consciousness itself, with the potential to change human perceptions on a planetary level, yet allowing each religion to pay its own karmic debt. It is a wonderful concept, a thought – the most powerful thing in the universe – that already, many individuals, in fact many many millions all over the world, are currently giving and receiving joy and unconditional love.

The concept that God is in each of us, that 'we' *are* all 'God' within ourselves, that deep within our hearts there lies a divinity, totally connected to everything that there is, was, or will be, is both an overwhelming and challenging thought. We must open our hearts and minds to its potential and accept the path of our soul, through reincarnation, back to the Godhead. It is the return journey, a journey of self, back to self, through the opportunity of life itself; the school of Planet Earth with its many lessons.

In his famous poem, *The Second Coming*, W.B. Yeats said, 'Things fall apart, the centre cannot hold. Mere anarchy is loosed upon the world'. This always has to happen in our individual lives as we make our own karma, just as it has to happen to whole civilisations – as in the Roman Empire. And so today, we are at the start of this cycle once again at the turn of another millennium. The crash is held off every month by clever monetary or military manipulation. But the Goddess is crying out, calling the angels and soon the great change will be upon us when 'the centre has given way'. Out of the abyss – the end of Christianity, the end of Islam – will come the rise of 'hermaphrodite', a balanced human being. This in essence, in human terms, is of new healing hands, fresh minds, a new innocence under the guardianship of vibrant cosmic forces, for the whole of Planet Earth in the New Age. The Messiah is with us already. There is little time – are you ready to change and go within?

168

Notes on a Limestone Cruciform Figure from Souskiou in Cyprus (c.2500–2000 B.C.)

Peter Dawkins

The figurine (diagram 118(1)) is basically in the shape of a cross. The cross is composed of two main elements:

(i) a 'T'-shaped lower part forming the body, arms and legs of a female or Goddess;
(ii) a phallus-shaped upper part forming the neck and head of a male or God.

The figurine clearly portrays the idea of the male lingam (Shiva) held in or penetrating or rising from the female yoni (Shakti). At a cosmological level this symbolises the principle of spirit (fire + air, or fiery breath) placed upon and penetrating matter (water + earth). It is equated with the fundamental principle of Feng-Shui (wind-water), or, as described in Genesis, the Holy Breath (Spirit) moving upon the face of the waters, from which love affair Light (the Son) and all subsequent creation came into being. This same symbology is to be found in the original symbol of the Tau Cross in the Mystery Schools, wherein the Tau (T) forms the manifest or phenomenal part of the cross, whilst the upper part of the cross remains invisible or spiritual, represented only by the Word (written as 'Tau' above the Tau Cross). In a dramatic portrayal of this, in Jesus' Crucifixion the written Word was represented by 'INRI', placed above his head on (or as) the upper part of the Cross. The male upper part of the Cross thus portrays the active spiritual principle of creation – the Creator or Heavenly Father, who fertilises the universal waters or substance with the Word. The female lower part of the Cross thus signifies the receptive material principle of creation – the matrix or Earth Mother, who gives birth to all forms of life within her womb and out of her substance.

The male lingam is single: the female yoni/body is divided by a central line, and is thus dual. Odd numbers are considered to be male in the Hermetic Pythagorean philosophy; whilst even numbers are female, 1 = the One, the Creator/Father God, male, 2 = the female, the Goddess/Earth Mother, with the duality required for phenomenal existence. Together they create the 3 = the hermaphrodite child, the light, Creation, known as the Son (or Sun). The male lingam can also be seen as the Son arising out of the womb/body/matrix of the Divine Mother. The Son is born in the Mother, in the divine waters, but must rise out of the waters into the fiery breath of the Holy Spirit in his evolution. The first birth or baptism is by water, but the second birth or baptism is by fire and holy breath. This same development is represented by the hill or pyramid arising out of the lake or sea, representing *Kheru* (Horus), the manifest 'Word' – the Christ, or *Maa Kheru*, 'the True Word' – Mercury. This is identical with the meaning of *Atlantis*, signifying 'the land or hill arising out of the waters'.

The same symbolism is used in the design of cathedrals, where the central part of the cathedral, representing the Christ, rises above and yet is at the same time supported by the outer church, representing the Mother. The Mother is at the same time the womb and the throne (i.e., the support or strength) of the Christ – the dark womb of the universe which enables the invisible light of the Father to become visible as the Son/Sun. The Father, related to the clerestory (i.e., the upper, 'Heavenly' part of the church) which allows light into the body of the church from above, is the holy wisdom which seeds the dark body (womb) of the church with light. The Son or Christ is the resulting beauty, the harmony of the light and dark, upper and lower, Heaven and Earth, Father and Mother, blended in mystical union.

The three Pillars of the Temple, corresponding to those of the Cabbalistic Tree of Life, are known as Wisdom, Strength and Beauty.

The figurine represents Atlantis, the Christ or Horus/Jesus, who is Mercury, the Hermaphrodite, in the process of being born from his Earthly Mother through the creative will and power of his Heavenly Father. The Mother is Aphrodite (Venus), the Father is Hermes (the single, male Mercury). Their child or 'Son' is Hermaphrodite (the male-female Mercury). The Father and Son are One. The figurine depicts the Mystical Marriage of spirit and matter; and the resulting birth or manifestation of the soul, the Light of Love.

The geometry of the figurine is remarkable and matches in meaning the natural symbology described above. The main geometric proportions are associated with the Trinity, the Golden Mean, Squaring the Circle and the 7-Pointed Star.

The Golden Mean. The figurine is based upon the Golden Proportion, associated symbolically with both Mercury and Venus. Its ratio is denoted as Phi (the twenty-first letter of the Greek alphabet). It is also known as the Fibonacci Series. It is a symbol of life, and in particular represents the ideal of universal Love, Harmony and Beauty. It is the proportion upon which the experience of knowledge (*logos*) is founded. Geometrically the Golden Proportion is inseparably related to the 5 function and the pentalpha.

The pentagram, pentalpha and number 5 are symbols of Venus (the planet Venus describes a five-fold geometry about the Earth in the course of eight years) and its emblem, the Rose. 3 is the number of Mercury (the planet Mercury describes a three-fold geometry about the Earth in one year). 8 describes the hermaphrodite Mercury. 8 is derived from 3 + 5, just as Hermaphrodite is born from the union of Aphrodite (Venus) and Hermes (Mercury).

The whole figurine is enclosed in a square of 16 × 16 units, which is equivalent to a chessboard of 8 × 8 double squares. the basic ground-plan of a temple

Diagram 118. *(1) 'Hermaphrodite' of Paphos (**Private collection**).*

(diagram 118(2)). Its enclosing circle (which fits inside the enclosing square) has a diameter of 16 and a circumference of 50 units, its centre being the heart centre of the figure. Thus the whole figure is heart-centred, emphasising the Love, Beauty, Harmony and Balance associated with the Heart.

50 is associated with the mystery of the Argonauts and of the star Sirius, a greater Sun to our solar system and thus a greater heart centre in the cosmos.

The proportion of head (face) to upper body (neck and heart) to lower body (heart to feet) is in the Golden Proportion series of 3:5:8. The proportion of the head to the rest of the body is 3:13. The proportion of the legs to the rest of the body is 3:13.

The inner circle (B, Z, D, Y) on the heart (C) has a diameter of 10, and its enclosing square (C, D, E, F) has an area of 10 × 10 = 100, and a perimeter of 40 (diagram 118(3)).

10 relates to the 10 Divine Principles of Life, and to the Tree of Life with its 10 Fruits.

40 is a particular number denoting a special period of time, a complete period or cycle. It consists of 4 × 10, which represents the 10 divine principles manifested throughout all four worlds of emanation, creation, formation and outer manifestation. This inner heart-centred circle and square contain the central part of the figurine's cross (i.e., excluding the head and legs), with its width denoted by the width of the outstretched arms. The central part of the cross is thus an equal-armed cross, or cross within a circle, whose measurement is 10 × 10, revealing that it is the Cross of Life.

The figurine thus depicts the Tree of Life (i.e., the 10 × 10 cross) at the centre of the Garden of Eden (i.e., the 16 × 16 square of the whole figurine).

Squaring the Circle. From the inner heart circle a based triangle (i.e., as per the Great Pyramid of Giza), whose base forms the horizontal diameter of the circle, marks with its apex the central point (X) of the face, on the bridge of the nose. A circle, diameter 3, drawn on this centre exactly outlines the inner head or face of the figurine. A heart-centred circle whose circumference passes

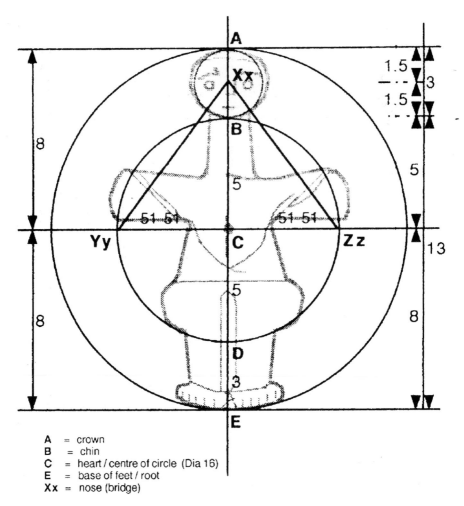

A = crown
B = chin
C = heart / centre of circle (Dia 16)
E = base of feet / root
Xx = nose (bridge)

Diagram 118. *(2) The Golden Mean.*

through this centre of the face provides the median heart circle, which is squared by the 10 × 10 heart square. The median heart circle has a diameter of 13, and a circumference of 40, which is equal to the perimeter of the 10 × 10 square.

The 10 × 10 square is the Square of Life containing the Cross or Tree of Life. The median heart circle is its corresponding Circle of Life.

13 is the number of the Holy Grail and of the Seat of the Grail Knight or King. The thirteenth Seat is the Kingdom or Queen, who is the Grail. She is the Mother of the Christ, the Son or Light (The Grail King), who lies within her womb as the child and sits on her lap as a king on his throne. She is also the Grail King's bride, wife and queen. The feminine part of the figurine depicts this Grail, the womb or seat of the manifested male aspect.

The proportion of the small face circle (A,B, centred on X) to the inner heart circle (B, Z, D, Y, centred on C) is identical to the proportion of the Moon to

172

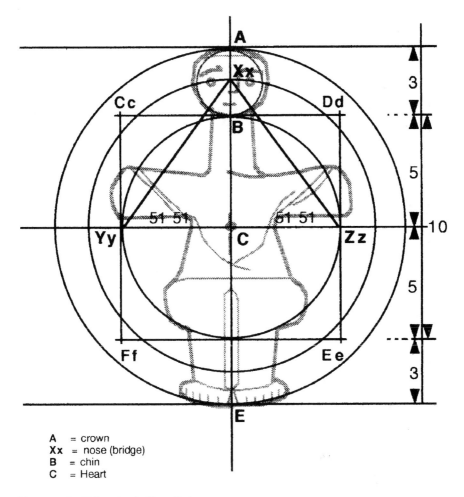

A = crown
Xx = nose (bridge)
B = chin
C = Heart

Diagram 118. *(3) Squaring the Heart Circle.*

the Earth, which perhaps indicates the linear character of the head and thus of the intellectual mind (which reflects the light or Wisdom of the Heart like a mirror or Moon), sitting on top of its Earth or body.

The Earth is thus contained within the 10 × 10 Square of Life (C, D, E, F), with its 10 × 10 Cross of Life marking the major compass points of the Earth, thereby giving the ancient sign of the cross within the circle which is used astrologically as a symbol to represent the Earth.

The drapery on the figure comes to a point at the figure's navel (L), which is the centre of another circle of life (P, B, Q, E,) whose diameter is 13 and whose circumference is 40 (diagram 118(4)). This circle accurately encloses all the body except for the head. The lines on which the drapery outlines were carved form two radii of this circle, at 90° to each other and 45° each to the vertical axis or spine of the figurine. Continued to their extremities they form

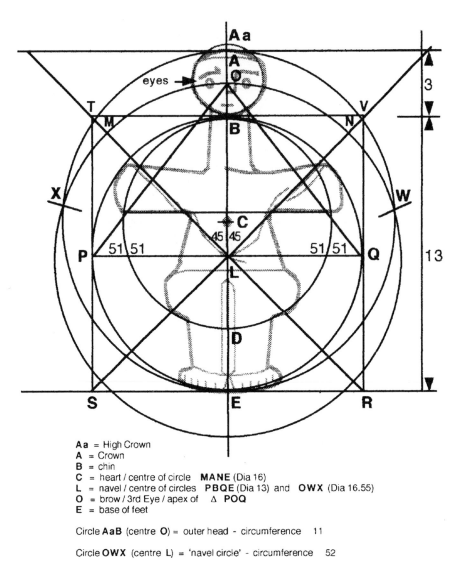

eyes →

Aa = High Crown
A = Crown
B = chin
C = heart / centre of circle **MANE** (Dia 16)
L = navel / centre of circles **PBQE** (Dia 13) and **OWX** (Dia 16.55)
O = brow / 3rd Eye / apex of △ **POQ**
E = base of feet

Circle **AaB** (centre **O**) = outer head - circumference   11

Circle **OWX** (centre **L**) = 'navel circle' - circumference   52

Diagram 118. *(4) Squaring the Navel Circle.*

the diagonals of a square (R, S, T, V) which squares the circle (O, W, X). The square (R, S, T, V) is 13 × 13, with a perimeter of 52. The circle (O, W, X) has a diameter of approximately 16.5, and a circumference of 52.

52 is the number of cards in a pack. It is a 13 based number, composed of 4 13, denoting the Grail manifested in all four worlds (depicted by the Four Suits or four alchemical elements).

The triangle (O, W, X) is defined by a second triangle (P, O, Q), whose apex (O) marks the brow centre or third eye of the figurine. The circle (O, W, X) passes through the two eyes of the figure on either side of this brow centre. A

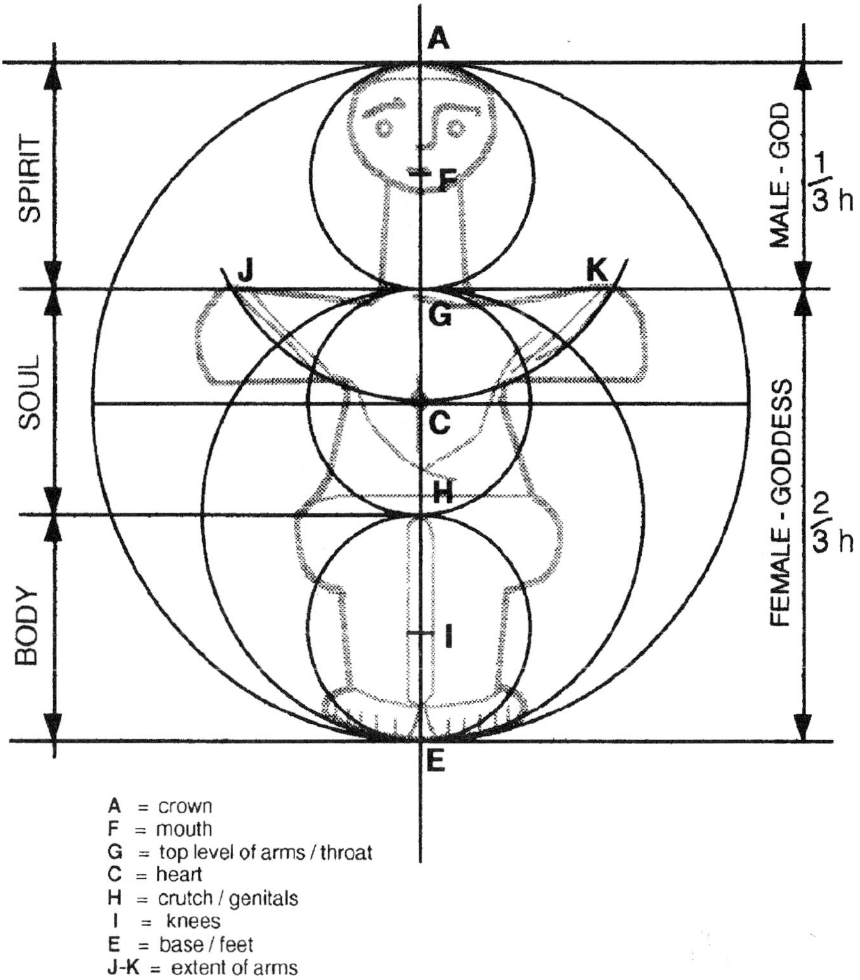
A
F
J
K
G
C
H
I
E
SPIRIT
SOUL
BODY
MALE - GOD
1/3 h
FEMALE - GODDESS
2/3 h
A = crown
F = mouth
G = top level of arms / throat
C = heart
H = crutch / genitals
I = knees
E = base / feet
J-K = extent of arms

Diagram 118. *(5) The Trinity.*

circle (A, B) centred on the brow centre (O) accurately defines the outer head of the figurine, and has a circumference of 11.

The Trinity. The diagonals of the navel circles (P, B, Q, E) (diagram 118(4)) cut the inner heart circle (B, Z, D, Y) at I and J, defining the upper limit of the outstretched arms, accurately divides the height of the figure into thirds, the height from the base to the line I,J (diagram 118(5)); being exactly double the height from the same line to the crown of the head – i.e., E-G:G-A:2:1. This 'Trinity' relates to the Golden Proportion, since $1 + 2 = 3$ is the starting point of the series.

The $1 + 2 = 3$ also refers to the Father or Spirit (1), the Mother or Matter (2), and the hermaphrodite Son (3), associated with the idea that the Tau (T) part of the cross represents the Mother, whilst the upper part of the cross (above the Tau) signifies the Father. The whole figurine is thus the Hermaphrodite, the Christ.

The whole trinitarian figure, when divided up into three parts (or circles), infers the idea of Spirit (above), Soul (middle) and Body (below). The soul and body belong to the female Goddess aspect (which is dual – 2), whilst the spirit belongs solely to the spiritual God-realm (which is single – 1). The hermaphrodite Mercury is all three – spirit, soul and body $(1 + 2 = 3)$ – hence the title of Mercury as Hermes Trismegistus ('The thrice greatest Hermes').

The Seven-Pointed Star or Heptalpha. The seven-pointed star is also to be found in the geometry of the figurine. There the upper $45°$ diagonals from the sacral centre (L) meet the figurine's enclosing heart-centred circle (at M and N). They divide the enclosing circle into one-seventh parts – i.e., the arc MA = arc AN = $\frac{1}{7}$ of the enclosing circle (A, N, O, P, Q, R, M) (diagram 118(6)). Two other points (Q and P) on this circle – points of the seven-pointed star – are defined by the outline of the body-waist of the figure and where the $45°$ diagonals from the navel intersect with the inner heart circle (at points Y and Z).

The heptalpha signifies the seven gifts of the spirit, the seven seals or chakras, the seven days of the week, the seven sacred planets, the octave of music. It also signifies the incarnation of spirit (3 – the Trinity) into matter (4 – the Elements). 7 is the number of the Earth revivified by the divine Current of Life.

In the figurine, centred upon the heart, the seven points of the heptalpha indicate the seven sacred planets and intelligences (Gods/Goddesses) which revolve around the sacred centre, the Sun or heart of the solar system.

The Heavenly Crown. The curve of the upper edge of the arms seems to be defined by an arc centred at A = H, 9 units above the crown (A) of the figurine, or 17 units above the heart centre (C). It may be that I have not found this centre accurately. The right-hand side of the figurine's neck finds this point (H) accurately, but it is not counterbalanced by the left-hand side (i.e., the neck of the figurine is asymmetrical).

As shown (diagram 118(7)), the arc has a radius of 14.8, being part of a circle whose circumference is 93. This may be a significant number for the figurine, but it is not as clear to me as all the other numbers are.

However, a circle centred on H which passes through the heart centre (O) of the figurine would have an approximate circumference of 108, which is the mystical number of all the names of God. $(108 = 3^3 \times 4 =$ the Trinity to the power of itself manifesting in the four worlds of existence). This of course is highly significant. If this is what is intended then it indicates that we are meant to understand that, symbolically, one of the 108 primary names or essences of God is implanted in the heart of the Hermaphrodite and that therefore the Hermaphrodite represents an Avatar and incarnation or manifestation of one of the 108 aspects of God – which is indeed what the hermaphrodite Mercury (or Christ) means.

Because of this, I believe that the centre (H) is accurately placed and the asymmetry of the neck is for a further reason which I have not yet deduced. The 'invisible' centre (H) therefore indicates the greater heart centre, the

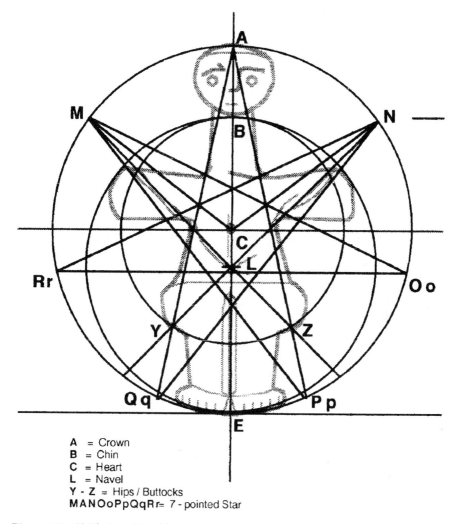

A = Crown
B = Chin
C = Heart
L = Navel
Y - Z = Hips / Buttocks
M A N O o P p Q q R r = 7 - pointed Star

Diagram 118. *(6) The Seven-Pointed Star.*

heart of the universe or Heart of God, which traditionally is described as being somewhere high above the head of a manifest person.

All in all this carved figurine is a remarkable work of art and seems to demonstrate a very high knowledge and technology in its makers. I can only conceive that the figurine was made from a template or drawing, as its symbolic numerology and geometry is so accurately constructed and portrayed. It is certainly a sacred object, almost certainly used in ritual, just as the lingam-yoni is used in India in fire ceremonies.

The correspondence of the geometric symbolism with the pictorial symbolism, which is highly accurate and carefully done, shows this figurine to be part of the long historical line of traditional sacred art created by initiates of the wisdom knowledge. It requires a profound knowledge and a high degree

177

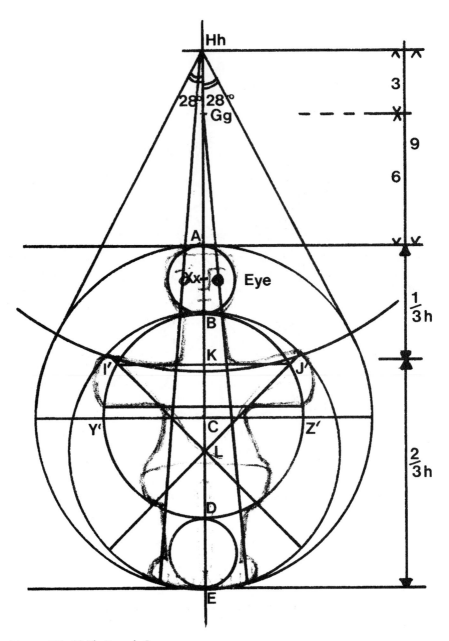

Diagram 118. *(7) The Heavenly Crown.*

of artistry (and appropriate technology). Such works of sacred art are designed to be useful, not purely decorative. Because of its symbolic meaning and high artistry, this figurine must have occupied a central place in some important ancient temple or sacred environment and a central role in any associated ritual like the icons of the Virgin and Child used in Christian churches.

APPENDIX B

The Mager Rosette

British Society of Dowsers

The Mager Rosette was invented by the famous French dowser, Henri Mager. The following is taken from the description in his book, *Water Diviners and Their Methods.*

For centuries dowsers have been able to determine suitable places for sinking wells for water supply, to find minerals or the most propitious place to build a dwelling.

The use of colour as an adjunct to the dowsing process (of which Henri Mager was a foremost exponent), greatly increases the range of information a dowser may obtain. In essence it relies upon the manifestation of sympathetic harmonies which appear to exist throughout all realms of nature.

The movement of his instrument will, to an experienced dowser, indicate a positive or negative response. If searching for underground water, then the instrument will be held in a neutral position as the search commences and will move to a positive mode when a source is crossed. Now it can be demonstrated that water, for example, has a resonance associated with particular colours which indicates the quality or purity of that water. As an example, good potable water is sympathetic to the colour violet, healing water to white and polluted water to grey. Dangerous water, both those containing poison or radiating noxious energies inimical to good health, respond sympathetically to black.

The Mager Rosette (colour plate 10) can be used in the following way. If dowsing with a pendulum, the colour to be tested can be held between the finger and thumb of the free hand. If dowsing with rods, then the appropriate colour can be held between finger tip and palm of one hand along with the rod or can be placed on the floor or ground over the discovered source and the chosen colour approached with the dowsing instrument.

If, for example, the colour violet is used then a positive response from water to that colour will indicate its excellent qualities. Likewise, other colours can be tested and a qualitative picture of water on a site can be built up.

In a similar way, metals or underground mineral veins can be tested. The following are typical sympathetic responses, red for iron, yellow for sulphur, green for arsenic, grey/red for lead, violet for copper and blue for cobalt. Other colour and mineral combinations can be discovered.

Another use of this versatile disc is in healing through colour where a person's need for a particular colour therapy can be determined by dowsing.

Personal experimentation will lead to a wide range of uses applicable to each person's field of interest.

Further information on **The British Society of Dowsers**, who run a programme of courses and lectures, and also issue regular magazines, can be obtained by sending a stamped, addressed envelope to:

Sycamore Barn
Tamley Lane
Hastingleigh
Nr. Ashford
Kent
TN25 5HW U.K.
Tel: 01233 750253

The **Irish Society of Dowsers** can be contacted:

c/o 4 Wade's Avenue
Dublin 5
IRELAND

The Mysterious Round Towers of Ireland Low Energy Radio in Nature

Prof. Philip S. Callahan, 1993

I spent the entire war at the secret ELF (extremely low frequency) radio range beam station installed at Belleek on the western Irish border. American and coastal command RAF aircraft navigated down the aerial beam highway to a safe landing in the north. It was as a technician at that low frequency station that I first became acquainted with the Irish round towers and ELF radio frequencies.

That is a 50-year-long story and involves the two major frequencies, of 310 KHz and 1,000 Hz, emitted from the crossed loops. The last such navigation aid in the U.S. was phased out in 1976.

Low frequencies were utilised in such systems because unlike high frequency radio, which is line of sight, low ELF and VLF frequencies follow the curve of the earth over land and sea. ELF waves also penetrate soil and water. High frequencies are absorbed by soil and water.

A strange thing about the round towers is the dirt that fills the base below the high doors. Each door has a different level of dirt filling the base as if they were 'tuned' like a pipe organ. It is fairly easy to get into the Alpha meditative state by chanting inside the towers that still have access in to them.

The fact that they have sound resonance is demonstrated both at Devenish and Kildare round towers. When the wind blows nothing is heard on the first floor but as one climbs the ladders to the top floor the hum of the breezes increases until it peaks on the top floor. There is no question that they are sound resonators.

Photos taken of the Scattery Island tower, which has no floors, show that the windows are arranged so that both light and air from the door and windows spiral up the shaft.

After many trips to Ireland since World War II, I have reached the conclusion that the structures were stone pipe organs for sound resonance from chanting monks, but could they also amplify electro-magnetic resonance? If so it would have to be in the radio region of the spectrum.

I do not know exactly when it happened; that is the way science develops, but I began to believe that radio waves travelling down my body from those wet antenna poles had actually tranquillised me. Could the round towers also emit tranquillising radio waves. If so, *where did they come from?*

Open Resonators

Over the years my work on insects centred on the resonant properties of the moth antenna, which, as it turns out, are covered with spine-like 'tower' forms, picket fence circles, cones, pyramids, etc., I was able to demonstrate conclusively, with spectrical experiments, scaled up models and Maxwell's antenna equations that such micron sized shapes are open resonators to frequencies generated by collision infra-red scatter from plants and insect scents.

Open resonators are fibres on which the waves travel on the surface instead of down the middle as in fibre optics which work in the visible region of the spectrum. If rods and spines can be open resonators for extremely short infra-red frequencies why can't standing stones, stone rings and tubular round towers be resonators for long wavelength radio? Round towers are the same length dimension as the towers and loops used in low frequency radio ranges.

My hypothesis made sense but did not explain why the radio frequencies were generated. I had postulated open resonator radio amplifier-antennas with no transmitter to oscillate and to produce such long wavelengths. Something important was missing!

The Picram

PICRAM is the word I use to describe a cloth ELF radio detector invented by me and my good friend Harry Kornberg. As is usual in the modern world it is formed by the first letter of the words: **P**hotonic **I**onic **C**loth **R**adio **A**mplifier **M**aser (patent pending).

Just as the Wright brothers developed and controlled flight by looking at nature – seagull wings – Kornberg and I developed the PICRAM by the same process – looking at flax (unbleached linen).

I have long known that raw flax was used by healers in Ireland to cure sprains, mumps and even certain types of arthritis.

A year or more of experimentation led to the development of a flax (plant fibre optic) wax coated open resonator doped with sea salt (anionic detector) and sandwiched between wool (condenser) plates. The designed cloth was connected to either a Tektronix 222 DC oscilloscope or Fluke 97 DC oscilloscope.

I had long before postulated that the towers were not transmitters but powerful amplifiers of radio resonance from the atmosphere generated by lightning flashes around the world. A year ago, a preliminary trip to Ireland with my Tektronix 222 demonstrated my hypothesis to be correct. I planned for a final trip with my PICRAM attached to the more sensitive Fluke 97 oscilloscope.

Round Tower Atmospheric Radio Amplifiers

W.O. Schumann, a German scientist, in 1952 calculated the cavity resonance between the earth surface and the ionosphere. He looked at the space between the earth and the ionosphere as being a sort of resonant cavity filled with low energy plasma called the atmosphere. The sky plasma is stimulated to 'light up' in the radio region by lightning flashes around the world. In 1962, H.L. Koenig measured these predicted ELF radio waves in the same region as the EEG (brain waves). In general, Schumann waves emit in harmonics from 1 to 70 Hz.

I immediately detected Schumann waves in free air with my PICRAM and since my 21b Fluke scope is DC operated I could measure such waves any place on earth. There is far more than Schumann frequencies involved, however, for we measured frequencies from the atmosphere clear out to 1 MHz (1,000,000 Hz). The round towers proved to be powerful amplifiers in the brain wave region, 2 to 24 Hz, electrical anaesthesia region, 1,000 to 3,000 Hz, and electronic induction heating region 5,000 Hz to 1,000 KHz.

Preliminary calculations demonstrate from 10 to 150 times tower amplification of these lightning stimulated atmospheric radio frequencies. My first experience of the power of lightning energy on living things is described in my published diary of my hike around the world in 1948 (*A Walk in the Sun*, 1988). In the jungles of South Asia I had actually watched bamboo shoots grow (as in time lapse photographs) during thunder storms.

The fascinating thing about round towers is that the main resonant amplified frequencies 4 to 10 Hz is in the meditative, alpha brain wave region, 2,000 Hz in the electrical anaesthesia region and 250 KHz in the electronic induction heating region.

Belleek Radio Range antenna emitted at 310 KHz, modulated by 1,000 Hz in the electronic induction heating and electrical anaesthesia region – no wonder I came down tranquillised, or drunk if one prefers, on the antenna poles in 1944.

It is fascinating that just above the surface of the ground to about 2 to 4 feet up there is a null of atmospheric frequencies and that they get stronger and stronger until at 9 to 15 feet above the surface they are extremely strong. The Irish monks were well aware of this for that is where they built their high doors! At every tower we measured there was a direct correlation between tower door height and the strongest waves.

At Scattery Island where the door is at ground level the strong waves began six inches to one foot above the island ground instead of nine feet and above! Round towers are well designed *atmospheric radio amplifiers*.

What It All Means

That the highly amplified waves occur in the meditative and electrical anaesthesia portion of the electro-magnetic spectrum is of utmost significance. In 1963, G. Walter researched brain EEG waves from 0.5 to 3 Hz (Delta region) and found anti-infectious effects. There is an elegant but short list of research projects demonstrating the beneficial effects of low ELF wavelengths on sick people.

J. Snape as early as 1869 demonstrated that pulsed ELF waves could be used to anaesthetise patients during dental extractions. A research group in Poland headed by W. Czaja, in 1986, demonstrated that 1,000 to 3,000 Hz enhanced the immune system of cattle. Although very little research has been accomplished in this field, and in fact it has been suppressed by the FDA there is no question about the healing potential of ELF wavelengths when generated at the correct frequency and waveform (just as important). Such waves definitely enhance the immune system. It occurs to the point where enhanced immune systems can destroy any virus (if nutrition is correct), or eliminate chronic diseases such as some arthritis. It is after all the immune system that heals, not drugs, or we scientists or physicians. The round towers are in reality healing chambers!

One of my favourite intact round towers is Rattoo in County Kerry. Carved into the wall of the top floor is the 'Sheila-na-gig'. The word is Irish and means 'pornographic'. The carving is not a 'dirty' carving but rather a stylised artistic work of a Celtic maiden in the upright (correct) birthing position. It may be a dirty representation to the vulgar but to me it is a beautiful sign that says 'delivery room'.

ELF radio waves penetrate soil and water. It is fairly simple to demonstrate the beneficial effects of lightning stimulated ELF radio on plants by merely planting vegetables or flowers around a small model of such a tower. The tower plants will have 2 to 6 times more fine rootlets on them.

Unfortunately, Ireland does not farm very much any more. It has been turned into one huge sheep ranch (to its own detriment) by the Common Market. One of the few large vegetable farms I found on my 1992 trip to Ireland was cultivated around the base of Rattoo round tower. The monks always planted their vegetable gardens at the base of the round towers.

The fact that there is a null radio gap above the ground tells a physicist in no uncertain terms that air flow and Bernouilli's principle (aircraft wings) are involved. Also the stimulation of radio waves, as is true of visible and IR photons, involves complex laser and molecular coherent scatter principles occurring in Schumann's earth-ionosphere atmospheric resonant cavity. But that is the subject of a far more complex paper or book.

APPENDIX D

Geopathic Stress and The Spiral of Tranquility™

Clive V. Beadon and Michael Poynder

With growing interest in alternative medicine and increasing involvement of ordinary people in all aspects of health, the term *geopathic stress* has come to be used to describe the cause of many different illnesses which are frequently stress-related and difficult to diagnose; M.E. and M.S. are cases in point.

We go out to the doctor's surgery or therapists' rooms expecting to find answers to our problems in the form of treatment, rarely stopping to consider if the cause of our illness stems from within ourselves or our environment. More often than not the cause is due to energy disruptions within our homes, particularly the place where we sleep.

Geopathic stress is caused by three different energy sources working in isolation or together:

(a) underground water-flows beneath the property/structure;
(b) para-magnetic force lines entering the property and splitting up into component rays;
(c) all forms of electrically powered equipment including televisions, computers, fluorescent lighting and not least, mobile telephones.

Underground water – Flowing through the earth, water is compatible to blood in our veins. It is the life-force of the earth, just as our bodies are similarly dependent on healthy blood to survive. The natural reaction of water energy in earth is to seek air, creating vibration in our atmosphere. When a structure is built above an underground water flow, this is restricted and disruptive vibrations are thus set up in the building: house, office, factory, farmyard, cowshed, etc.

Instead of energy activating at a constant benign 8 Hz, the natural 'beat' of the earth which parallels natural brain wave patterns, surrounding energy is split into different vibrations that can be demonstrated by a competent dowser as separate colours of the light spectrum. These lines can then be related to a diagnoses of the physical state of the occupants of the property.

If two underground water courses conjunct under a property, a spiral or vortex of disrupted energy will evolve and the disruption is accentuated and multiplied, forming a circle about the point where the two lines meet. The depth of the water source gives the radius of the disrupted circle above, at ground level. This deeply affects the health of those who live and sleep within its radial influence and compounds any pre-existing health problems.

For example, if one is sleeping over or above an underground source of running water, troubled sleep may result in growing anxiety and, where the source is polluted, be it an underground flow of water or a water-table, the body's immune system can be affected over a period of time. As illustrated in Chapter XIII, if one is sleeping over any of these lines of separate colour, the related chakra will be disrupted accordingly and that area of the body will be liable to associated illness or 'dis-ease'. For example, an indigo/violet line may cause head problems such as migraines and subsequent stress; a green line may cause heart problems; a red line anxiety and/or anger, etc.

Water ebbs and flows in the earth with the phases of the moon, contracting and expanding just like the tides. Of course, the flow changes with rainfall and the seasons. This natural fluctuation also causes changes to the energy levels above ground and therefore in those of human beings.

Paramagnetic Lines – The entire planet is covered with billions of paramagnetic $\oplus$ force flow lines as narrow as centimetres and as wide as many metres. Originally, these natural magnetic environmental *energy lines* formed a web-like net of geometrically shaped 'Star' patterns, interlocking with each other to form a fine unseen energy network around the world – lines that course and flow and vibrate everywhere like unseen 'cables'. At some time in the past, undoubtedly due to the activities and inventions of mankind, the balance of these patterns was disturbed, resulting in the network disintegrating to form unbalanced energy lines over large areas of the Earth's surface. In remote areas of the globe, over deserts and oceans, parts of the original network still exist, enlightening us to the true form of these natural patterns which once surrounded us.

To a diviner (a dowser in simplistic terms is concerned with water and a diviner with everything else), these energy lines can again be annotated in colour-like strands of energy linked together: red/black/white/black/red. These are the 'Dragon Lines' of Feng Shui – a practice that is only relevant and really successful with the assistance of a dowser. When these lines cross an underground water-flow and where the water is in conjunction, already forming a circular pattern of energy, the circle is accentuated by earth magnetism and comes alive as a vibrant force-field.

The red and black lines form clockwise and anti-clockwise flows around the circle with the central white energy going through the circle, seemingly as a connective link. Hence a 'fairy line' or the path of ghosts and poltergeists in folklore!

The priests of the Stone Age knew about these circular energy formations and used the pendulum with their clairvoyant perceptions to work and build in harmony with nature, forming power sites indeed. This is the origin of the layout of the ancient stone circles and the placement of standing stones.

However, like underground water-flows, the Earth's paramagnetic flow lines can be easily disrupted and fractured into the component nine-colour vibrations of the spectrum: black, red, orange, yellow, green, blue, indigo, violet and white – giving us the 'rainbow' colours with the addition of black and white. By comparison to the human body: from 'below', the base chakra (black), to 'above', the crown chakra (white) – from darkness to light or symbolising matter into spirit, when in harmony and balance.

Where a paramagnetic line meets an obstruction such as a house, a large stone, a monument or perhaps a well, it breaks down into its component colours in a shattered pattern rather like a pane of glass 'starring' when hit by a stone. Each line of the star forms a disrupted colour resonance, i.e., all are at different ULF (ultra low frequency) Hz levels instead of the balanced natural standard planetary beat of 8 Hz.

These subsequent disrupted lines flowing through a property are the cause of many distressing unrecognised or undiagnosable states that doctors are unable to pinpoint or treat: "have another pill and your headache/heartache/stomach ache/prostate problem, etc. etc. will go away". It does, but only temporarily of course until the pill wears off. The disruptions remain and the cause has been neither understood nor treated successfully. Where these unbalanced lines of energy occur in concentrations, they can give rise to discomfort and disquiet, impinging on an individual's subconscious mind. Humans and animals seem to become subject to stress symptoms, and where this occurs, as with underground water flows, general health and sleep patterns often appear to be affected.

The classic example of a misdiagnosed human state is where a vagrant green and vagrant yellow line flow together through the cot of a young baby. The yellow 'stops' the solar plexus chakra and the green, the vital resonance of the heart chakra – resulting in a *cot death*. The armour of light (protective aura) of a baby does not form until the fontanel (cap stone of the brain cairn) closes over about six months after birth.

The late Clive Beadon and the author have written papers on this subject and while evidence exists to demonstrate that this tragic experience is neither mere coincidence nor the fault of the parents and can often be prevented by counteracting geopathic stress, sadly the authorities refuse to listen or accept this diagnosis, considering it too 'far out'.

A combination therefore of underground water and disrupted magnetic flow lines (confused with and wrongly termed 'ley' lines) causes *illness* and *stress* in the home, singularly affecting one, more or all of the occupants, depleting the aura and immune system.

Electromagnetic Energies – Mankind, through the use of *electricity*, has unwittingly created harmful electromagnetic energies that affect some although not all of us; encountered in our everyday lives through the use of televisions, computers, microwave ovens, fluorescent lighting and particularly mobile telephones. Until electricity was discovered only 120 years ago and put into our houses, human beings could cope reasonably well with the disruptions from underground water flows and fragmented Earth energy lines, provided they weren't destroying themselves with poor diet or alcohol. Moreover, houses themselves were not then constructed with concrete, plastics and external glass but made of natural materials

– mud and wooden floors, stone walls, etc. – with a vibrational frequency resonating to that of the Earth itself.

It is these energy fields, especially those from harmful sources, that reach out to our subconscious minds over much greater distances, distracting our thoughts, concentrations and dreams. For example, the twin beam-like rays from the front and back of a television set or computer terminal can be easily picked up and identified by a diviner, and registered by some sensitive people, over a distance of some 50 to 100 or more feet from the source.

Well-known electrical fields exist under pylons and cables of the National Grid system. Water or Earth energy lines crossing through these strong fields acquire some of the grid's negative characteristics, carrying them many miles further afield. When a house lies on the track of these particular energies, the occupants of the property can feel restless and under constant pressure, unable to find the peace and tranquility they should hope to experience in their own homes.

Electricity, coursing through these fractured lines – both water and magnetic – accentuates the Hz levels to the point where the human immune system begins to break down. Not just from the 240v ring mains in our houses but from the electricity operating familiar everyday appliances. All of these devices emit concentrated high Hz waves, pulsing out into our environment and upsetting our own electrical and magnetic 'balance' which, as we have already mentioned, used to be 'in tune' with nature.

To understand what is happening with geopathic stress today, we need to draw a parallel with the tobacco industry from 1940–80s: 'Tobacco does not harm your health . . . there is no evidence that nicotine causes cancer' etc. etc. But now we know that it does. Currently, the electronic industry is saying that mobile telephones, computers, powers lines, aerial masts etc. *do not* have any harmful effects on health, that there is no risk – relax and all will be OK.

This is rubbish! There *IS* mounting evidence that cathode ray transmissions from everyday appliances deplete the healthy quality of our *blood*, causing the breakdown of the immune system – which creates *stress* and in turn may lead to illness and 'dis-ease': M.E., M.S., cancer, heart disease, etc. The USA and some EEC countries now acknowledge electrical fields from pylons and power cables as directly related to cancer and heart disease and their planning authorities frequently choose not to build these areas.

Considerable research by doctors and scientists internationally has been published concerning the hidden dangers of mobile (cell) telephones, even when on 'stand-by' let alone 'send' or 'transmit' mode. When in use it has been shown that up to 80% of the microwaves from these sophisticated radio transmitters enter the head and brain.

STOP PRESS

Mobile Phones Damage Immune System

Radiation from handsets used by more than 19 million Britons can wreck the ability of white blood cells to fight disease and cancer tumours.

There are several (plug-in) electrical anti-geopathic stress instruments now on the market. However, they are generally of limited effectiveness and range, largely because they rely on household electricity for their use. Other methods incorporate some weird ideas such as putting copper rings or aluminium sheets around the bed.

Some inexperienced 'experts' of practices such as Feng Shui, believe that by moving furniture around and changing colour schemes, the effects of geopathic stress can be counteracted. While Feng Shui can be a valuable tool, without dowsing ability the potential harmonisation is generally ineffective. This practice is frequently misunderstood and misapplied and largely produces a 'feel good' factor, favouring our emotional responses and interior design foibles of fashion – how can one balance underground water, perhaps 60 feet below ground level, just by moving the sofa? Neither does a pot plant nor a crystal, specially chosen on an emotional level and superficially placed do the trick – disruptions caused by underground water or magnetic flows remain.

A device called the **Spiral of Tranquility**[TM] (colour plate 11), a unique hand-crafted model encapsulating carefully selected gemstones positioned between two copper spiralled rings and measuring $2\frac{1}{2} \times 2\frac{1}{2} \times 2\frac{1}{2}$ inches, shields the damaging effects of common electrical/electronic appliances and corrects the Earth's unbalanced energy lines within its immediate vicinity.

The **Spiral** is designed for the home and will cover an area of some fifty yards square. The small **Pendant**, crafted along the same lines, meets the same requirements and fulfils the same function. It is designed for travel or for the workplace and corrects the environment over an area of some ten square yards. The ranges depend on the confines around them.

The **Spiral** and **Pendant** have been specifically designed to re-balance vagrant geopathic forces and lock them back into their original 'Star' pattern. By neutralising and dispersing others, the environment can be cleared of such disruptive and pollutant energies and sources of stress permanently removed.

No specific healing properties or miracles are claimed for these devices, but in providing an improved environment, anyone currently receiving treatment should find that it is enhanced and more effective; thus their health benefits, and positive results are experienced in many areas of daily life.

The **Spiral of Tranquility** is the result of many years of experimental work, carried out by its inventor, Clive Beadon, with the assistance of Geoffrey King in the early years. Beadon's final model of the **Spiral** is Mark No. 56 and its manufacture was completed over 20 years of research. He stated before his death, on 16 September 1996, that he had fulfilled all he set out to achieve – to harmonise all these vagrant energies encountered in the home. Beadon's work has been passed on to the author to continue in his memory and for the benefit of the environment.

The **Spiral of Tranquility** has recently been scientifically tested by the recognised and independent **Roger Coghill Laboratories**, Pontypool, Gwent, Wales. The effect of disruptive influences from mobile telephones on blood lymphocytes (white corpuscles – the 'soldier' blood cells) has have been examined and the results given in a report that makes fascinating but frightening reading.

These tests demonstrate the effectiveness of the **Spiral** as a harmoniser of geopathic stress influences in the home and workplace. The report concludes that the **Spiral** acts as a significant shield to all these disruptions, and specifically from the most harmful emissions – those from mobile telephones:

> *The radiation from some TACS mobile phones even on stand-by is capable of adversely affecting human peripheral blood lymphocytes* **in vitro**. *This adverse effect is mitigated to a significant extent by a device called the* **Spiral of Tranquility**.

The **Pendant** has been stringently tested by **Mr G.W. Crockford**, a Fellow of The Ergonomics Society and Member of The British Occupational Hygiene Society and Earth National Institute of Risk & Safety Management. His comprehensive report states:

> *The* **Pendant** *affects and controls by attracting to itself magnetic fields associated with running water, earth energies and electrical appliances. It is concluded that the* **Pendant** *influences and controls the magnetic fields in its environment. This control may extend to a number of metres about 10 m.*

Following new research by the author since the first edition of this book, and as a result of tests undertaken by Mr Crockford examining the effectiveness of the **Pendant** in a range of magnetic fields in the environment, it is now recommended that the **Pendant** is put on a 9ct gold chain (which contains approximately one-third gold, one-third copper and one-third silver, and is therefore *not* pure gold) for even greater effectiveness – thereby mitigating the absence of the copper rings.

The unique **Spiral of Tranquility & Pendant** are trademarked and registered in the UK and now also backed-up by stringent laboratory testing. *It really works*!

A FREE Brochure is available on receipt of an A5 stamped, addressed envelope to:

The Spiral of Tranquility
PO Box 3747
WEYMOUTH
Dorset DT3 5YD U.K.

Tel/fax: + 44 01305 816644

Agencies are offered to alternative medical practitioners.

To obtain a copy of the **Spiral Report** by **The Coghill Research Laboratories** or the **Pendant Report** by **Mr G.W. Crockford**, please send a cheque for £3.00 and £3.50 respectively, together with an A4 s.a.e. (50p).

Finally, hundreds of letters are on file praising the benefits **The Spiral of Tranquility** has brought to people with many different physical, emotional and mental problems. Here is a quotation from Ms Leslie Kenton, an internationally acclaimed author (*Passage to Power* and *Journey to Freedom*) and broadcaster on all aspects of health and healing, and particularly topics of interest to women:

I have followed Wing Commander Clive Beadon's work for many, many years, watching his **Spiral of Tranquility** *go through many metamorphosis, each time I believe, becoming more effective than the previous. I am delighted that Clive's work continues. Being someone who travels a quarter of a million miles on jet plane a year, I must say that I delight in the help that the little* **Spiral of Tranquility Pendant** *gives me while travelling, and I certainly recommend it to others in the help it gives me, in avoiding jet lag and maintaining mental and physical balance. I highly recommend it to anyone.*
(Leslie Kenton, Pembrokeshire, Wales)

Bibliography

ANDERSON, Flavia (1987) *The Ancient Secret*. R.I.L.K.O. Books, distributed by Thorsons, U.K.

BAUVAL, Robert & GILBERT, Adrian (1994) *The Orion Mystery*. W. Heinnemann Ltd., London, U.K.

BEADON, Clive V. (1978) *Earth Stars*. Lecture Notes, British Society of Dowsers, Sycamore Barn, Tamley Lane, Hastingleigh, Nr. Ashford, Kent TN25 5HW, U.K.

CALLAHAN, Philip, S. Prof. (1984) *Ancient Mysteries, Modern Visions*. Acres, Kansas City, U.S.A.

COTTERELL, Maurice (1988) *Astrogenetics*. Brooks Hill Robinson, Saltash, Cornwall, U.K. (out of print).

CRITCHLOW, Keith (1979) *Time Stands Still*. Gordon Fraser, London, U.K. (out of print).

DAWKINS, Peter (1981) *The Cycles of Initiation*. Francis Bacon Research Trust (F.B.R.T.), Castle Ashby, Northampton, U.K. Journal Series 1, Vol. 1.

DAWKINS, Peter (1982) *The Virgin Ideal*. Ibid. Journal Series 1, Vol. 2.

GILBERT, Adrian & COTTERELL, Maurice (1995) *The Mayan Prophecies*. Element Books, Shaftesbury, Dorset, U.K.

GRUBER, Elmar & KERSTEN, Holger (1995) *The Original Jesus*. Element Books, Shaftesbury, Dorset, U.K.

HANCOCK, Graham (1995) *Fingerprints of the Gods*. W. Heinnemann, London, U.K.

HEATH, Robin (1992) *Sun Moon Man Woman*. Bluestone Press, Cwm Degwel, St. Dogmaels, Cardigan, Wales, U.K.

HERITY, Michael (1974) *Irish Passage Graves*. Irish University Press (I.U.P.), Dublin (out of print).

HERITY, Michael (1993) *Gleanncholmcille*. Na Clocha Breaca, Dublin, Ireland.

JOWETT, George (1975) *The Drama of the Lost Disciples*. Covenant Publishing, London, U.K. (out of print).

KASHMIRI, Aziz (1973) *Christ in Kashmir*. Roshni, Srinagar, Kashmir.

KERSTEN, Holger (1990) *Jesus Lived in India*. Element Books, Shaftesbury, Dorset, U.K.

LAWLOR, Robert (1982) *Sacred Geometry*. Thames & Hudson, London, U.K.

LOMAX & KNIGHT (1996) *The Hiram Key*. Century Publishing, London, U.K.

MAGER, Henri (1931) *Water Diviners and Their Methods*. G. Bell & Sons, London, U.K. (out of print).

MAVOR, James, W. Jnr. *Gallarus Oratory and the Dingle Peninsular*. Journal of Ancient Sites Research Society, Longhill, Rowley, Massachusetts, U.S.A.

POYNDER, Michael (1997) *Pi in the Sky*. The Collins Press, Cork, Ireland.

SCHONFIELD, Hugh, J. (1991) *The Passover Plot*. Element Books, Shaftesbury, Dorset, U.K.

THEIRING, Barbara (1993) *Jesus the Man*. Corgi, U.K.

References

CHAPTER I

Diagram 3	Cyprus Museum, Souskiou.
Diagram 7	Michael Herity, *Irish Passage Graves*, I.U.P., Dublin, Ireland, 1974.

CHAPTER II

B&W plate 1	Commissioners of Public Works, Dublin, Ireland.
Diagram 14	Op. Cit.
Diagram 17	British Museum, London.
Diagrams 19 & 20	Robin Heath, *Sun Moon Man Woman*, Bluestone Press, Wales, 1992.
Diagram 21	Keith Critchlow, *Time Stands Still*, Gordon Fraser, London, 1979.

CHAPTER III

Diagram 27	John Michell, *View over Atlantis*, Garnstone Press, London, 1972.
Diagram 33	Fountain International, Amsterdam Group, Holland.
Diagram 35	National Museum of Ireland.
Diagram 39	Andrew Sinclair, *The Sword and the Grail*, Century, London, 1992.

CHAPTER IV

Diagrams 43 & 44	Robert Webster, *Gems*, Butterworths, London, 1975.
Diagram 45	National Museum of Ireland.
Table 1	Clive Beadon.

CHAPTER VII

B&W plate 3	British Museum, London.

CHAPTER VIII

Diagram 55	Clive Beadon, *Earth Stars*, Lecture Notes, British Society of Dowsers.

CHAPTER IX

Diagrams 57 & 58	National Museum of Ireland.
Diagram 63	Op. Cit.
Diagram 64	James W. Mavor Jnr., *Gallarus Oratory and the Dingle Peninsular*, Journal of Ancient Research Society, Longhill, Rowley, Massachusetts, U.S.A.
Diagram 66	Op. Cit.
Diagram 68	Op. Cit.
Diagram 69	Prof. Philip, S. Callahan.
Table 2	James. W Mavor Jnr., Ibid.
Diagrams 70 & 71	Prof. Philip S. Callahan, *Ancient Mysteries, Modern Visions*, Acres, Kansas City, U.S.A., 1984.
Diagram 73	Michael Herity, *Gleancholmcille*, Na Clocha Breaca, Dublin, Ireland.

CHAPTER XI

Diagram 80(1–9)	Peter Dawkins, researched for Michael Poynder, *Pi in the Sky*, The Collins Press, Cork, Ireland.
Diagram 89	Cairo Museum, Egypt.

CHAPTER XII

Diagrams 113 & 114	Olivia Dewhurst-Maddock.

APPENDIX A

Diagram 118(2–7)	Peter Dawkins, researched for Michael Poynder, *The Lost Magic of Christianity*, The Collins Press, Cork, Ireland, 1997.

APPENDIX B

Diagram 119	Henri Mager, *Water Diviners and Their Methods*, G. Bell & Sons, London, 1931.